Robert A. Byers

dBASE III PLUS™
for Every Business

ASHTON·TATE®

ISBN: 0-912677-86-4

Published by Ashton-Tate Publishing Group
20101 Hamilton Avenue, Torrance, California 90502-1319

10 9 8 7 6 5 4 3 2   *87 88 89*

Ashton-Tate, dBASE, dBASE II, and dBASE III are registered trademarks of Ashton-Tate Corporation. dBASE III PLUS, dBASE Tools, dBLINKER, dBRUN, dBRUN III PLUS, and RunTime are trademarks of Ashton-Tate Corporation.

The software, computer, and product names mentioned in *dBASE III PLUS for Every Business* are manufacturer and publisher trademarks and are used only for the purpose of identification.

IBM-PC and Personal Computer AT are registered trademarks of International Business Machines Corporation.
Lotus and 1-2-3 are a registered trademarks of Lotus Development Corporation.
WordPerfect is a registered trademark of Satellite Software, Inc.
WordStar is a registered trademark of MicroPro International Corporation.
Quicksilver is a trademark licensed to WordTech, Inc. by Quicksilver Software, Inc.
Compaq is a registered trademark of Compaq Computer Corporation.
Epson is a registered trademark of Epson Corporation.
Clipper is a trademark of Nantucket, Inc.

Senior Editor: Karen Bergen   Production Manager and Text Design: Rachel Mahler
Editor: James S. Bradbury   Production Editor: Kathryn M. Schmidt
Design Director: Thomas Clark   Assoc. Prod. Editor: Pamela A. Gausman
Cover Illustration: D.A. Gray Bare   Production Coordinator: Lilo Kilstein

Acknowledgment

Writing this book has been fun as well as challenging. Part of the fun comes from the friends and associates who have made contributions. As usual, Bill Jordan of Ashton-Tate deserves credit for seeing the enterprise through to a successful outcome. Thanks also go to Robert Hoffman and Brenda Johnson-Grau of the Ashton-Tate Publishing Group, who did their usual brilliant job of editing and assembling the technical material into good English.

The original programs themselves were reviewed and tested by Steve Kurasch, Richard Malm, Kathy Rowe, and J. Starnes. Thanks to all of you. Testing programs is hard and often tedious work that takes a great deal of time. I really appreciate their help.

Thanks also go to my very dear friend, Charlene Ebert, for her patience and understanding these past few months. A very special thanks goes to my daughter and girl Friday, Lauren, who typed much of the manuscript, tested and helped debug the programs, proofread the manuscript diligently, and made many good suggestions.

While writing this revision, it's been my pleasure to work with a new group of talented people. Lisa Potter, my assistant, helped prepare the manuscript. Ralph Davis did a remarkably thorough job of technical editing and review. Karen Bergen and James Bradbury skillfully folded in the new and revised material.

Robert A. Byers

A disk of the programs for
dBASE III PLUS for Every Business

If you wish to order a program disk for *dBASE III PLUS for Every Business*, please send $25.00, plus $2.00 postage and handling to:

Ashton-Tate Publishing Group
20101 Hamilton Avenue
Torrance, CA 90502-1319

Att: Maxine Harris

CONTENTS

APPENDIXES

Introduction

This book is intended for people who want to write computer programs using dBASE III PLUS.™ It is intended to serve as a sequel to *Everyman's Database Primer Featuring dBASE III PLUS*. It is not intended for the first-time user. To gain the most from this book you need to have completed the *Primer*, have some background in either dBASE II® or dBASE III,® or have programming experience.

The bulk of this book covers the development of a business system using dBASE III PLUS. You get to see the dBASE III PLUS commands used in context. The text explains the program itself, how it was designed, and why specific commands were used. Although these programs will function in a business environment, they are intended as a teaching tool. In many cases, you will find that you would choose to implement a program in another way. One of the challenges in writing the book was to use all of the dBASE® commands and functions at some point in the business program. The book's purpose (and mine) is to give you an insight into how to get the most from dBASE III PLUS.

Insofar as possible, I have attempted to promulgate good programming practices and programming style in the development of these programs. dBASE is an informal environment; consequently those practices that are rigidly enforced by more formal languages are not mandatory—nor are they always possible. However, since it is to your advantage to acquire good programming habits, you should pay attention to these lessons in style.

The book is divided into three sections. The three chapters in Section One review dBASE III PLUS fundamentals and provide the foundation for the remainder of the book. There are no references back to the *Primer* or to the dBASE III PLUS manual. The book can be used "stand-alone," although it is always a good idea to have additional references available.

The second and largest section consists of nine chapters that describe the application of dBASE III PLUS to a series of business problems. We build a foundation for a business software system with a series of programs for customer files, mailing lists and labels, and inventory management. With this foundation we then attack the more dynamic problems associated with sales order entry, order fulfillment, and billing.

The programs in the second section have a dual function. Each solves a simple business problem, and all showcase the dBASE III PLUS programming language. In doing so, they provide the reader with programming examples. The primary purpose of the programs is to show the reader how to go about writing a dBASE III PLUS program to solve a specific problem. The software system itself does not purport to be complete. It will serve as a model that you can use to build your own viable business program.

The text and programs are illustrated by screens and figures. When appropriate, bold type is used to help you distinguish between the program response and user input. The programs are all presented in lowercase type with the names of data items (variables, fields, and files) in uppercase. The use of lowercase is not mandatory—it just makes the programs easier to read.

The last section consists of five chapters, dealing with special topics and tricks, and generic discussions of such things as getting the most from the **report** command and dealing with the date as a data type. The reader should look for tricks in coding in the programs themselves.

The emphasis in the book is really on learning by doing—most of us learn best when we are actually trying to accomplish something. One of the best ways to learn is to look at how someone else has solved a problem and then to adapt that solution to meet our needs. Our adaptation itself becomes unique and may, in turn, become the model for the next problem solver.

AUTHOR'S NOTE

Those readers who are unfamiliar with computers should read, or have read, a basic computer text such as *Everyman's Database Primer* before undertaking this book. Beginners should start at the beginning of this book and read the material carefully. If you are an experienced computer user, but are unfamiliar with dBASE III PLUS, you should review the introductory material in Chapters One and Two. Experienced dBASE users can safely skip to Chapter Three, where the discussion on dBASE III PLUS programming begins.

SECTION ONE

Fundamentals

CHAPTER ONE
Database Basics

Record keeping is a major part of the operation of most organizations. Businesses keep records on customers, employees, inventory, taxes, payrolls, sales, purchases, and so on. Schools keep records on students, teachers, and class attendance. Clubs keep track of membership, meetings, and dues. Records such as these constitute the *database* of an organization.

In the past, the database was kept on paper and was stored in ledgers and cabinets. Clerks were employed just to file and retrieve these paper records. Today, records are increasingly kept as electronic images in a computer. A *database management system* (DBMS) is used to store and retrieve these electronic records. The computer and a database management system, such as dBASE III PLUS, allow you to deal with larger amounts of data than you could manually.

dBASE III PLUS is unusual in that it is both a database management system and a computer language. As a DBMS, it can be used directly from your keyboard to help you keep track of business records. As a computer language, it allows you to write simple programs to make record-keeping even more efficient.

The dBASE combination of DBMS and language is particularly easy to learn and use. You can learn it a little bit at a time—as you are using it. You can make practical use of dBASE even while you are learning. With other computer languages such as FORTRAN, COBOL, or even BASIC, you have to spend a large amount of time learning the fundamentals before you can accomplish anything productive.

dBASE III PLUS BASIC TERMINOLOGY

dBASE III PLUS is a relational database. Relational means that *data* is stored in tables of rows and columns (shown in Figure 1-1). Each row is a *record*. Each column is a *field*. Column titles are *fieldnames*. The width of a column is its *fieldwidth*. The kind of information stored in a field is its *fieldtype*.

Each database table is stored on the computer's disk as a disk file. Each disk file has a name, its *filename*. Rules for filenames are established by your computer's operating system.

Filenames

Filenames may have *eight* or fewer characters. They can contain letters, numbers, and underscores.

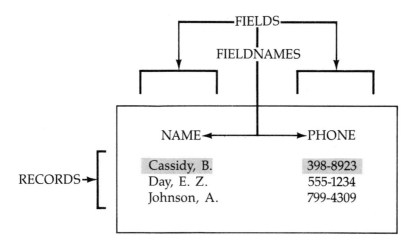

Figure 1–1: Basic database.

Fieldnames

The rules for fieldnames (column titles) are similar to those for filenames. But fieldnames may have up to *ten* letters, numbers, and underscores. They must begin with a letter and may not contain embedded blank spaces. In the sample database, the fieldnames are NAME and PHONE.

Fieldwidth

The fieldwidth is simply the number of characters that can be entered in the column.

Fieldtype

The fieldtype identifies the kind of data to be stored in a field. dBASE has five fieldtypes: character, date, logical, memo, and numeric.

Character fields: These fields can contain letters, numbers, blank spaces, and symbols. Most database fields fit this description. For example, zip code fields are normally character fields even though they contain only numbers, because no arithmetic calculations are performed. Character fields can be as wide as 254 characters.

Date fields: These fields contain only dates, which are stored in the form *mm/dd/yy*. Date fields are set automatically by dBASE III PLUS to eight spaces.

Logical fields: dBASE sets these fields to one character automatically. These fields can store only True/False (T and F) or Yes/No (Y and N) values.

Memo fields: These are variable-length fields which are used to store large blocks of text, such as memorandums, letters, abstracts, and so on. Memo fields can contain up to 4096 bytes. Memo field data is actually stored in a second file, a *database text file*, which is separate from the database file. Each memo field uses ten characters within the database file to *point* to the location of the text data in the database text (.DBT) file.

Numeric fields: These fields store numbers that can be used in calculations. Numbers can be either integers or decimals, but the field width has to account for the decimal point and all digits to the right of the decimal point. For example, the number 1.25 requires a field width of at least 4 to allow for the decimal point.

Relations

Two or more database files can be used together. Suppose that you have one database file of students and another of teachers (see Figure 1–2). We can find Tommy Jones's teacher by searching the teacher file for the teacher with the same room number as Tommy. When we do this we are relating the information in one table to that in another.

When two or more database files are used together in this way, the files are called *relations*. All of the relations together make up the database.

Student's Name	Room	Grade
Aardvark, Angela	13	1
Bottle, John	26	1
DeWire, Barbara	15	2
Jones, Tommy	20	3

Teacher's Name	Room	Grade
Armalite, Edward	25	1
Newton, Katherine	16	2
Plato, Peter	20	3
Shakespeare, Judith	13	1

Figure 1–2: Relational database example.

BASIC COMMAND VOCABULARY

Commands allow you to create, change, manipulate, and extract information from database files. dBASE III PLUS offers the user a choice between entering commands directly by typing in the command or indirectly by selecting the commands from a series of "pull down" menus. Even though dBASE III PLUS offers menu selection, it is primarily a command-driven DBMS. Since this is a book on programming, we'll ignore the use of menus and focus on dBASE commands—what they are and how they work. You can issue dBASE commands either from the keyboard or from command files (programs). Twenty-four of the most basic dBASE commands are shown below. Each of these commands is a verb whose dBASE meaning is close to its ordinary English meaning.

append	edit	recall
average	find	replace
browse	index	report
copy	list	select
count	locate	sort
create	modify	store
delete	pack	sum
display	quit	use

Many of these commands can be used with optional modifiers—words and clauses to specify more precisely what the command is to do. The syntax of a dBASE command consists of the command verb and all of its optional words and clauses. The complete syntax for all dBASE commands is shown in Appendix B. For the remainder of this chapter we will be demonstrating command syntax informally; there will be a more formal discussion of the dBASE tools in Chapter Two.

To demonstrate the use of these basic commands, let's create and use the database shown in Figure 1–3. Although this database contains only five records, it is adequate to demonstrate the basic database operations, which are the same whether there are 5 records or 500,000.

PART NAME	QTY	MIN STOCK	UNIT PRICE
HAMMER, 16 OZ CLAW	6	6	10.88
WRENCH, 5/8 BOX	4	6	4.29
WRENCH, 3/4 BOX	8	5	6.19
HAMMER, 10 OZ BALL	5	3	8.15
PLIERS, 8 IN GAS	11	5	3.89

Figure 1–3: Sample database.

GETTING INTO dBASE III PLUS

The dBASE III PLUS program consists of several disk files that come on two floppy disks and can also be copied to a hard disk. The principal files are DBASE.EXE, DBASEINL.OVL, and DBASE.OVL. There are other disk files that come with dBASE that are useful, but not necessary. These include HELP.DBS and ASSIST.HLP, which contain the text of help messages; you will not need either of these files while working with this book. If you will be using dBASE on a computer with only floppy disks, I would recommend that you copy the file DBASE.OVL to a disk which also contains the DOS file COMMAND.COM. This disk will remain in your A disk drive while you are using the dBASE program, and COMMAND.COM will allow you access to the DOS commands from within dBASE.

There are two other files, CONFIG.SYS and CONFIG.DB, that will be of much more interest to you. To use the programs in this book, CONFIG.SYS *must* be on the root directory of the disk used to boot your computer and must contain the following two statements:

```
FILES = 20
BUFFERS = 15
```

Without this file you would be able to use only three files from within dBASE. DOS (your operating system) normally allows you to use eight files, but five of these are taken back for the computer's I/O, your screen, keyboard, and so on. With CONFIG.SYS you can have up to 15 open files.

The file CONFIG.DB is used to custom configure dBASE and is discussed in Appendix C. dBASE III PLUS normally "comes up" in the Assistant, a system of menus that make it easier for the beginner to use dBASE. In this book we want to work directly with the command language. To enable dBASE to "come up" ready to accept commands from the keyboard, edit the file named CONFIG.DB, and remove the following two statements:

```
COMMAND = ASSIST
STATUS = ON
```

The first of these causes dBASE III PLUS to start up in the menu mode. The second creates a status bar across the bottom of the screen.

To load dBASE you must be *logged* to the disk drive with the file DBASE.OVL. DBASE.EXE can be on any other disk drive, and, because the program will reside in your computer's memory, its disk can be removed from the computer once the dBASE program has loaded. The disk containing DBASE.OVL must remain in the computer.

If dBASE is in disk drive A and you are logged to A, type **dbase** after the operating system prompt and press the **Return** key.

```
A> dbase
```

When dBASE has loaded, a screen display showing the license agreement appears. The cursor is located at the bottom of the screen just after a dot (if you have removed the configuration commands as described above). This dot is called the *dot prompt*. You can enter commands only at the dBASE dot prompt. If you have not removed the configuration commands as described above, you will be in the menu-driven Assistant. To get to the dot prompt, press the **Esc** key a couple of times.

GETTING OUT OF dBASE III PLUS

To exit from dBASE, type the command **quit** after a dot prompt. Then press the **Return** key, which tells dBASE to *do* what you've just typed. When entering commands from the keyboard, finish each command by pressing the **Return** key. Because dBASE commands can be of different length, you must signal the end of the command.

. quit

Always exit from dBASE with **quit**. This command closes all open files and exits from dBASE in an orderly manner. Exiting by some other means (such as turning off the computer) can result in data loss.

CREATING A DATABASE

To create a database, type the command **create** immediately after the dot prompt; dBASE responds by asking for a filename.

. create
Enter the filename: HARDWARE

Entering a legitimate filename, such as HARDWARE, calls up a data-entry screen for defining the fields in the database. The fields are defined by simply filling in the blanks. The completed entry screen for the sample database called HARDWARE is shown as Figure 1–4. These field definitions constitute the *structure* of the database.

The box at the top of the screen shows you which keys can be used to help with data entry. Press function key **F1** (on the IBM® PC) to toggle this *help menu* on and off.

The Control Key

Note the caret (**^**) symbol in the help menu of Figure 1–4. This symbol indicates the **Ctrl** key, which is used in the same manner as the shift key. It gives a third meaning to many of the keys on the keyboard. Hold it down while pressing the key shown after the caret symbol. For example, **^U** means hold down the **Ctrl** key and press the **U** key. **^U** deletes the field to which the cursor is positioned.

To define a field, enter its fieldname, fieldtype, and fieldwidth. To enter a fieldtype, press the key for the first character of the fieldtype (**C** for character, **D** for date, **L** for logical, **M** for memo, and **N** for numeric). The number of decimal places is entered only for numeric fields. If it is more than 0, the decimal point and the number of decimal places must be included in the fieldwidth.

When all of the fields in the structure are defined, press the **Return** key when prompted to define another field. This tells dBASE that you have finished defining the structure.

dBASE asks whether you wish to enter data at this time. Type **Y** to begin data entry.

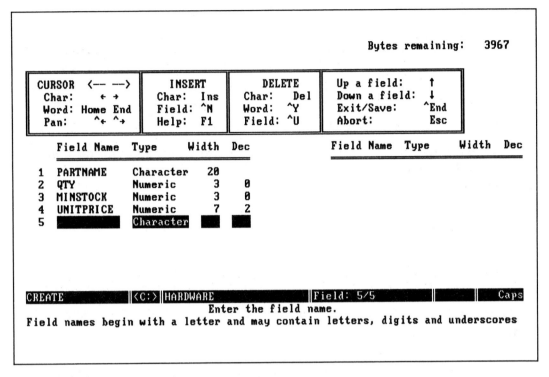

Figure 1–4: Screen to create sample database.

This places you in the append mode—as if you had issued the **append** command (see below). Pressing any other key returns you to the dot prompt.

USING A DATABASE

To work with a particular database file, type the **use** command followed by its filename.

. use HARDWARE

This command closes any database file that you have been using and opens the named database file—in this case, HARDWARE.

Adding Records: Append

To add new records to the database file that you are using, type the **append** command:

. append

This command presents you with a full-screen data-entry form. The data-entry form for the sample database HARDWARE is shown in Figure 1–5.

After you type **append**, the cursor is positioned at the beginning of the first field (PARTNAME) of the new record. To enter data, type it in as desired. The cursor will

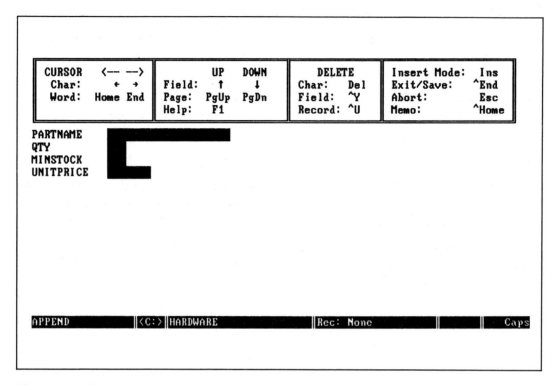

Figure 1–5: Data-entry screen.

move only within the screen areas that are in reverse video. Use the arrow keys to move around within the record, the **PgUp** key to go back to a previous record, and the **PgDn** key to return to the current record. **F1** toggles the help menu on and off.

When data entry for a record is complete, a blank new record is automatically presented. As each record is added to the database it is assigned a *record number*. To exit from **append**, press the **Return** key when prompted to enter a new record. Enter the data from Figure 1–3.

Changing the Database: Modify Structure

The **modify structure** command allows you to alter a database's structure. It produces the same screen display as the **create** command (see Figure 1–4). You can use it to change field definitions, add fields, and delete fields; however, if you change a fieldname during a **modify structure**, you cannot add or delete fields at the same time.

The **modify structure** command takes a copy of the database's *structure* into memory. Once the modification is complete, dBASE copies the data from the file into the new structure and renames the old file .BAK. There *must* be room on the disk to hold both the new version and the old version of the file; otherwise you will get a DISK FULL error message during the modification.

Changing the Record Content: Edit, Browse, and Replace

One of the reasons for storing data electronically is that the data becomes easy to change. Three of the 24 basic commands that can be used to change record contents are **browse**, **edit**, and **replace**.

Edit: This command begins editing with the *current record*—that is, the record in use when the **edit** mode was entered. To edit a particular record, use **edit** followed by the record number. For example, to edit record 4 use:

. edit 4

As in the **append** mode, the arrow keys move the cursor within the reverse video area. To go back a record, press **PgUp**. To move forward a record, press **PgDn**. To stop editing, press **Ctrl-End**. To toggle the help menu on and off, press **F1**.

You can specify which records you want to edit by describing those records as part of the command. For example, to edit only those records where the field PARTNAME contains the word HAMMER, use:

. edit for PARTNAME = "HAMMER"

Note that the word HAMMER is enclosed in quotes. These quotes are *delimiters*, and must be used to set off *character strings*, such as HAMMER, that occur in commands. Use either single quotes, double quotes, or square brackets. However, be sure to use the same symbol to begin and end the character string.

Browse: This is a full-screen editing command that combines editing with data display. Figure 1-6 shows **browse** being used with the HARDWARE database.

The current record is shown in reverse video. To edit this record, simply type in the new information. Use the **Up Arrow** and **Down Arrow** keys to select a desired record. When the database has more records than can fit on a single screen, use **PgUp** and **PgDn** to select new display screens. Options available with **browse** are shown on the help menu which can be toggled on and off with function key **F1**.

Replace: This command allows you to make changes in the contents of specified fields and records. To increase all prices stored in the field UNITPRICE by 10 percent, use the command:

. replace all UNITPRICE with UNITPRICE * 1.1

The asterisk is the symbol for multiplication in dBASE.

Viewing Data: List and Display

List and **display** allow you to view the contents of your database. **List** displays the entire database without interruption, whereas **display** shows only the current record. Optional modifiers can be added to the **display** command to show more than a single record. For example, to display all records, use **display all** as shown in Figure 1-7. When multiple records are displayed by this command, the screen display pauses after every screenful and shows the message "press any key to continue . . . ."

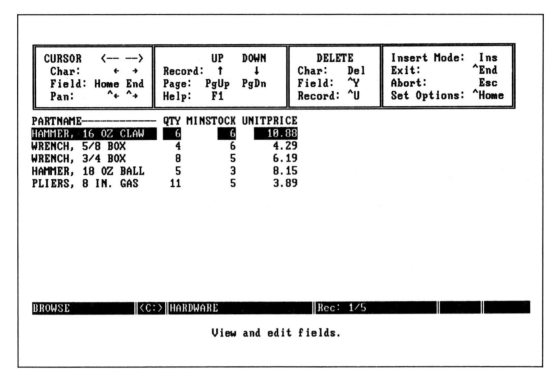

Figure 1–6: Browse used with the HARDWARE database.

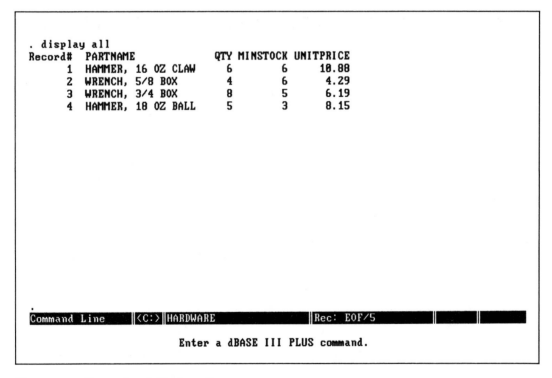

Figure 1–7: Example of display all.

Use the **for** clause to specify which records are to be displayed. Figure 1–8 shows how to use this clause to select records. The first example specifies the records where the content of the field PARTNAME begins with HAMMER. The condition PART-NAME = "HAMMER" is evaluated for *every* record in the database, and only those records for which the condition is true are displayed. The second example specifies the records where the content of the field QTY is less than the content of the field MINSTOCK.

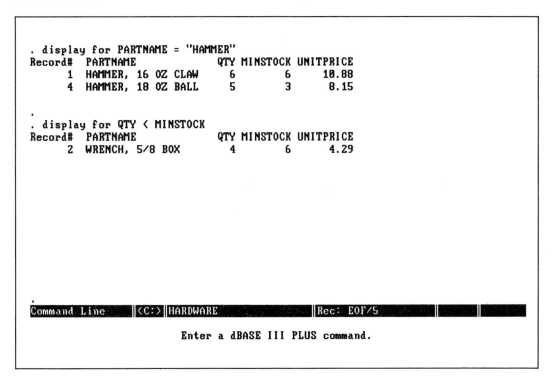

```
. display for PARTNAME = "HAMMER"
Record# PARTNAME              QTY MINSTOCK UNITPRICE
      1 HAMMER, 16 OZ CLAW      6        6     10.88
      4 HAMMER, 18 OZ BALL      5        3      8.15


.
. display for QTY < MINSTOCK
Record# PARTNAME              QTY MINSTOCK UNITPRICE
      2 WRENCH, 5/8 BOX         4        6      4.29
```

```
.
Command Line    ||<C:>||HARDWARE                ||Rec: EOF/5       ||      ||

            Enter a dBASE III PLUS command.
```

Figure 1–8: Example of for clause in command.

The display can be also limited to selected fields or expressions, as shown in Figure 1–9. This example displays the result of an operation involving two fields. The content of the field QTY is multiplied by the content of the field UNITPRICE. An expression can consist of fields, constants, and operations involving fields.

List and **display** are also used to display the structure of the database. Figure 1–10 shows the result of the command **display structure** for the HARDWARE database. The date shown in the structure is the last time the database was changed in any way. Note that the record size is one greater than the sum of the fieldwidths. This is because dBASE uses one byte of overhead for each record in the database to identify whether or not the record has been marked for deletion.

Removing Records From the Database: Delete, Pack, and Recall

Records are removed with a two-step process. A record is marked for removal by

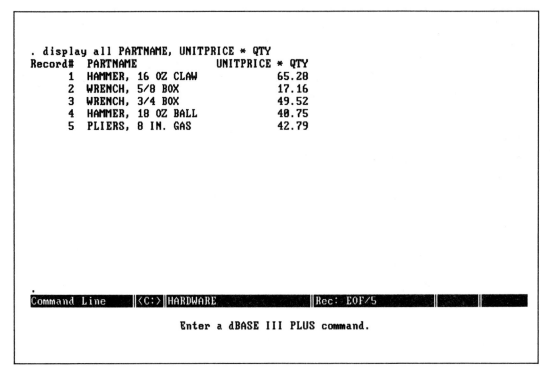

Figure 1–9: Display selected fields.

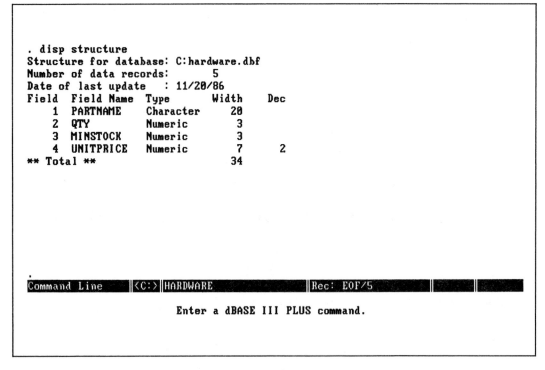

Figure 1–10: Display structure for HARDWARE database.

the **delete** command, which adds an asterisk (∗) to the beginning of the record. Records that are marked for deletion (deleted) are removed from the database by the **pack** command. **Pack** adjusts the positions of remaining records by copying them into the space formerly occupied by removed records. A record that has been marked for deletion can be unmarked by the **recall** command. Some examples of the **delete** command are:

. delete
. delete next 3
. delete for PARTNAME = 'HAMMER'
. delete all

To undo these commands we use the **recall** command:

. recall
. recall next 3
. recall for PARTNAME = 'HAMMER'
. recall all

The deletion and removal of a record are shown in Figure 1-11. Note that records 4 and 5 have become records 3 and 4 after the **pack** operation.

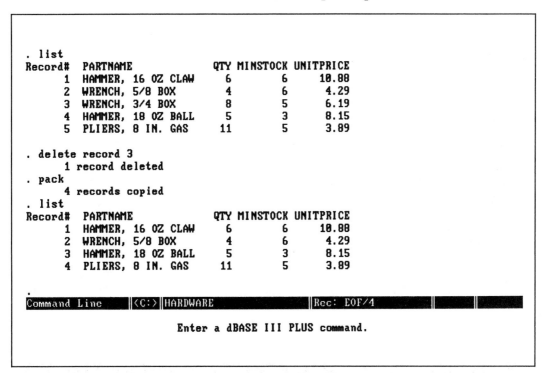

Figure 1-11: Deletion and removal of record.

Copying All or Part of a Database: Copy

The **copy** command lets you copy specified records and fields or an entire database.

The examples below illustrate the **copy** command by copying from our sample database HARDWARE to the new database named DEMOCOPY.

```
. copy to DEMOCOPY
. copy fields PARTNAME, QTY to DEMOCOPY
. copy next 5 to DEMOCOPY
. copy for PARTNAME = 'HAMMER' to DEMOCOPY
```

To copy only the structure of your database, add the word **structure** to the command.

```
. copy structure to DEMOCOPY
. copy structure fields PARTNAME, QTY to DEMOCOPY
```

Extracting Information: Average, Count, and Sum

To extract information from the database, use the commands **average**, **count**, and **sum**. The **average** command provides the average value of a numeric expression involving a field.

```
. average QTY
. average QTY, QTY*UNITPRICE
. average QTY, QTY*UNITPRICE for PARTNAME = "HAMMER"
```

The **count** command provides a number representing the quantity of records meeting a condition.

```
. count
. count for PARTNAME = "HAMMER"
```

The **sum** command adds the contents of fields (or expressions involving fields).

```
. sum QTY
. sum QTY, QTY*UNITPRICE
. sum QTY, QTY*UNITPRICE for PARTNAME = "HAMMER"
```

Ordering Records: Sort and Index

Records are stored in the database in the order they were appended, but this order is not always the best one for their use. Two commands are provided to rearrange records: **sort** and **index**. Either of these commands can rearrange the database in alphabetical, chronological, or numeric order.

Sort: The **sort** command makes a copy of a database, in which the records are permanently sorted by the content of the specified fields. All or part of a database may be sorted. Records can be sorted in either ascending or descending order, and the sort order can be independently specified for each key field. Figure 1–12 illustrates the use of the **sort** command by showing our hardware database sorted by PART-NAME.

Note that the record numbers in the sorted file have been reassigned from those in the original file (see Figure 1–11.) The physical order of the records in the sorted

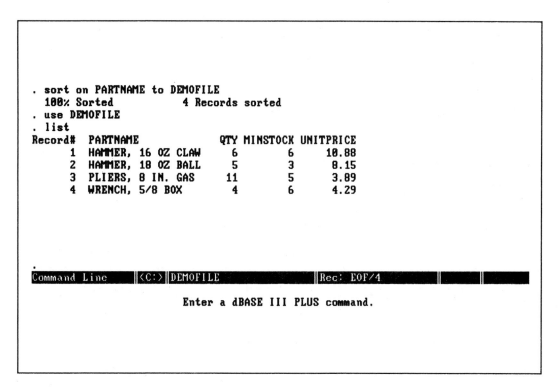

```
. sort on PARTNAME to DEMOFILE
  100% Sorted          4 Records sorted
. use DEMOFILE
. list
Record# PARTNAME              QTY MINSTOCK UNITPRICE
      1 HAMMER, 16 OZ CLAW      6        6     10.88
      2 HAMMER, 18 OZ BALL      5        3      8.15
      3 PLIERS, 8 IN. GAS      11        5      3.89
      4 WRENCH, 5/8 BOX         4        6      4.29




.
Command Line      ‖<C:>‖DEMOFILE              ‖Rec: EOF/4      ‖      ‖    ‖

         Enter a dBASE III PLUS command.
```

Figure 1–12: Example of sort command.

file matches the logical order (alphabetical, chronological, or numeric) of the sort key (the fields that the file was sorted on).

Index: Indexing, an alternative to sorting, creates a new file called an index file. It is not a copy of the database. When used with the database, an index file causes the records to *appear* to be sorted in logical order. In Figure 1–13, the database of Figure 1–5 is indexed on the field PARTNAME. Note that the records now appear in alphabetical order, yet the record numbers are not sequential. The database itself has not been changed.

While an index file is in use, all access to the database is through the index. Records are searched in the index order, not in record number order. Some database operations will appear to be slower when an index file is being used, because there may be more movement of the disk head than when using the unindexed database.

There are a number of advantages to indexing over sorting. You can maintain up to seven index files on a database at one time. All indexes that are in use are updated whenever a change is made to one of the key fields by adding, editing, or removing records. Records can be used in the desired order simply by selecting the appropriate index file. In addition, use of an index file gives you direct access to records by the index key.

To use existing index files with a database, add the list of index files to the **use** command. Index filenames are separated by commas (that is, delimited by commas).

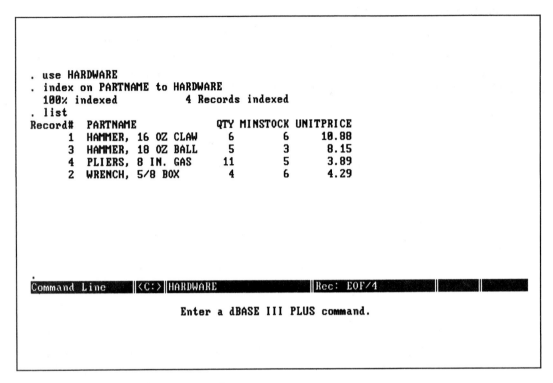

Figure 1-13: Using index command.

. use HARDWARE index HARDWARE, SOFTWARE, . . .

The controlling index is the first index file named in the list.

Locating Records: Locate and Find

Two commands are used to locate a particular record: **locate** and **find**. **Locate** is the most general and can be used with any field or combination of fields. *Find can be used only to find a record based on an index key.*

. locate for PARTNAME = "PLIERS"

Locate *rewinds* the database to the beginning. The records are searched and examined sequentially in either actual (physical) or indexed (logical) order until a record is found that matches the specified condition. If the database is large, the search can be time-consuming.

. find PLIERS

Find searches the index file for the character sequence immediately following the command verb. (Note that delimiters are not used with the **find** command.) The index file is technically called a *modified B tree*, which is a structural arrangement that can be searched very quickly. Virtually direct access is provided to the record by **find**.

Writing Reports: Report

The **report** command provides a powerful method for preparing formal formatted reports on the contents of the database; an example is shown in Figure 1-14. A report is prepared by means of a *report form*, which is a disk file that contains only the answers to simple questions about the report format and content.

```
Page No.        1
04/08/85
                         SAMPLE DATABASE REPORT

PART NAME                QTY    MIN UNIT PRICE  STOCKVALUE
                              STOCK


HAMMER, 10 OZ BALL        5      3        8.15       40.75
HAMMER, 16 OZ CLAW        6      6       10.88       65.28
PLIERS, 8 IN GAS         11      5        3.89       42.79
WRENCH, 5/8 BOX           4      6        4.29       17.16
*** Total ***
                         26                        165.98
```

Figure 1–14: Example of a dBASE report.

Report forms are created by means of the **create report** command. This menu-driven command activates a series of screen forms as shown in Figures 1-15, 1-16, and 1-17. The first screen, Figure 1-15, is concerned with the title and format of the report—that is, how big the margins are, and whether or not the report is to be double-spaced.

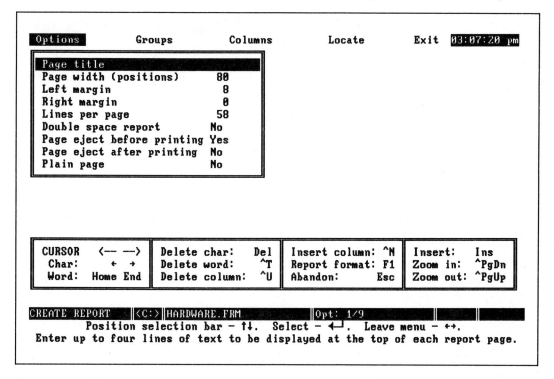

Figure 1–15: First report screen.

The second screen is concerned with subtotalling.

The third screen, Figure 1–17, is used to define the columns that make up the body of the report. This screen repeats as each column is defined by content, title, and size. For numeric fields, you can elect to total or not and select the number of decimal places to be displayed. To direct a report to the printer, use the command:

. report form to print

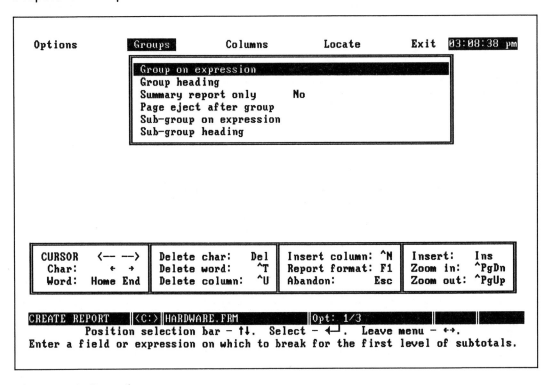

Figure 1–16: Second report screen.

USING MULTIPLE DATABASE FILES

dBASE III PLUS allows you to use as many as ten database files at a time. Each file occupies a separate work area, designated as *work area 1* through *work area 10* (or A through J). One database file and its associated index files can be open in each of the ten work areas. The total number of files of all types that can be open at the same time is 15. Suppose we have two database files: STUDENTS and TEACHERS. We want both of these files to be open at the same time.

. select 1
. use TEACHERS
. select 2
. use STUDENTS
. select TEACHERS
. select 2

```
   Options          Groups        Columns          Locate        Exit  03:09:57 pm

                            Contents
                            Heading
                            Width                        0
                            Decimal places
                            Total this column



      ┌─Report Format─────────────────────────────────────────────────────────────
      >>>>>>>>────────────────────────────────────────────────────────────────────




   CREATE REPORT      <C:> HARDWARE.FRM                   Column: 1
        Position selection bar - ↑↓.  Select - ↵.  Prev/Next column - PgUp/PgDn.
        Enter a field or expression to display in the indicated report column.
```

Figure 1—17: Third Report Screen.

First, select a work area. Open the database file with **use**. Once a file is open in a work area you can select the work area by either the database filename or work area identifier. Each work area has its own record pointer, which means that when you leave a work area the database in use will remain at its current record until you return.

dBASE AS A PROGRAMMING LANGUAGE

This quick overview of the basic dBASE III PLUS vocabulary shows that the individual commands are simple and powerful. These commands are *non-procedural*. You tell dBASE what you want done, not how to do it. Conventional programming languages such as BASIC, PL/1, FORTRAN, and COBOL are *procedural*; that is, you have to provide a sequence of instructions (a program) to accomplish the results that we have achieved with simple one-line commands.

dBASE III PLUS has procedural features, too. It is a structured language similar in some ways to languages such as PL/1 and Pascal. It also includes many of the teaching features of BASIC and the command lexicon (vocabulary) is similar to that of BASIC.

dBASE III PLUS is interpretive. This means that it always reads the English commands and interprets them, which allows us to set up pieces or sections of a program directly from the keyboard to test our methodology and syntax. Conventional languages must compile programs into machine symbols so that the computer reads them directly. Before you can test an operation or series of operations you must enter them into a program and compile them. Interpreting the commands makes dBASE run slightly slower than a conventional language, but helps the programmer run significantly faster. There are now compilers available for dBASE. This gives you the best of all worlds: an interpreter to use for developing programs and a compiler to transform the developed program into a more smartly-executing program.

Some experts have estimated that between 50 and 80 percent of programs written in the conventional languages are devoted to the tasks of storing and managing data, preparing reports, and handling screens. This is the hard stuff that most programmers hate. dBASE does much of this routine work for you, thereby cutting the overall programming task by as much as 80 percent.

What are dBASE's disadvantages? For one, dBASE does not provide all of the math functions. If transcendental and trigonometric functions are necessary for your work, dBASE may not meet your needs.

A second disadvantage is that interpretive dBASE programs are often slower when compared to their counterparts written in C or COBOL. This is part of the trade-off: You trade speed for power and ease of use. Speed is important on mainframe computers where time translates directly into dollars. Mainframe operations costs will often run around 56 cents per CPU seconds, but you need to pay programmers to make the program efficient.

On the microcomputer you're concerned with your own efficiency. If a program is too slow, it can be irritating at times but is of little economic importance. Also, speed is relative. Adding two numbers together in dBASE III PLUS takes about seven milliseconds. That's slow by computer standards; however, it is pretty fast to the microcomputer user. Finally, well-written programs in dBASE will compare favorably (overall) with business programs written in traditional languages. The really time-consuming operations—sorting, searching files, and so on—are as fast in dBASE as in any other language.

All in all, for the computer beginner, dBASE is a terrific first language. Much of the dog work of programming is already done for you: dBASE takes care of managing data files, screen handling is simple and direct, and the report writer will produce much of the needed paper output—freeing you to concentrate on learning how to produce a custom business application.

dBASE III PLUS is economical for the experienced programmer. He or she can write better applications programs in less time with dBASE. The code is self-documenting and easily maintainable. An experienced programmer should become proficient in dBASE in about a week; programmers' time is money, and using dBASE will result in improved productivity. Even if you should, at some point, need to recode the programs to a traditional language, you can still use dBASE as a design language. Most design languages are little more than syntax checkers. You can use dBASE to test your program logic. After all, design and testing are the time-consuming elements in programming; coding (especially recoding) is of relatively little consequence.

A SHORT HISTORY OF dBASE

dBASE's legacy dates back to the mid-1960s and a management information system called RETRIEVE, which was marketed by Tymshare Corporation. The Jet Propulsion Laboratory in Pasadena, California, used RETRIEVE until the late 1960s, when it purchased three UNIVAC 1108 computers. Jeb Long, then a new programmer at JPL, was assigned the task of writing a program which would perform the same functions as RETRIEVE. The new file-management system that Long developed was called JPLDIS. This system continued to evolve over the next several years and is still used on many UNIVAC 1100–class computers.

In the late 1970s, Wayne Ratliff, a friend of Jeb Long's, became interested in microcomputers. Wayne was an experienced programmer who had worked at JPL on the Viking Mars Lander under a contract with the Martin Marietta Corporation. For a very short time, his interest focused on winning the office football pool. Soon, however, he became interested in the commercial aspects of a microcomputer database management system. And he developed a system which, to the user, was very much like JPLDIS.

Wayne marketed this microcomputer version of JPLDIS himself, under the name VULCAN. VULCAN rapidly evolved to the point where it had its own personality and character, but customer sales did not follow: by 1980, there were only about 60 customers of VULCAN. Entrepreneurs George Tate and Hal Lashlee entered the scene—after seeing an ad for VULCAN in *BYTE* magazine. VULCAN soon had a new name: dBASE II. A new company, Ashton-Tate, was formed to market it.

dBASE II enjoyed tremendous success in the marketplace. It was a product built around the limitations of 8-bit CP/M computers. After some work, Wayne developed a concept that would retain much of the virtue of dBASE II but would use the power available in 16-bit microcomputers. Ashton-Tate assembled a team of experts largely recruited from JPL, led by Wayne Ratliff, to develop this next generation microcomputer database management system: dBASE III. This new program was subsequently upgraded again to dBASE III PLUS. dBASE III PLUS is easier to use and much more powerful than dBASE II. Far from being a simple upgrade of the popular dBASE II, dBASE III and dBASE III PLUS are entirely new products that borrow the best of dBASE II.

CHAPTER TWO
The Tools

This chapter provides a brief overview of the dBASE III PLUS toolkit, which is particularly suited for business applications because of dBASE's ability to organize and manipulate tables of data. The discussion of each of the tools is brief; it is not intended to replace the dBASE manual.

The dBASE III PLUS tools consist of the dBASE program itself, several kinds of special purpose disk files, memory variables, the dBASE commands and functions (that is, the language), and a pull-down menu system for the interactive user. Taken altogether, dBASE has become as much a language as BASIC, C, or Pascal. You will find it easier to use and, generally, more powerful than these more-traditional languages.

To use the programs in this book, the file CONFIG.SYS *must* be on the root directory of the disk used to boot your computer and *must* contain the following two statements, as discussed in Chapter One.

```
FILES = 20
BUFFERS = 15
```

This version of CONFIG.SYS lets you use up to 15 files at a time within dBASE III PLUS. Should you intend to use the **run** command from within dBASE, increase the *files* value to 25 or 30.

A special version of CONFIG.DB supplied with dBASE III PLUS causes dBASE to "come up" in the menu-driven ASSIST mode and turns on a status bar at the bottom of the screen. To use dBASE as a programming language, discard this version of the file and create another based on the sample shown in Appendix C.

dBASE III PLUS DISK FILES

dBASE III PLUS provides nine different kinds of disk files that have some use in programming. Each kind of file has a specific purpose. There are a handful of other file types provided by dBASE III PLUS, but these additional files have little or no value in programming.

All dBASE III PLUS files have a user-supplied name of up to eight characters plus a dBASE-supplied three-character file identifier. The dBASE-supplied file identifiers for each of the dBASE file types are shown on the next page.

dBASE III PLUS File Type	File Identifier
Database	DBF
Database Memo	DBT
Format	FMT
Index	NDX
Label Form	LBL
Memory	MEM
Program	PRG
Report Form	FRM
Text Output	TXT

Only the eight-character user name is necessary when referring to dBASE files. dBASE assumes an identifier based on the command used. For example, to open the database file EXAMPLE.DBF the proper command is:

. use EXAMPLE

dBASE assumes the .DBF file identifier, because the **use** command opens only database files.

You can override dBASE III PLUS and assign your own file identifier; but, if you do, you must use the complete filename, including the file identifier, in all references to the file. If the file EXAMPLE.DBF is renamed as EXAMPLE.86, the command to open this database file becomes:

. use EXAMPLE.86

Database (.DBF) Files

As discussed in Chapter One, database files store data in tables (files) of rows and columns. Each row is a record, and each column is a field. Column titles are fieldnames, and the width of a column is its fieldwidth. The kind of information stored in a field is its fieldtype. The five distinct field types in dBASE are character, data, logical, memo, and numeric. These are described in detail in Chapter One.

Each database file can contain up to one billion records or two billion bytes. A record can contain up to 128 fields or 4,096 bytes. As each record is added to a database file it is assigned a record number. The database file contains a header which describes each of the fields. It also contains any number of data records (up to the limits of the system).

Database Memo (.DBT) Files

Each memo file is an auxiliary file to a database file of the same name. The file identifier must *always* be .DBT and the name must *always* match the database filename.

The memo file, which is created automatically, contains the contents of memo fields named within the database file.

Index (.NDX) Files

Index files allow records in a database file to be used in the alphabetical, chronological, or numeric order of a key, regardless of the physical order of the database records. These files translate the content of a key to a physical position in the database file, and provide direct access to the records by means of the key.

Each index key is limited to 100 characters. A key can be part of a field or can include parts or all of several fields, but the larger the key, the slower the indexing operation. To create an index to organize a database file, called CUSTOMER, alphabetically by the content of the field NAME, use:

. index on NAME to CUSTNAME

The command to use the existing index files CUSTNAME and ZIPCODE in conjunction with the database file CUSTOMER is:

. use CUSTOMER index CUSTNAME, ZIPCODE

Up to seven index files can be used simultaneously with a database file. The first file named controls the access to the database file. All open index files will be automatically updated whenever changes are made to the database file.

Program (.PRG) Files

Program files contain legitimate dBASE III PLUS command statements and nothing else. They are ASCII files and can contain only characters from the basic (not the extended) ASCII table in Appendix A. Program files can be created and modified by means of the internal dBASE III PLUS word processor (**modify command**) or with any external word processor that can work with ASCII files (most can).

Report Form (.FRM) Files

These are special files that are used by the **report** command to prepare formatted reports. Report form files are created by **create report** and changed by **modify report**. Unlike dBASE II report files, dBASE III PLUS report files are *not* ASCII files and they cannot be modified by a word processor.

Label Form (.LBL) Files

These are special files that are used by the **label** command to print mailing labels. Label form files are created by **create label** and changed by **modify label**. These label form files are not ASCII files.

Format (.FMT) Files

These are special files that produce custom screen forms for data entry. Format files, which are actually limited program files, may contain only three different dBASE III PLUS commands. They may be used only in conjunction with the **append**, **change**, and **edit** commands. These files may be created and changed by means of the internal screen editor **modify screen** or by any text editor.

Text Output (.TXT) Files

Text output files are ASCII files and contain only characters from the standard ASCII tables (see Appendix A). They can be read into a dBASE III PLUS database as a special form of the command **append** or can be created from a database by a special form of the command **copy**. In this context, they are used to transfer data between dBASE III PLUS and external files such as word processors and spreadsheets. They are also used to record dBASE processing, either from the keyboard in the query mode or from dBASE III PLUS programs.

Memory (.MEM) Files

These files are used to save dBASE III PLUS memory variables as a disk file. They are created by the command **save** and read back into memory by the command **restore**. Memory files are not ASCII files.

Other dBASE Disk Files

There are a number of other disk files that can be used by dBASE. These include Query (.QRY), View (.VUE), Catalog (.CAT), and Backup (.BAK) files. They can be valuable when using dBASE III PLUS in its interactive mode, but have little or no value in dBASE programming.

MEMORY VARIABLES

Memory variables provide the ability to store data items outside of the database file structure. These data items, which are normally stored temporarily in the computer's main memory and discarded upon exiting from dBASE, can be saved in memory (MEM) files.

As in all languages, memory variables let us assign a label (a name) to individual data items. Unlike most languages, dBASE has an informal technique for creating memory variables. All you have to do is assign a label (a name) to a data item. The data type and size are determined by the content of the variable. For example: To create a memory variable named NUMBER1 which contains the value 3, we use either of the following commands:

NUMBER1 = 3
store 3 to NUMBER1

There are four types of memory variables (datatypes): character, date, logical, and numeric. These are similar to the fieldtypes of the same names.

- Character variables contain letters, numbers, blank spaces, and symbols. The maximum size of a character variable is 254 bytes.
- Date variables contain only dates, which are are stored in the form MM/DD/YY.
- Logical variables are automatically one character wide. They can store only representations for True/False (.T. and .F.) or Yes/No (.Y. and .N.).
- Numeric variables are used to store numbers to be used in calculations. Numbers can be either integers or decimals.

Names for memory variables can contain up to ten characters, which can be letters, numbers, and underscores. They must begin with a letter. If a memory variable and a database field have the same name, the field takes precedence. The memory variable can be identified explicitly by using the symbol M-> in front of the variable name. For example, if a database has a field NAME and there is a memory variable NAME we can call the memory variable by:

M->NAME

This method is somewhat awkward. It's a lot easier to avoid using duplicate names. A simpler scheme is to add an additional letter such as an M to the beginning of a memory variable name, so that MNAME is the memory variable corresponding to a field NAME.

Memory variables can be either *public* (meaning global) or *private* (meaning local). Variables created within a program are PUBLIC to all programs called by (below) the originating program. They are not available to programs above the originating program. In this case, the variable is destroyed when the subroutine returns to the calling program. A variable may be declared public—in which case, it is available to all programs.

To hide a variable from a subroutine (and hence prevent conflict with a variable of the same name), declare the variable private upon entering the subroutine. Variables created within a program are automatically discarded when exiting the program unless they have been explicitly labeled as public.

WORK AREAS

dBASE III PLUS has ten independent work areas, which can each contain an open database file. This means you can have up to ten database files at any one time. The same database file cannot be open in two work areas at once.

Each work area can have up to seven open index files and a format file. The work area can also have an active record filter as well as a linkage to a database file that is currently in use in another work area. The total number of open files for all work areas together is limited to 15, although there are commercial programs which will allow you to increase this limit to 20.

Only the database in the currently selected work area can be directly repositioned. A file in another work area can be repositioned only when the second file has been linked to the active file and the active file is repositioned. The command to switch between work areas is **select**.

THE dBASE III PLUS LANGUAGE

The dBASE III PLUS language is composed of commands, functions, and operators. *Commands* are verbs, such as **count** and **display**, that can be tailored to a specific need by additional optional words and clauses. *Functions* are specialized tools to be used in conjunction with commands. For example, the **sqrt( )** function calculates the square root of a number. *Operators* allow you to perform other arithmetic as well as logical and relational operations.

Arithmetic Operators

dBASE III PLUS can perform the four basic arithmetic operations: addition, subtraction, multiplication, and division. Functions are also provided to perform higher-level math. Symbols used for the mathematics operators are:

+ addition	=	equal
− subtraction	#	not equal
* multiplication	< >	not equal
/ division	< =	less than or equal
< less than	> =	greater than or equal
> greater than	( )	parentheses for grouping
** exponentiation		

Logical Operators

dBASE III PLUS can handle the standard logical or Boolean operators:

.not.
.and.
.or.

The following command illustrates the .and. Boolean operator:

. display for ROOM="3" .and. GRADE="5"

This command displays all database records where the content of ROOM is 3 and the content of GRADE is 5.

String Operators

Three operators are provided to help with string manipulation:

- + Concatenation (joining)

  "alpha"+"bet" = "alphabet"

- − String concatenation with blanks moved to right

  " alpha "−"bet" = "alphabet "

- & Macro operator: substitutes contents of memory variable

FUNCTIONS

Functions, which are used only with commands, perform commonly-needed operations that would be difficult (if not impossible) to accomplish without them. Functions are provided to support programming in five areas: time and date, character string manipulation, math, character conversion, and to perform specialized tests. All functions end with parentheses, which may contain an argument.

Date and Time

cdow(Date( ))	Calendar day of the week (for example, Tuesday)
cmonth(Date( ))	Calendar month (for example, January)
ctod('01/01/85')	Character to date conversion
date( )	System Date in form mm/dd/yy
day(Date( ))	Day of the month
dow(Date( ))	Day of the week (for example, Tuesday = 3)
dtoc(Date( ))	Date to character conversion
month(Date( ))	Month of the year (for example, 1)
time( )	System time (HH:MM:SS)
year(Date( ))	Year of the date (for example, 1985)

Character String Manipulation

at(string1,string2)	Returns the starting position of string 1 in string 2
left(string,n)	Extracts the first n characters from the indicated string
lower('ALPHA')	Converts to lowercase (for example, alpha)
ltrim(string)	Removes leading blank spaces
replicate(character,n)	Reproduces a character n times
right(string,n)	Extracts the last n characters from the indicated string
space(n)	Produces n blank spaces

stuff(string1,*x*,*n*,string2)	Replace *n* characters in string 1 with string 2 beginning at position *x*
substr(string,*a*,*n*)	Extracts the *n* character substring beginning with character position *a* of the indicated string
trim(string)	Removes trailing blank spaces
upper('alpha')	Converts to uppercase (for example, ALPHA)

Mathematical Functions

abs(*x*)	Absolute value of *x*
exp(*x*)	Calculates the value e^x
int(*x*)	Discards decimal places from *x*
log(*x*)	Calculates the natural logarithm of *x*
max(*x*,*y*)	Returns the larger of *x* and *y*
min(*x*,*y*)	Returns the smaller of *x* and *y*
mod(*x*,*n*)	Returns the remainder of *x/n*
round(*x*,*n*)	Rounds *x* to *n* decimal places
sqrt(*x*)	Calculates the square root of *x*

Character Conversion

asc('L')	Returns the ASCII code value of a letter
chr(*n*)	Returns the character corresponding to the ASCII code *n*
str(*n*,*x*,*y*)	Converts a number *n* to a character string of length *x* having *y* decimal places. The value *y* is optional.
val('123')	Returns the numeric value of a string

Specialized Tests

bof( )	True if beginning of file
col( )	Screen column cursor position
deleted( )	True if deleted record
diskspace( )	Remaining space on disk (bytes)
eof( )	True if end of file
error( )	Returns numeric code for last error
file('filename')	True if file exists
found( )	True if last search command was successful
iiff(true exp,exp1,exp2)	Single line equivalent for **if** command
isalpha(character)	True if character is a letter
iscolor( )	True if graphics monitor
islower(character)	True if character is lowercase
isupper(character)	True if character is uppercase
len('string')	Returns length of character string

lupdate( )	Returns date of last update
message( )	Returns error message
pcol( )	Printer column position
prow( )	Printer row position
reccount( )	Number of records in database file
recno( )	Current database record number
recsize( )	Size of database record (bytes)
row( )	Screen row cursor position
type('memvar')	Data type of memory variable

COMMANDS

The commands can be grouped into a number of functional categories, as listed below. An individual command can belong to more than one category. The complete syntax of each dBASE III PLUS command is listed in Appendix B.

- Creating database files
- Creating other files
- Choosing databases
- Changing database files
- Sorting and indexing
- Extracting information
- Viewing data
- Data entry
- Positioning
- Programming support
- Memory variables
- General file operations
- Special function
- Processing parameters

Creating Databases

These commands are used to create new database files:

create
copy
copy file
import
join
sort
total

Only **create** can originate a completely new database. The remaining six commands create database files from existing databases.

Creating Other Files

These commands are used to create special-purpose, non-database files:

> **create report**
> **modify report**
> **modify file**
> **create label**
> **modify label**
> **create/modify view**
> **modify command**
> **create screen**
> **modify screen**
> **copy file**
> **index**
> **save**
> **create/modify query**
> **export**

Create and **modify** are identical commands when used with **report**, **label**, **screen**, **query**, and **view**.

Choosing Databases

Two commands are used to choose a database file:

> **use** *FILENAME*
> **select** *WORK AREA*

Use closes the active database file and opens the file named in the command. Up to ten database files can be open at any time, each in a separate dBASE III PLUS work area.

Select switches between work areas either by specifying the work area number or the ALIAS for the file open in the desired work area:

select 2

or

select EXAMPLE

Changing Databases

A database can be changed in two ways. The basic structure of the file can be altered or the content of existing records can be modified using the following commands:

Change Structure	Change Content
modify structure	browse
append	change
insert	edit
delete	read
recall	replace
pack	update

Commands to change structure:

Modify structure: Allows redefinition of existing file structure. Changes the fieldnames, fieldtypes, and fieldsizes.

Append: Adds records to the end of the database.

Insert: Inserts a record inside the database.

Delete: Marks a record for deletion.

Recall: Removes the record deletion mark (undeletes).

Pack: Removes all records marked for deletion and renumbers all remaining records.

Commands to change record content:

Browse: Full-screen editing window onto multiple records.

Change: Full-screen editing.

Edit: Full-screen editing.

Read: Full-screen editing; used with the **get** command to edit either fields or memory variables.

Replace: Direct replacement of field content.

Update: Batch updating of selected fields and records.

Sorting and Indexing

These commands sort or index database files:

> **sort**
> **index**
> **reindex**

Sort: Makes a copy of the database. The records in the copy have been sorted by one or more keys. The sort order can be alphabetical, numerical, or chronological for each key.

Index: Creates a file relating dBASE record numbers to a key. A database used with an index file appears to be sorted by the expression. Index files are used only in conjunction with database files.

Reindex: Reindexes any open index files in the active work area.

Extracting and Displaying Information

The following commands as well as the full screen editing commands **browse**, **change**, and **edit** can be used to extract and display data:

> **?**
> **??**
> **average**
> **count**
> **display**
> **label**
> **list**
> **report**
> **@ row,col . . . say**
> **@ row,col . . . get**
> **sum**

?: Displays specified data items. Used alone, the **?** displays a blank line.

??: Same as the **?** except the **??** does not issue a carriage return or a linefeed. Used to display data items beginning at the current position of the print head or the cursor.

Average: Averages contents of numeric fields or expressions involving fields.

Count: Counts database records.

Display: Displays all or part of the database, pausing after each screenful.

Label: Prepares labels from database content.

List: Displays all or part of the database without pausing.

Report: Prepares standardized reports on the content of a database.

@ Row,col . . . say: Displays items beginning at the named row and column.

@ Row,col . . . get: Displays a single field or memory variable at the named row and column. Items displayed with **get** can be edited by use of the **read** command.

Sum: Adds contents of fields or expressions involving fields.

Positioning Commands

The following commands are used to position the database:

find
seek
locate
continue
goto
skip

Find: Positions the database to the first location of a specified key field; uses an INDEX file to perform the positioning.

Seek: Positions the database to the first location of a specified key field; uses an INDEX file to perform the positioning.

Locate: Positions the database to first location of the specified parameter; does the positioning by means of a sequential file search.

Continue: Positions to the next occurrence of parameter specified in the last **locate**.

Goto: Positions the database directly to the specified record number.

Skip: Moves forward or backward a specified number of records. **Skip** is a relatively slow way to move as each record must be examined for deleted status.

Printing

Commands to route data to the printer or to aid in printing and print formatting are:

set print on/off
set printer to *device name*
set device to print/screen
set margin to *n*
eject

Data-Entry Commands

Commands that are normally used for data entry are:

accept
browse
change
edit
input
read
set format to
wait

Accept: Prompts a user to enter character data into a single memory variable.

Browse: Full-screen editing window onto multiple records.

Change: Full-screen editing.

Edit: Full-screen editing.

Input: Prompts a user to enter numeric or logical data into a single memory variable.

Read: Full-screen editing; used with the **get** command to edit either fields or memory variables.

Set format to: Calls up special screens to be used with **append**, **change**, **edit**, and **read**.

Wait: Prompts a user to enter a single keystroke into a one-character memory variable.

Programming Support

These commands are included in the language as programming constructs:

> **cancel**
> **do** *PROGRAM*
> **do** *PROGRAM* **with** *parameter*
> **do while** / **enddo**
> **do case** / **endcase**
> **exit**
> **if/endif**
> **loop**
> **note** or *
> **parameter**
> **return**

Cancel: Terminates programs in use; returns user to the keyboard.

Do: Executes a dBASE program.

Do with parameter: Calls a dBASE program and passes processing parameters.

Do case / **endcase:** Selects one of a set of choices.

Do while / **enddo:** Repeats the commands between the **do while** and the **enddo** as long as a condition remains true.

Exit: Escapes from a **do** loop.

If/endif: Executes the commands between the **if** and the **endif** if a condition is true. Can be used with an optional **else** clause: **if/else/endif**.

Loop: Loops back to the beginning of a **do** loop.

Note or *:** Comment lines.

Parameter: Assigns names to parameters passed by the calling program.

Return: Terminates the program in use; goes back to the calling program.

Memory Variables

These commands can store data directly into memory variables or are designed to manipulate memory variables:

> **accept**
> **average to**
> **call with**
> **clear all**
> **clear memory**
> **count to**
> **display memory**
> **input**
> **private**
> **public**
> **read**
> **release**
> **restore**
> **save**
> **store**
> **sum to**
> **wait**

Accept: Stores keyboard input of character data to a memory variable.

Average to: Saves the result of the averaging operation.

Call *PROGRAM* **with** *MEMVAR*: Calls the named assembly-language program and passes parameters to the program by means of a memory variable. Results are passed back to dBASE in the same variable.

Clear all: Closes all files and destroys all memory variables.

Clear memory: Destroys all memory variables.

Count to: Saves the result of the counting operation.

Display memory: Displays all memory variables.

Input: Stores keyboard input of numeric or logical data to a memory variable.

Private: Hides memory variables from a subroutine.

Public: Declares memory variables to be global.

Read: Allows full-screen data entry into memory variables displayed by means of @ . . . **get**.

Release: "Erases" memory variables.

Restore: Reads a disk file containing memory variables back into memory.

Save: Saves memory variables to a disk file.

Store: Stores an item as a memory variable.

Sum to: Saves the result of the summing operation.

Wait: Halts program execution until a key is pressed. Key value can be entered into memory.

Debugging Commands

These commands are of help when debugging dBASE III PLUS programs. Other kinds of help can be obtained from commercially-available programs—such as Ashton-Tate's *dBASE Programmer's Utilities*.

> **display history**
> **resume**
> **set debug on/off**
> **set dohistory on/off**
> **set echo on/off**
> **set history to**
> **set step on/off**
> **set talk on/off**
> **suspend**

Display history: Displays contents of history buffer—last executed commands.

Resume: Resumes program execution after temporary suspension with **suspend**.

Set debug: Routes debugging output to the printer.

Set dohistory: Turns on recording of command lines during program execution.

Set echo: Displays each command line as program executes.

Set history to: Sets the size of the command history.

Set step: Places program execution in a line-by-line mode.

Set talk: Displays response to each command.

Suspend: Suspends program execution.

General File Operation and Utilities

These commands provide information about files or operate on files:

> **copy file**
> **clear all**
> **close**
> **copy to**
> **dir**
> **display status**
> **display structure**

> **erase**
> **rename**
> **set alternate**
> **set catalog**

Copy file: Makes a duplicate copy of the named file. The file may not be open when copied.

Clear all: Resets dBASE. Closes all database files and support files and destroys all memory variables.

Close: Closes specified file types (e.g. **close alternate**).

Copy to: Use this variation of the copy command to transfer data from dBASE to Lotus® 1-2-3® and other programs.

Dir: Displays disk directory information.

Display status: Displays database files in use, index files used with the databases, the index keys, and the status of dBASE processing parameters.

Display structure: Displays the structure of the database file in use.

Erase: Allows you to delete a named file.

Rename: Changes name of specified file.

Set alternate: The **to** option lets you specify the name of the active alternate file. On/off toggles screen output (except for @ . . . **data**) to the named disk file. Alternate files have a .TXT file extension.

Set catalog: The **to** option specifies which catalog is to be used. If the specified catalog does not exist, it will be created. The **off** option allows you to create and use files without their being added to an open catalog. The **on** option adds new files to the open catalog.

Special Function Commands

> **call**
> **load**
> **quit**
> **text/endtext**

Call: Calls an assembly-language program.

Load: Loads an assembly-language program.

Quit: Exits from dBASE.

Text/endtext: Displays a block of text without delimiters.

dBASE III PLUS Processing Parameters

These are processing parameters that can be controlled by the user. Parameters take two forms: **set . . . to** or **set . . . on/off**. The **set . . to** parameters are not invoked unless the user takes a specific action. The **set . . . on/off** parameters are pre-set in dBASE III PLUS. The pre-set, or *default*, value is in capital letters in the description below:

Set alternate on/OFF: Toggles on and off output directed to the alternate file.

Set alternate to: Saves screen output to named disk file.

Set bell on/OFF: Turns warning bell on and off.

Set carry on/OFF: Writes content of last entered record into new record during **append**. Useful when there is little change from record to record.

Set catalog ON/off: Turns the cataloging function on and off.

Set catalog to: Selects the specified catalog.

Set century on/OFF: Toggles display of century years on and off.

Set color to: Sets screen attributes.

Set confirm on/OFF: Normal operation is to move automatically to the next item in full-screen entry. Confirm requires a **Return** to advance an item.

Set console ON/off: Stops display of data on the terminal.

Set date: Selects date format.

Set debug on/OFF: Routes command lines and control lines from **set step ON** to a printer. Used when debugging programs with full-screen operations.

Set decimals to: Controls the number of decimal places that are normally displayed for the results of calculations.

Set default to: Allows setting of default disk drive which is different from the logged drive.

Set deleted on/OFF: Hides deleted records.

Set delimiters on/OFF: Turns special screen delimiters on and off.

Set delimiters to: Permits specification of characters to delimit full-screen video data areas.

Set device to: Switches @ . . . **say** output between screen and printer.

Set dohistory on/OFF: Enables recording of commands issued by dBASE programs.

Set echo on/OFF: Displays command lines from programs.

Set escape ON/off: Prevents use of the escape key to abort a command or program.

Set exact on/OFF: The equal sign in character-string comparisons normally means *begins with*. This command forces a complete and exact equality.

Set fields on/OFF: Activates or deactivates field list selected with **set fields to**.

Set fields to: Only specified fields can be accessed.

Set filter to: Hides database records that do not meet the filter specifications.

Set fixed on/OFF: Determines whether or not the number of decimal places displayed after a calculation is a fixed number.

Set format to: Allows selection of format files for full-screen editing.

Set function n to: Allows the assignment of character sequences to specified function keys.

Set heading ON/off: Turns on and off normal display of column headings in **display**, **list**, **sum**, and so on.

Set help ON/off: Determines whether or not a user will be offered help from the file HELP.DBS upon error.

Set history ON/off: Turns recording of keyboard commands on and off.

Set history to: Specify the number of commands to be recorded.

Set index to: Allows selection of index files.

Set intensity ON/off: Toggles reverse video on and off.

Set margin to: Sets the left print margin.

Set memowidth to: Sets the size for displaying memo field data.

Set menu ON/off: Determines whether or not the help menus of key assignments will be shown for full-screen commands.

Set message to: Displays the specified message at the bottom of the screen.

Set order to: Change the controlling index without opening and closing index files.

Set path to: Allows specification of directories to be searched for a file.

Set print on/OFF: Turns the printer on and off.

Set printer to: Routes printed output to a specified device (LPT1, LPT2, COM1, COM2).

Set procedure to: Opens the named procedure file.

Set relation to: Specifies how two database files are to be linked.

Set safety ON/off: Determines whether or not a user will be warned about possible destruction of data as a result of a command.

Set scoreboard ON/off: Determines whether dBASE III PLUS status messages appear on the top line of the screen (the status line).

Set status on/OFF: Enables display of status bar on line 22.

Set step on/OFF: Allows you to step through a program one command line at a time.

Set talk ON/off: Toggles normal dBASE III PLUS response to commands on and off.

Set title ON/off: Enables prompting for catalog title.

Set typeahead to n: Specifies the size of the typeahead buffer.

Set unique on/OFF: Determines whether or not records with duplicate keys will be included in an index file.

Set view to: Opens the specified view file.

This overview of the tools with which we will be working has been brief. To recap, the dBASE III PLUS toolkit consists of the various dBASE files and the command language, which is made up of commands, functions, and operators. Functions and operators are used in conjunction with commands to specify exactly what we want dBASE to do. This can all be put together in a variety of ways. See Appendix B for a complete listing of the dBASE III PLUS functions, operators, and commands.

CHAPTER THREE
Beginning to Program

If you're new to programming, you will find that it's not really difficult—"even a grown-up can learn to do it." If you are already familiar with the fundamentals of programming with dBASE III PLUS, skip this chapter and move on to Chapter Four.

Suppose you have a database that contains information about students in grades 1 through 6. This database, which we'll call SCHOOL, has a number of fields. One of the fields is the student's grade, which we'll call GRADE. From time to time we need a count of the students in each of the six grade levels. One way of counting the students is to use the **count** command directly from the keyboard, as in Figure 3–1.

```
. use SCHOOL
. count for GRADE='1'
      78 records
. count for GRADE='2'
      81 records
. count for GRADE='3'
      79 records
. count for GRADE='4'
      74 records
. count for GRADE='5'
      80 records
. count for GRADE='6'
      81 records
```

Figure 3–1: Example of dBASE count command.

A simple program for counting students is shown in Figure 3–2. This program consists of exactly the same commands that you used when performing this task from the keyboard. The big difference is that with a program you do the typing only once. After that you get your tabulation by telling dBASE to use the program. If your program name is COUNTER, you have dBASE run this program with

. do COUNTER

To write the program, enter **modify command** at the dot prompt. dBASE will ask you for a filename. Programs are disk files. All disk files need filenames. Your program name can consist of letters and numbers. It can be up to eight characters long, and it cannot contain embedded blank spaces.

. modify command
Enter the filename: COUNTER

```
use SCHOOL
count for GRADE='1'
count for GRADE='2'
count for GRADE='3'
count for GRADE='4'
count for GRADE='5'
count for GRADE='6'
```

Figure 3–2: Example of simple counting program: COUNTER.

dBASE adds the four-character extension .PRG to the filename. The .PRG file extension indicates that this disk file is a program.

When you have entered the filename, press the **Return** key. The screen will clear. Write your program by typing in the commands one line at a time. Do not type in dots to simulate the dot prompt. If you make a mistake, use the arrow keys to move the cursor to the error and retype. Press **Ctrl-End** when you are finished. This step saves the program on the disk.

In its standard keyboard mode, dBASE III PLUS conducts a dialogue with you. You type in a command, it displays a response. Both the command and the response are visible on the screen. However, when you run a program, the commands are not displayed—only the responses are. The computer execution of the sample program appears in Figure 3–3.

```
.do counter
    78 records
    81 records
    79 records
    74 records
    80 records
    81 records
```

Figure 3–3: Execution of COUNTER program.

To view your commands as they are executed in a program, use the additional command **set echo on**. This command tells dBASE to display the command on the screen. Once echo is set on, dBASE will echo all commands (including those from the keyboard). At the end of your program use **set echo off**. Figure 3–4 incorporates the **set echo on/off** command. The result of this program appears in Figure 3–5.

Echo is one of many processing parameters that can be controlled by means of the **set** command. **Set echo on** is most often used for debugging (finding and fixing errors in) programs. There are better ways to label the results of a command.

Memory variables (memvars) provide one of the better ways. dBASE allows you to store up to 256 items (memory variables) in the computer's main memory at any

```
set echo on
use SCHOOL
count for GRADE='1'
count for GRADE='2'
count for GRADE='3'
count for GRADE='4'
count for GRADE='5'
count for GRADE='6'
set echo off
```

Figure 3–4: First revision of COUNTER program.

```
count for GRADE='1'
    78 records
count for GRADE='2'
    81 records
count for GRADE='3'
    79 records
count for GRADE='4'
    74 records
count for GRADE='5'
    80 records
count for GRADE='6'
    81 records
```

Figure 3–5: Response of modified COUNTER program.

one time. These memory variables are stored temporarily; they are forgotten (discarded) when you leave dBASE. You can store numbers, dates, and text in memory variables. Commands that can be used to create and store data in memory variables include **average**, **count**, **store**, and **sum**. For example, you can store the number 275 to the memory variable SIZE with

. store 275 to SIZE

dBASE III PLUS takes your variable and squirrels it away somewhere in memory. You can retrieve this variable and use it simply by employing its name. The rules for memory variable names are the same as for fieldnames: They can contain up to ten letters, numbers, and underscores; they must begin with a letter. If a database field and a memory variable have the same name, dBASE will assume you want the field.

Figure 3–4 showed you how to display commands from a program with **set echo on**. Figure 3–6 demonstrates how to do the reverse and turn off the dBASE conversation mode. To tell dBASE to "shut up," use **set talk off**. This command turns off the conversational mode. Once talk is off, dBASE produces displays only with commands that are provided for that purpose. Remember to set talk on again when you return to the interactive mode.

Figure 3–6 saves the result of each counting command in a memory variable. The content of each variable is displayed, along with a text label, by the **?** command. The result that is produced by this program is shown as Figure 3–7.

```
set talk off
use SCHOOL
count for GRADE='1' to GRADE1
count for GRADE='2' to GRADE2
count for GRADE='3' to GRADE3
count for GRADE='4' to GRADE4
count for GRADE='5' to GRADE5
count for GRADE='6' to GRADE6
? GRADE1, 'IN GRADE1'
? GRADE2, 'IN GRADE2'
? GRADE3, 'IN GRADE3'
? GRADE4, 'IN GRADE4'
? GRADE5, 'IN GRADE5'
? GRADE6, 'IN GRADE6'
set talk on
```

Figure 3–6: Counting program with set talk off.

```
.do COUNTER
      78 IN GRADE 1
      81 IN GRADE 2
      79 IN GRADE 3
      74 IN GRADE 4
      80 IN GRADE 5
      81 IN GRADE 6
```

Figure 3–7: Response of counting program with set talk off.

One thing to bear in mind when designing programs is speed of access to the records. Each time we count the students in a grade, dBASE has to read our entire database. In the programs in Figures 3–2, 3–4, and 3–6, the database is read six times—once for each grade. If a database is large, reading it can take some time. The time required depends on the size of the database and the specific computer system. Computers with hard disks will read the same size database considerably faster than computers with only floppy disks—usually about ten times faster.

Suppose we have a 160,000-byte database and a computer system that reads the database at 1600 characters per second. Counting the students in a grade takes 100 seconds. Counting the students in all six grades takes ten minutes.

Whether ten minutes is good or bad depends on how often one wants to count the students. If it's only once or twice, we'll accept the ten minutes and let it go at that. But, if we want a class count more often, we will want the result much faster. We can do our counting on a single pass through the data.

If our database is sorted by GRADE or if it has been indexed on GRADE, we can make use of the arrangement of the data to speed up our program. (You probably won't save time—unless the database is already sorted or indexed—because sorting and indexing take time.)

The program in Figure 3–8 produces the same result as the program in Figure 3–6: the response in Figure 3–7. All the records for each grade are grouped together. We take advantage of the record grouping by using **while** instead of **for** in each counting command. The **while** condition starts with the current record and processes only as long as the content of the database matches the **while** condition. By counting in this way, we process each student's record only one time, as opposed to six times—when the **for** clause was used.

```
set talk off
use SCHOOL index GRADE
count while GRADE = '1' to GRADE1
count while GRADE = '2' to GRADE2
count while GRADE = '3' to GRADE3
count while GRADE = '4' to GRADE4
count while GRADE = '5' to GRADE5
count while GRADE = '6' to GRADE6
? GRADE1,'IN GRADE1'
? GRADE2,'IN GRADE2'
? GRADE3,'IN GRADE3'
? GRADE4,'IN GRADE4'
? GRADE5,'IN GRADE5'
? GRADE6,'IN GRADE6'
set talk on
```

Figure 3–8: Counting from indexed database file.

INDEXING

When we use an indexed file (as in Figure 3–8), each individual operation will be slower than if the file were not indexed—because we access the records in a "logical" sequence. This sequence is different from the physical arrangement of the records on the disk, resulting in more movement of the disk head (hence slower operation). Sequential operations like counting can be much faster in a sorted file than in an indexed file.

There are two basic kinds of database access: sequential and direct. In *sequential access*, we leaf through the database a record at a time. Most of the high-level commands in dBASE III PLUS (**list**, **count**, **sum**, and so on) operate sequentially. *Direct access* allows us to go directly to any record—provided we know which record we want to go to.

PROCEDURAL AND NON-PROCEDURAL PROGRAMMING

The first programs in this chapter were non-procedural. We simply told the computer what we wanted and it figured out how to do it. As we have progressed, we have become more concerned with how we do things, and the programs have become much more procedural. The next example of counting the students is entirely procedural: We tell it *how* to count; not just *what* to count. The basic tools are **do while/enddo** and **if/endif**. These are sometimes called *programming constructs*. To truly customize an application, we nearly always need to write programs that are some combination of procedural and non-procedural.

The construct **do while/enddo** causes the commands between **do while** and **enddo** to be repeated as long as the expression after the **do while** is true. The construct **if/endif** causes the commands between the **if** and the **endif** to be executed only when the expression after the **if** is true.

The program in Figure 3–9 examines every record in the database one record at a time. It does not require any special ordering of the database records. The GRADE field is examined and the content of the appropriate memory variable is increased by one. Then the database record pointer is advanced to the next record (**skip**) and the process is repeated. When we run out of records, the process is halted and we generate the display. The term **eof( )** after **do while** becomes true when the end of the database is reached.

The program sets the initial value of the variables GRADE1 through GRADE6 to zero. Once a variable has a value, you can add to it. The expression used after the **if**, GRADE='n', compares the content of the field GRADE with the grade of interest. In the context of this program, count for GRADE='1' is equivalent to:

```
do while .not. eof( )
   if GRADE='1'
     store GRADE1 + 1 to GRADE1
   endif
   skip
enddo
? GRADE1
```

Writing programs is a matter of putting commands together to solve problems, and complicated problems can usually be solved by breaking them down into several simple problems. Difficulties encountered in programming solutions to complex problems usually have little to do with the complexity of programming, but rather with our grasp of the problem itself.

Quite often there are any number of possible programming solutions to any particular problem. The approach selected is often a matter of personal choice. Other factors governing the selection of an approach might include the number of times the program will be used, who the program is for, and the need for program speed.

```
set talk off
use SCHOOL
store 0 to GRADE1,GRADE2,GRADE3,GRADE4,GRADE5,GRADE6
do while .not. eof()
        if GRADE= '1'
           store GRADE1+1 to Grade1
        endif
        if GRADE= '2'
           store GRADE2+1 to Grade2
        endif
        if GRADE= '3'
           store GRADE3+1 to Grade3
        endif
        if GRADE= '4'
           store GRADE4+1 to Grade4
        endif
        if GRADE= '5'
           store GRADE5+1 to Grade5
        endif
        if GRADE= '6'
           store GRADE6+1 to Grade6
        endif
        skip
enddo
? GRADE1, 'IN GRADE1'
? GRADE2, 'IN GRADE2'
? GRADE3, 'IN GRADE3'
? GRADE4, 'IN GRADE4'
? GRADE5, 'IN GRADE5'
? GRADE6, 'IN GRADE6'
set talk on
```

Figure 3–9: Procedural approach to counting problem.

New programmers should not worry about writing so-called elegant programs. There is no better program than one that works. There is an old story about a consultant who visited a corporation that was having problems with a major computer software system. On the way home, the solution to the problem came to the consultant. The consultant called the chief programmer at the corporation and explained the solution. The solution required that the software be rewritten in a manner different from that which the corporation had been using. The chief programmer countered with a list of reasons why their existing program was "Better" than the one the consultant was suggesting. The consultant listened to all of this and replied, "But mine works."

SECTION TWO

Business Applications

CHAPTER FOUR
A Business Example

Let's develop a set of programs for a hypothetical small business. These programs will demonstrate the dBASE III PLUS language in a practical context. The discussion of the programs will cover design considerations, coding, and style. All of the dBASE III PLUS programming tools will be used at least once; some of the tools will be used over and over again. As we proceed, basic patterns for the structure of dBASE programs will become apparent. Look at these examples on two levels: first, as a solution to the specific business problem; then, as a solution to a generic problem.

For the next several chapters, we will pretend to be a small book distributor who buys books from publishers and resells them to book stores. Much of the day-to-day activity of our book business has to do with record keeping for a variety of purposes. The "business systems" for which we keep records include:

- Customer files
- Mailing lists and labels
- Inventory management
- Sales order entry
- Order fulfillment and invoicing
- Payments received
- Accounts receivable

ABOUT PROGRAMS

A program is a disk file that contains only legitimate dBASE commands. The program name is its disk filename. The program name should end with the file extension .PRG, which tells dBASE that it is a program. You can write (or edit) a program from within dBASE III PLUS by using the command **modify command** followed by the program name. To create (or change) the program MENU.PRG, use:

. modify command MENU

The screen will clear and you will be in dBASE's built-in word processor.

dBASE Word Processor

Enter your commands, a line at a time. When finished, press **Ctrl-End** to save the file. To abort editing, press **Esc**. dBASE assumes the file ends with the .PRG extension and automatically adds the extension to the name. Incidentally, you can use the dBASE III PLUS editor for creating or changing other text files by adding the file extension yourself:

. modify command MENU.TXT

dBASE programs are ASCII files. You can write or edit a dBASE program by using an external word processor or text editor only if the editor has a mode (usually called a non-document mode) for editing ASCII files. Many editors add hidden characters to a file for the editor's own use in formatting and processing the file. dBASE doesn't tolerate these extra characters. If you do use an external editor, consult the editor's user manual to make sure that you are using the correct mode.

You can call a dBASE program from within dBASE by using the **do** command from either the dBASE prompt or from within a program. To have dBASE execute the program MENU, use

. do MENU

You can execute a dBASE program from the operating system only by calling the command file in conjunction with calling dBASE.

A> dBASE MENU

You can have dBASE III PLUS always execute a specific program at start up by including the statement

command = do *PROGRAM NAME*

in the CONFIG.DB file.

Your program does not have to end in the .PRG extension. You can actually choose any file extension that you wish. However, if the extension is not .PRG, you must enter the complete filename when referring to the file. For example, you might want to have two versions of a program. One version is a working operational program, the other is a new version that is being developed. To have dBASE run the new version (MENU.NEW), use:

. do MENU.NEW

Naming Your Programs

It's good practice to name your programs so that you can easily identify the software system to which they belong. This method will help you manage your disk directory. Disk directories can contain an enormous number of filenames. By following a method for naming files, you can more easily determine which files belong and which files are just excess baggage.

We're going to name our main menu program MENU. Programs that are called from this menu will be named MENU1, MENU2, and so on. Programs called from a submenu will be similarly tagged. For example, programs called from MENU1 will be named MENU11, MENU12, and so on. Programs subordinate to a menu selection will be named with the calling program name followed by a letter. For example,

MENU36 may call the programs MENU36A, MENU36B, and so forth. Figure 4–1 shows a diagram of our program names. The letters S and P indicate screen formats and print formats respectively. MENU1S is a screen program used with programs called from MENU1. Finally, the name SETUP is used for initialization programs.

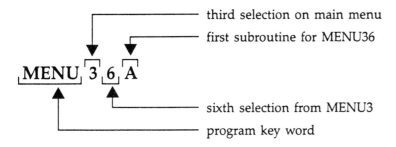

Figure 4–1: Diagram of program names.

In chapters to follow, we will develop the sections of the business system in the order that they appear on the main menu. This procedure allows us to develop the simplest items first. It also allows us to do our development in a natural order. For example, we will need the CUSTOMER file and the INVENTORY file before we can develop Sales Order Entry.

When we write programs, or have them written for us, we must begin with a clear idea of what we want the programs to do. Only then can we develop and customize the software to meet our exact needs. It takes time and effort to develop good software. This time and effort is justified only if the programs are useful and increase the efficiency of the people who use them.

We're going to implement software to do the record keeping for each of these business systems. The approach we're going to take is called *structured programming*. This method uses a system of small, simple modules that together perform the needed functions. Each module is a program that does one part of the overall job. The modular approach allows you to build a system one piece at a time. It has the added advantage of making it easy to make changes to the system.

We're going to start at the top and work our way down. This is commonly called top-down design. I'm always amazed when people find it necessary to codify common sense. The starting point is to develop a program to display the list of business systems and provide a way to choose which of the systems we want to work with. This is a menu program.

The menu program serves to tie all of the individual programs together into a single coherent package: a menu system. A diagram of a simple menu system is shown as Figure 4–2. NASA-sponsored studies have shown that the best menu designs have between five and nine items on a menu. This doesn't mean that you should add menu items if you have less than five or delete items if you have more than nine; it just means that you should think about what you are doing. Design your system to work with people. Think about how these people will react to your displays.

You might also think about the software that you didn't like to use yourself.

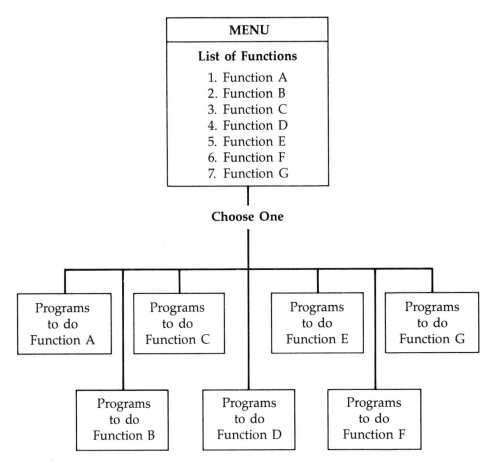

Figure 4–2: Diagram of simple menu system.

When there are a lot of selections, creating a main menu is useful. A main menu is a "menu of menus." This approach is our choice for the bookseller's system. A diagram of this menu system is shown in Figure 4–3. This diagram resembles an organization chart. This system is called a hierarchical system because it uses programs that are arranged in a hierarchy, that is, a ranked series. The principal advantage of a hierarchical system is that it is simple and direct. It is easy to add (and delete) programs in a hierarchical system.

In the hierarchical menu, you can move along a path that connects the programs in the hierarchy. For example, if Menu 2, the Customer File Menu, is selected, you will be presented with a list of the functions that can be performed from that menu. When an item is chosen, we are actually calling a program to perform the task—such as adding new records to a customer database.

A hierarchical menu system does not allow you to go directly from a program in the Customer File Menu to one in the Sales Order Menu. When you finish using

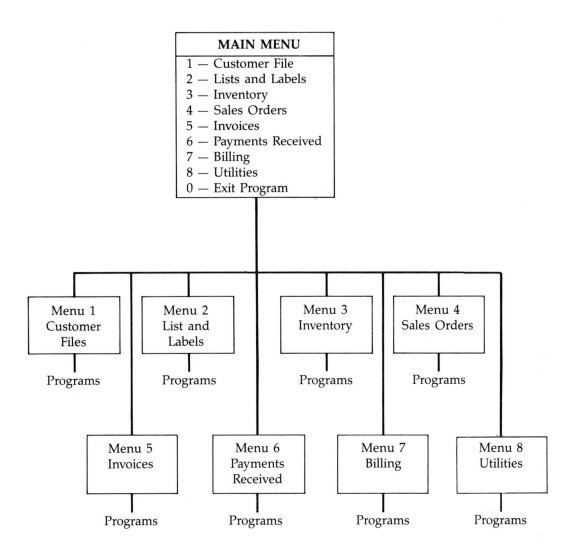

Figure 4–3: Book distributor's menu system.

a program, you are automatically returned to the menu from which the program was selected. To select a program from another menu, you must return first to the main menu, select the menu that contains the program you want, and then select the desired program from the submenu.

The advantage of using a menu system is apparent: It provides a way of remembering which program, out of all of the programs on the disk, is the particular one we want to use. It also indirectly documents your software system. A properly-designed menu-driven system allows a user to perform complex tasks on the computer with very little training. If you do your job right, the user will look on your menu as a natural way to work with the computer.

Let's begin the actual programming of the main menu and the submenus. When we bring up our main menu program, we wish the screen display to resemble Figure 4-4. Our next step is to develop a program to provide this display—as well as the means for a user to select an item from the display. The program shown in Figure 4-5 will do it.

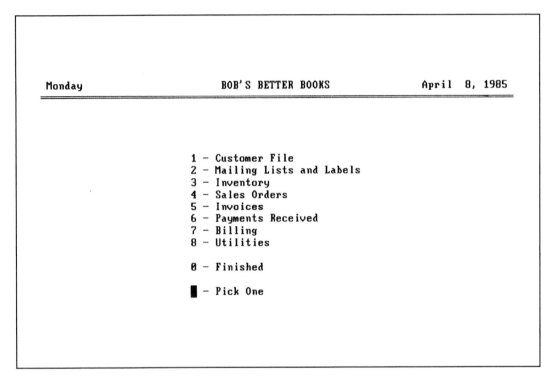

Figure 4-4: Screen display for main menu.

THE MAIN MENU PROGRAM

Let's take a look at this program. As it stands, the program is brief. That's good. Try to keep each of your programs to less than a page. Use as many subprograms as you need. This makes it easier to understand your program.

There are three parts to most programs: the initialization (setup), the main body of the program, and the program shutdown. In this program the initialization is accomplished by the commands that occur before the statement **do while**. The main body of the program lies between **do while** and **enddo**. The program shutdown in this case consists of the single command **quit**. Now, let's look at the commands.

The asterisk (*)

Lines beginning with the asterisk are non-executable statements. Use the * to insert comments into programs. Many programmers make a big production out of com-

```
* MENU.PRG - - main menu program for bookstore 10/1/86
set default to C
set path to C:\BOOK\PROGRAMS, C:\BOOK\DATA
do SETUP
do while .T.
   clear
   @  2,2  say cdow(date())
   @  2,26 say "BOB'S BETTER BOOKS"
   @  2,78 - len(CDATE) say CDATE
   @  3,1  say BAR

   @  8,26 say '1 - Customer File'
   @  9,26 say '2 - Mailing Lists and Labels'
   @ 10,26 say '3 - Inventory'
   @ 11,26 say '4 - Sales Orders'
   @ 12,26 say '5 - Invoices '
   @ 13,26 say '6 - Payments Received'
   @ 14,26 say '7 - Billing'
   @ 15,26 say '8 - Utilities'
   @ 17,26 say '0 - Finished '
   @ 19,26 say '  - Pick One'

   CHOICE = ' '
   do while .not. CHOICE $ '01234567'
      @ 19,26 get CHOICE
      read
   enddo

   if CHOICE = '0'
      quit             && use cancel till program set is complete
   endif               && then change to quit if desired

   do MENU&CHOICE

enddo
```

Figure 4–5: Main menu program.

menting programs. Unfortunately, most program comments merely state the obvious and serve only to clutter up the program code. Embedded comments make it harder for you to read the code.

Don't comment on the obvious. Save your comments for the tricky stuff. Don't put your comments in the middle of the program. Group them at the beginning or the end. Do add a comment that contains the filename and the date you changed or created the file. You'll find this useful when you find a printout of code and haven't the foggiest idea of what it is or when it was valid.

Set default to C:

dBASE III PLUS can be on a disk drive other than the one that contains your program. **Set default** tells dBASE to assume that the files you use are on the named drive (in this case, the C drive) unless a drive identifier is included in the filename.

This command is one of the many **set** commands that control dBASE processing parameters. The status of these processing parameters, as well as status information on the open databases and associated index files in the various work areas, can be displayed with the command **display status**.

Set path to C:\BOOK\PROGRAMS, C:\BOOK\DATA

Set path tells dBASE to search the specified directories (in order) if a file is not found on the working directory (that is, the directory you are using). Your operating system uses a hierarchical directory system. A representative directory system is shown as Figure 4–6. A disk directory can contain both files and subdirectories. The top-most directory is called the root and is designated by the backslash (\). This is normally the directory you end up in when you start up your computer. You do not need to use subdirectories for this or any other program.

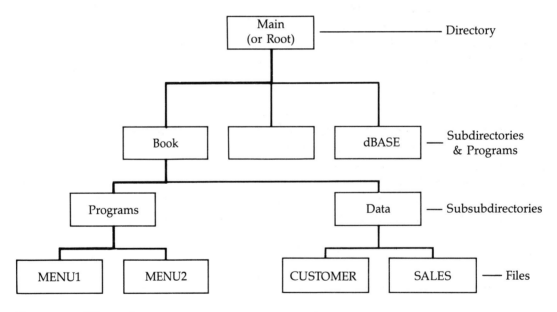

Figure 4–6: Directories.

However, subdirectories can help you manage your disk files. If you have a large number of disk files, you would benefit by organizing your disk into subdirectories. Subdirectories are created from the operating system with the **mkdir** command. To create the directories BOOK\PROGRAMS and BOOK\DATA, use the DOS commands:

```
mkdir \ BOOK
mkdir \ BOOK \ PROGRAMS
mkdir \ BOOK \ DATA
```

To write programs that are to be contained in \BOOK\PROGRAMS, use

. modify command \ BOOK \ PROGRAMS \ *PROGRAM NAME*

The subdirectory names are pathnames. Pathnames beginning with a slash are absolute pathnames; they trace a path from the root directory. Pathnames without the starting slash are relative and trace a path from the current directory.

Place default and path statements at the beginning of your software system. This gives you the opportunity to place all of your files in convenient locations and to relocate these files without the need to change disk and path identifiers throughout your programs. This makes your program much more maintainable. On the other hand, you can pick up program speed by specifying the complete pathname (that is, \BOOK\PROGRAMS\MENU) for each file in your program.

Do SETUP

Complete the system setup with the program SETUP. This program is shown as Figure 4-7. We could include all of the items in the setup file as program statements in the program menu. I prefer using a separate setup file in most cases. Use this file to open your database files and their associated index and format files, set your processing parameters, and declare all of your system memory variables.

Do while .T.

The commands between a **do while** and its companion **enddo** are repeated as long as the expression following **do while** is true. The .T. is a logical True and is always true. The command we have used really means *do forever*. **Do while/enddo** is usually referred to as a **do** loop. In this program there are two **do** loops: an outer and an inner. **Do** loops cannot cross. Note that we have added a comment after the last **endif**. You can add text on the lines containing **endif** and **enddo**—after the command.

Clear

This command erases the screen.

@ . . . Say . . .

The lines beginning with @ . . . **say** display the item following the word **say** on the screen. The numbers following the @ symbol are the screen row and column positions for the item. There are 24 usable rows on your screen (numbered 0–23). Avoid using row 0. dBASE III PLUS uses row 0 for many status messages. There are 80 columns on your screen (numbered 0–79). When more than one item is to be displayed with a single @ . . . **say**, the items must all be of the character data

```
* Setup.prg   Initialization for Menu.prg          01/15/85

clear
? 'loading initial databases'

clear all

set bell off
set device to screen
set escape off
set function 2  to chr(0)
set function 3  to chr(0)
set function 4  to chr(0)
set function 5  to chr(0)
set function 6  to chr(0)
set function 7  to chr(0)
set function 8  to chr(0)
set function 9  to chr(0)
set function 10 to chr(0)
set help off
set margin to 10
set menus on
set procedure to MENUPROC
set safety off
set status off
set talk off


select 1
     use CUSTOMER index CUSTID,CUSTNAME
select 2
     use CONTROLS
select 3
     use INV index ISBN alias INVENTORY

public ANSWER, BAR, BELL, CDATE, CHOICE, INKEY

A     = date()
BAR   = replicate(chr(205),78)
BELL  = chr(7)
CDATE = cmonth(A) + str(day(A),3)+','+str(year(A),5)
store space(1) to ANSWER, CHOICE
```

Figure 4–7: SETUP.PRG.

type and are concatenated (connected by + signs). The first four lines beginning with the @ . . . **say** are used to display the page heading.

Date( )

This is the system date expressed as mm/dd/yy. It has a date data type. In this set of programs we have assumed that your computer has a clock/calendar. If you are going to use your computer for serious business purposes and you do not have a clock/calendar, go out and buy one. Many business transactions depend upon the proper date stamp.

Cdow(date( ))

The **cdow( )** function is used to output the calendar day of the week (for example, Monday) for a date. The item included within the parentheses is called an *argument*. The argument with the **cdow( )** function must be a date variable.

"BOB'S BETTER BOOKS"

Note that single quotes enclose all other text (character strings) that are displayed in this program. Double quotes were used in this case to allow the display of a single quote (the apostrophe in Bob's).

78 – len(CDATE) say CDATE

First of all, the variable CDATE was created in the program SETUP. This variable contains a calendar date in the form January 20, 1985. We want the right edge of this variable (the 5 in 1985) to be positioned on screen column 77. The number of characters in CDATE will vary with the month and day of the year. To display this date in its proper position we need to know how many characters are in the variable CDATE. We get this number with the **len( )** function. The display position of CDATE is then column 78 minus the number of characters in CDATE (**len(CDATE)**).

@ 3,1 say BAR

We want to draw a double line under the title. This is accomplished by displaying the variable BAR, which is created in the program setup.

CHOICE = ' '

This command creates a memory variable named CHOICE and stores a single blank space in it. CHOICE is a character variable. An alternate statement is **store ' ' to CHOICE**.

Do while .not. CHOICE $ '01234567'

This **do** loop prevents the program from accepting an entry for which there is no corresponding menu item. You could translate this code as: "Do the following until the contents of the variable CHOICE are contained in the character sequence 01234567." This is equivalent to saying:

do while .not. (CHOICE='O' .or. CHOICE='1'... CHOICE='7')

Which one do you prefer?

@ row,column get CHOICE

This command is similar to the @ . . . **say** command. It is used to display a memory variable or a data field directly on the screen at the specified row and column. The display created by a **get** is in reverse video.

Read

This command places the cursor at the beginning of the first item displayed with the **get** command—here, the variable CHOICE. This allows you to type directly into the variable from the keyboard. Only printable characters can actually be entered into the variable from the keyboard. dBASE may act on control characters but filters them and prevents their actually becoming a part of the variable. The **read** command will cause the program to pause at this point until the user makes a keyboard entry.

Quit

Quit closes open files of all types and executes an orderly exit from dBASE III PLUS. While you are developing the program, substitute the command **cancel**. The **cancel** command aborts all programs in process and returns control to the keyboard.

```
if CHOICE = '0'
  quit
endif
```

The **if** command is sometimes referred to as a switch. It executes the commands between **if** and **endif** only when the expression following the word **if** is True. The expression in this example is CHOICE='0'. If the variable CHOICE contains a 0, we want the computer to execute all of the instructions to the **endif**.

The zero is contained within delimiters. This is because our variable CHOICE is a character string; entering a number doesn't change the variable type. A number can be either a character or a number, but we need to tell the computer which it is.

Usually, you would add an **if/endif** for each of the menu possibilities. There would be a whole sequence of **ifs**, each of which would look like:

```
if CHOICE='1'
  do MENU1
endif
  .
  .
  .
if CHOICE='7'
  do MENU7
endif
```

The program would examine each **if** sequentially until a condition was satisfied. Then the commands inside the **if/endif** would be executed. When finished, the program would continue to check **ifs** until the **enddo** was reached. We've used a much less cumbersome approach to select a program.

Do MENU&CHOICE

dBASE interprets the characters following a command, such as **do**, literally. We use the ampersand (&) to tell dBASE to substitute the contents of a memory variable instead. For example, if the variable CHOICE contained the character 1, dBASE would interpret this command as **do MENU1**. This procedure is called *macro substitution*.

This scheme works because of the clever structure that we have given to the filenames. If we had used the more common (and casual) approach to naming the programs (ADDCUST, EDITCUST, or ADDINV), we would have been forced to use either cascaded **ifs** or **do cases**. It is important that the **do MENU&CHOICE** statement follow the block of commands beginning with **if**. Were the positions reversed, we would get an error message when the zero was selected (there is no file named MENU0).

> **Note:** This scheme works only if your program is going to be used with the dBASE interpreter. If you will be compiling your program or using the dBASE RunTime™ products (see Chapter Seventeen), you must use the more conventional **do case**, in which you must explicitly identify each possible action. You'll need to take similar action for each menu program in this book.

THE SETUP PROGRAM

Let's take a look at the SETUP program. We first clear the screen, then display the message: loading initial databases. Next, we close all open databases and associated files (if any) and release all memory variables (if any). Then we set all of the dBASE processing parameters to the desired states. After that, we select the database files and indexes that are to be used initially. Finally, we create those memory variables that will be used throughout the system. When using a large number of **set** commands, it is good practice to arrange them in alphabetical order.

? 'loading initial databases'

The **?** command is a display command. It can be used to display any legitimate dBASE III PLUS expression. Expressions can consist of fields, memory variables, and text. Text, such as "loading initial databases" must be enclosed in quotes. The quotes may be either single or double, but remember to use the same one to close the character sequence as you did to open it. If you are opening several databases and their index files, there can be a prolonged hesitation. Sending little messages like this one reassures the user that something is actually going on.

Clear all

This command sets dBASE III PLUS to the state that existed when dBASE was first entered. All database files are closed and their associated index and format files are closed. All memory variables are discarded. The selected work area is work area 1.

Next, we want to set all of the dBASE III PLUS processing parameters to a desired state. dBASE sets these parameters to values that are convenient when working from the keyboard. It's good practice to set these parameters in alphabetical order.

Set bell off

dBASE rings a bell whenever a data field is filled during full-screen data entry. Some users find this annoying. In addition, we want to "ring the bell" only when there is an error of some kind.

Set escape off

The **Esc** key will interrupt program execution. This can be disconcerting to the user. **Set escape off** "disconnects" the escape key. A word of advice: Enter this command as a comment until all of the programs in the system are working correctly. Once you are sure that your software works properly, remove the asterisk. Otherwise, you will become very tired of using **Ctrl-Alt-Del** as an escape.

Set function n to chr(0)

This command effectively disconnects the function key from your computer by storing the "null" character to the function key. It is a good idea to do this unless you have your own specific purpose for these keys. dBASE preloads the function keys with character sequences, and pressing them can have unpredictable results in your programs. But dBASE won't let you disconnect function key **F1**; it's there for help whether you need it or not. However, it won't get in your way either.

Set help off

This command prevents dBASE from asking the user: "Do you want some help? (Y/N)" in the event of an error.

Set margin to 10

The standard printer margin for dBASE III PLUS is 0 (no left margin). For most of our printing routines, we will want a left margin of ten character spaces. You might want to increase this margin when using smaller print.

Set menus on

This command provides a help menu for use with full-screen operations such as **append, browse, create,** and **edit.**

Set procedure to FILENAME

A procedure file is a special kind of program file. It can contain up to 32 procedures. Each procedure must have a procedure name. This name can be up to ten characters long. A procedure itself can be identical to any other program, but it must begin with the statement **procedure PROCEDURE NAME** and end with the statement **return**.

In our business system, the procedure file is named MENUPROC.PRG. The file extension for procedure files is .PRG, just as for regular program files. Procedures are useful for small utility programs that need quick response. Procedure names are distinguished in this book from regular programs by names that describe their functions.

The entire set of procedures is opened by the **set procedure** command. The use of a procedure does not count as an additional file opening. When the procedure file is opened, dBASE scans the file and creates a table in memory that contains the names of these procedures and their disk addresses. A procedure takes precedence over a program file with the same name.

To better illustrate the procedure file, let's make procedures out of the code to produce the screen heading and the code to make a menu selection in the menu program. These provide good examples of procedures. Procedures should consist of functions that will be used repeatedly throughout the set of programs. The procedure file then becomes a library of these small subroutines. Incidentally, there is no rule that says they must be small.

Use **modify command** to create a file named MENUPROC.PRG. Then enter the procedure into the file so that it looks like Figure 4–8.

As the complete program set is developed, we will be adding procedures to this file. The complete procedure file MENUPROC is shown in the appendixes. As in this case, a procedure file can become very large. The file size of programs that can be edited by **modify command** is limited to 4096 bytes. When a procedure file will be larger than 4096 bytes, use an external word processor. You can check on the size of your procedure file by using the dBASE **dir** command:

. dir MENUPROC.PRG

```
procedure BANNER
   parameter BANNER
   @ 2,2
   @ 2,2  say cdow(date())
   @ 2,(80-len(BANNER))/2 say BANNER
   @ 2,78 - len(CDATE) say CDATE
   @ 3,1  say BAR
return

procedure CHOICE
   parameters COL, RANGE
   CHOICE = ' '
   ROW = row()
   do while .not. CHOICE $ RANGE
     @ ROW,COL get CHOICE
     read
   enddo
return
```

Figure 4–8: Initial procedure file: MENUPROC.PRG.

The two procedures (shown in Figure 4–8) are slightly different from the original program (MENU.PRG). The changes allow the procedures to be used in a variety of applications. These two procedures will be discussed later in the chapter.

Set safety off

dBASE III PLUS normally provides a warning when you attempt to overwrite a file or otherwise destroy data inadvertently. A user feels very insecure when asked "File already exists—do you want to overwrite?" **Set safety off** leaves the decision as to what to do with a file to the programmer.

Set status off

The status line, as shown in the screen examples in Chapter One, is normally turned off. It is turned on by means of the optional file CONFIG.DB. To protect your programs from displaying the status line, always use **set status off** at the beginning of the program.

Set talk off

Normally, you should use **set talk off** early in your program. When you are using dBASE III PLUS from the keyboard, all commands produce some response. This isn't desirable for commands in programs. With **talk off**, the dBASE side of this conversation is shut off. Nothing will be displayed on the screen or the printer unless you take overt action in the program to cause the display. Of course, error messages from both dBASE III PLUS and your operating system will be displayed if and when errors occur. **Talk** is set back on with **set talk on**.

Select n

dBASE has ten independent work areas. When you enter dBASE you are automatically in work area 1. Each work area can contain a database file, a format file, and up to seven index files. Each work area also has an independent record pointer that keeps track of the current record for the database in use in that work area. Remember, you are only allowed a total of 15 open files of all types because of restrictions placed by the operating system.

The **select** command allows you to switch between work areas. Initial selection of a work area is by work area number. Later selection may be by either the work area number or the work area *alias*. The alias is the name of the database being used in the work area or a special name assigned when the database was opened.

Use FILENAME index [list of index files] alias NAME

This command closes any open files in a work area and opens the named database file and the named index files (if any). The index filenames must be separated by commas (comma delimited). The first index file in the list is the controlling index. The optional alias name can be up to 10 characters in length.

Until the data files are created, you can try the program by adding an * in front of the **use** commands. Remember to remove the asterisks when the files have been created so that the commands will actually open the files. The three files that we have chosen to open in this program are files that are used in most of the menu systems.

Public ANSWER, BAR, BELL, CDATE, . . .

dBASE III PLUS memory variables are normally available to the creating program and all programs below the creating program. Variables are normally discarded when a program is exited. To prevent these variables from being discarded when we leave SETUP, the variables ANSWER, BAR, BELL, CDATE, and so forth are declared public. A variable must be declared public before it is assigned a value.

It's a good idea always to list memory variables in alphabetical order. This becomes helpful whenever you must deal with a large number of variables. Similarly, it is easier to keep track of public variables when they are all declared in the same program.

A = date( )

This command creates a memory variable named A, and stores the current system date to A. **Date( )** is the date function. A is simply a convenience variable to be used later in the expression for CDATE. The system date, **date( )**, is in the form *mm/dd/yy*.

BAR = replicate (chr(205),78)

The variable BAR is used to produce the double line bar at the top of most of our screens (see Figure 4–4). The variable is created by means of the **replicate** function, which produces a specified number of copies of a specified character. In this example, we make 78 copies of the double bar character.

The **chr(n)** function produces the ASCII character corresponding to the number inside the parentheses. **Chr(65)** is a capital A. **Chr(7)** is the bell. **Chr(205)** is a double line. The function is most valuable when we want to produce a symbol or action for which there is no keyboard character. A complete ASCII table is included in this book in Appendix A.

BELL = chr(7)

Chr(7) is the ASCII control code that rings the bell. Although we could use the control code directly when we want to ring the bell, the code is more readable by using the variable BELL to ring the bell.

CDATE = cmonth(A) + str(day(A),3)+' , '+str(year(A),5)

This memory variable stores the system date in the form *month day, year*. Here we've used the functions **cmonth**, **day**, **year**, and **str**. Cmonth( ) outputs the month in calendar form. **Day( )** outputs the day of the month as a number. **Year( )** outputs a four-digit number that represents the year (for example, 1985). To combine all of these items into a single variable they must all be character expressions. Then they can be concatenated. **Str( )** transforms a number to a character string. The number in the expressions indicates the number of characters that are included in the string.

Store space(1) to ANSWER, CHOICE

Store provides another way to create a memory variable. It should be used when storing the same value to multiple memory variables. This particular command stores a single blank space to the variables ANSWER and CHOICE.

THE REVISED MENU PROGRAM

The revised menu program, MENU.PRG, is shown in Figure 4–9. The lines of code that were formerly used to display the page heading and perform the menu selection have been replaced by the two lines:

```
do BANNER with "BOB'S BETTER BOOKS"
do CHOICE with 26,'012345678'
```

The items after the word *with* are called *parameters*. We can translate the command as: "Do the named procedure using the following parameters." These commands not only call the procedures, but also pass needed parameters to those procedures.

If these parameters are to be passed, the first executable line (the first non-comment line) of the receiving program or procedure must begin with the word *parameter* (as do the two procedures shown in Figure 4–8).

```
parameter BANNER
parameters COL, RANGE
```

Parameters passed from the calling program become memory variables in the receiving program. Variable names are assigned in the order that the parameters were passed. You can assign these variables names with impunity. These newly-created variables "hide" any existing variables having the same name. In the second of these examples, the number 26 and the character string "012345678" are passed to the procedure CHOICE. The parameter statement in CHOICE receives these two variables and stores the number 26 in the numeric variable COL and the character string "012345678" in the character variable RANGE.

If you examine these procedures (subroutines), you will find that the code differs slightly from the code in the original menu program. This is done to make their use more general (the purpose of a procedure). BANNER is to be used with many dif-

```
* MENU.PRG

set default to C
set path to C:\BOOK\PROGRAMS, C:\BOOK\DATA
do SETUP
do while .T.
   clear
   do BANNER with "BOB'S BETTER BOOKS"

   @  8,26 say '1 - Customer File'
   @  9,26 say '2 - Mailing Lists and Labels'
   @ 10,26 say '3 - Inventory'
   @ 11,26 say '4 - Sales Orders'
   @ 12,26 say '5 - Invoices '
   @ 13,26 say '6 - Payments Received'
   @ 14,26 say '7 - Billing'
   @ 15,26 say '8 - Utilities'
   @ 17,26 say '0 - Finished '
   @ 19,26 say ' - Pick One'

   do CHOICE with 26,'012345678'

   if CHOICE = '0'
      cancel
   endif
   do MENU&CHOICE

enddo
```

Figure 4–9: Finished version of MENU.PRG.

ferent screen titles. The line that displayed BOB'S BETTER BOOKS has been changed to display the content of a memory variable named BANNER. The content of this variable is centered by the expression **(80-len(BANNER))/2**.

In the CHOICE procedure, you will note the line **ROW = row( )**. When we exit from **read,** the cursor moves to the bottom line of the screen. By using ROW within the procedure, we avoid having the variable CHOICE displayed on the bottom of the screen—if we have entered a non-allowed selection. This command line stores the current row position of the cursor to the memory variable ROW.

Now, we have our main menu program, MENU.PRG, an initialization program, SETUP.PRG, and the beginning procedure file, MENUPROC.PRG. These three pieces form the top level of our overall set of programs. They provide us with a road map to guide the design of the remainder of our business system. In addition, they illustrate the use of both top-down design and structured programming techniques. And they have provided the vehicle to demonstrate a large number of dBASE III PLUS commands. Study these programs for both structure and style, as well as coding techniques.

CHAPTER FIVE
The Customer File

Our book dealer needs one set of programs to help keep customer records. These records contain the company name, address, phone number, and contact—together with other related information such as current credit standing. These records need to be accessed by the customer's name.

Businesses keep records about their customers, suppliers, and employees. Schools keep records on students and staff. Governments keep records on everyone. These records are usually kept in files called *name files* because they are primarily accessed by a name. In this chapter we will develop programs to add, edit, delete, remove, and view records stored in a name file.

These records often need to be related, as in our case, to records stored in other files—such as in Sales Order Entry or in Accounts Receivable. A name does not provide a satisfactory link between data files. Names are not usually unique. There may be more than one customer with the same name. Our book dealer, for example, has 73 different customers with the name "Book Nook" alone.

To reliably link customer records to records in other files, we use a customer number. This is a unique number that is assigned to each customer. No two customers can have the same customer number. As each customer is added to the database, the program assigns a unique customer number. Our book dealer has chosen to use numbers that are separated from each other by 17. This offers some protection when customer numbers are entered manually—a single-digit entry error will not result in a valid customer number. An interesting alternative method for assigning customer numbers is to use the date and time (to the second) when the customer was added. Date and time are both available from the computer's clock, relieving us of the need to keep track of the last number assigned.

Our book dealer has two database files in his customer system: CUSTOMER and CONTROLS. The database plans for these files are shown as Figures 5–1 and 5–2. Additional fields can be added to these files at any time. To create the files in the subdirectory \BOOK\DATA, use the full pathname:

```
. create c:\BOOK\DATA\CUSTOMER
. create c:\BOOK\DATA\CONTROLS
```

Index files provide direct access to data records. Our book dealer needs direct access to customer records by both customer name and customer number. Two index files are created and maintained to provide this direct access. The file CUSTNAME provides access by name; CUSTID provides access by customer number. Other index files will be created ad hoc when they are needed.

DESCRIPTION	FIELDNAME	FIELDTYPE	FIELDWIDTH
Customer Name	NAME	Character	30
Attention	ATTN	Character	30
Street Address	ADDRESS	Character	25
City	CITY	Character	20
State	STATE	Character	2
Zip Code	ZIP	Character	5
Telephone Number	PHONE	Character	14
Customer Since	DATE	Date	8
Customer ID Number	CUSTID	Character	6
Credit Standing	CREDIT	Character	1

Data size . . . . .142 Bytes
File to be indexed on: CUSTID to CUSTID
NAME to CUSTNAME

Figure 5–1: CUSTOMER database plan.

DESCRIPTION	FIELDNAME	FIELDTYPE	FIELDWIDTH
Customer ID Number	CUSTID	Numeric	6
Last Customer Edited	LASTEDIT	Character	6

Data Size . . . . .13 Bytes

Figure 5–2: CONTROLS database plan.

An index file can be created for an empty database file. To place the index files in the subdirectory \BOOK\DATA, use the full pathname when creating the index file:

```
. index on NAME to C:\BOOK\DATA\CUSTNAME
. index on CUSTID to C:\BOOK\DATA\CUSTID
```

The CONTROLS database keeps track of the last customer number assigned and the customer ID number for the last record edited. This database will contain a single record. Assign the initial value of 100000 to the field CUSTID. The field LASTEDIT is initially blank.

THE CUSTOMER FILE MENU

The customer system provides the means for the user to add, edit, delete, and view customer records. A menu, shown in Figure 5–3, provides a way to select among the options. The menu program MENU1.PRG is shown in Figure 5–4.

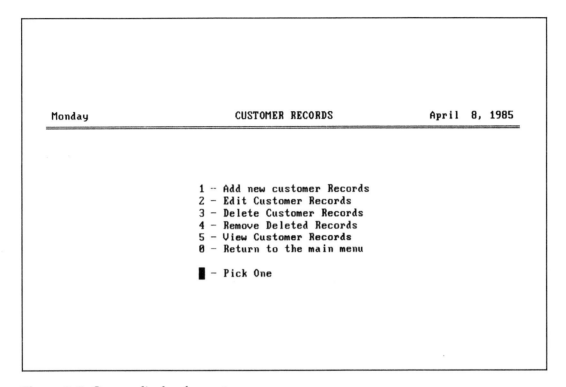

```
Monday                    CUSTOMER RECORDS              April  8, 1985



                    1 -- Add new customer Records
                    2 - Edit Customer Records
                    3 - Delete Customer Records
                    4 - Remove Deleted Records
                    5 - View Customer Records
                    0 - Return to the main menu

                    ▌ - Pick One
```

Figure 5–3: Screen display for customer menu.

The customer menu program establishes the initial conditions for customer records
and provides a way to select among the six menu options. When we first bring up
this menu and the customer database is empty, the only choices provided are to add
records or return to the main menu.

Select CUSTOMER

The first step is to establish the initial conditions. We select the CUSTOMER file.
Once a file has opened in a work area, we can use the alias (alternate) filename with
the **select** command. If no alias name is given, the filename itself becomes the default
alias.

Set index to CUSTNAME,CUSTID

We use the **set index** command to make sure that both indexes are open and that
they are in the proper order. This step keeps us from having to keep track of what
we do with these indexes in the other parts of the overall system.

Do while .T.

This command (do forever) keeps us in this menu until we make a decision to return

```
* MENU1.PRG

select CUSTOMER
set index to CUSTNAME,CUSTID

do while .T.
   clear
   CHOICE = space(1)
   CHOICES=  '01'

   do BANNER with "CUSTOMER RECORDS"
   @  8,26 say '1 - Add new customer Records'

   if .not. (eof() .and. bof())
      @  9,26 say '2 - Edit Customer Records'
      @ 10,26 say '3 - Delete Customer Records'
      @ 11,26 say '4 - Remove Deleted Records'
      @ 12,26 say '5 - View Customer Records'
      CHOICES = CHOICES + '2345'
   endif

   @ 13,26 say '0 - Return to the main menu'
   @ 15,26 say '  - Pick One'

   do CHOICE with 26, CHOICES

   if CHOICE = '0'
      return
   endif
   do MENU1&CHOICE

enddo
```

Figure 5–4: Menu program for customer records system: MENU1.PRG.

to the main menu. Whenever we finish with one of the first five selections we automatically return to this menu. Selecting option 0 will return us to the main menu program.

Do BANNER with "CUSTOMER RECORDS"

This calls the procedure BANNER that was developed in the last chapter. BANNER displays the legend at the top of the screen.

If .not. (eof( ).and. bof( ))

When the database is empty, both the end-of-file function **eof( )** and the beginning-of-file function **bof( )** are true. This is the only time that will ever occur. We have decided to prevent the user from attempting to edit, delete, remove, or view records when the database is empty. We can read this **if** statement as "if there are records in the database, execute these commands." When the database is empty, the screen displays only the two selections: "Add new Customer records" and "Return to the main menu." An alternative test for an empty database is to use the **reccount** function, which returns the number of records in the database.

Do CHOICE with 26, CHOICES

This command calls the procedure CHOICE that was developed in Chapter Four. CHOICE allows you to make a menu selection from among the options stored in the variable CHOICES. As we enter the loop, we initially store only the two possibilities, items 1 and 0, to the controlling variable CHOICES. If there are records in the database, the **if** statement adds the remainder of the options to the variable.

Return

The **return** command terminates the program and takes you back one program level. In this case, **return** takes us back to the main menu program.

ADDING RECORDS TO THE CUSTOMER DATABASE

What do we want the program to do? dBASE III PLUS has a command, **append**, that allows a user to add records to a database. We use a program because we want to do more than just add records. We want this program to:

- Display the last customer record entered.
- Accept a candidate customer name.
- Search the database and display information from records that match the candidate name.
- Provide a way for the user to enter the record even if potential duplicates exist.
- Provide a data-entry screen form for the customer data.
- Assign the customer identification number.
- Automatically enter the customer number and the date into the new customer record.

Our program to accomplish all of this, MENU11.PRG, is shown in Figure 5–5. Figure 5–6 shows the data-entry screen for customer records. The program to create the data-entry screen, MENU1S.PRG, appears in Figure 5–7.

BANNERMSG = 'Add New Customer Records'

The banner at the top of the screen is produced by the procedure BANNER, which requires that we pass it a banner message as a parameter. BANNER is called from general-purpose programs such as the MENU1S.PRG screen program, which can

```
* menu11.prg       Adds Records To Customer Database     1/15/85

BANNERMSG = "Add New Customer Records"
if reccount() > 0
     go reccount()
endif
do MENU1S
clear gets
do while .T.
   MNAME   = space(30)
   OKTOADD = 'N'
   @ 23,2 say "Enter the new customer's name" get MNAME picture '@!'
   read

                        if MNAME = space(30)
                             exit
                        endif

   seek trim(MNAME)

   if found()           && alternate: if .not. eof()
      clear
      @ 1,1 say 'Records matching the new customer name are: '
      display off NAME,ADDRESS while NAME = trim(MNAME)
      wait "Add the name anyway (Y/N)? " to OKTOADD
      go top
   endif

   if .not. found() .OR. upper(OKTOADD) = 'Y'
      append blank
      replace NAME with MNAME, DATE with date(), ;
              CUSTID with str(CONTROLS->CUSTID,6)
      select  CONTROLS
      replace CUSTID with CUSTID + 17
      select  CUSTOMER
      do MENU1S
      read
   endif

enddo
use CUSTOMER index CUSTNAME,CUSTID
```

Figure 5–5: Data-entry program: MENU11.PRG.

be called from several menu selections. The memory variable BANNERMSG contains the banner message to be used by BANNER when the screen program is called from this menu selection. (See Figures 5–6 and 5–7.)

If reccount( ) > 0
  go reccount( )
endif

This command block positions the database to the last record added, allowing us to display the record with the program MENU1S. We have to test for the existence of records—we cannot use the **go** command in an empty database. The **reccount** function gives us the number of records in the database.

MEMORY VARIABLES

This loop uses two memory variables: MNAME—which has 30 spaces—and OKTOADD. Each variable is reset on each pass through the loop.

@ 23,2 say . . . get MNAME picture '@!'
read

This displays a message on the bottom of the screen together with the blank memory variable MNAME. You can combine the **say** and **get** on the same line. The **get** must follow the **say**. The term **picture '@!'** forces all of the characters entered into MNAME to uppercase, including the data entered after the **read** command. The **read** command causes the program to pause for keyboard input to the variable.

If MNAME = space(30)
  exit
endif

Here we test to see whether a candidate name was entered into MNAME. If not, we assume data entry is over and return to the menu. This test provides for our escape from this **do** loop.

Seek trim(MNAME)

Seek evaluates the following expression and searches the index file for the first matching record. The **trim( )** function discards any trailing blank spaces in the variable MNAME for this search (MNAME still contains those blanks). If MNAME contained only the letter A, the search would find the first database record beginning with the letter A. Searching for "JOHN SMITH" would find those records beginning with "JOHN SMITH." However, a search for "JOHN SMITH INC." would not find "JOHN SMITH." Read this command as: "Search for the first record beginning with the trimmed contents of MNAME." If we omit the **trim( )** function, the search would be for a record that exactly matched MNAME, including trailing blank spaces.

If found( )

Read this command as: "If a matching record is found." If the **seek** is successful, the database will be positioned to a matching record and the **found** function will be true. Otherwise, the database will be positioned to the end-of-file; the **found** function will be false, while the **eof( )** function will be true. We can use either the **found** or **eof( )** function to determine if the **seek** was successful.

Display off . . . while

If a record is found, any additional matching records will be in adjacent records in the index list. The **off** in this command indicates that record numbers are not to be displayed. We chose to use **display** rather than **list** because **display** causes the listing of possible duplicates to pause after every screenful, giving the user a chance to read the list.

Wait . . . to OKTOADD

Wait displays the message on the screen and stores the next keystroke to the named memory variable. If no message is specified, the default message "Press any key to continue . . . " is displayed. For no message, use a blank space.

Go top

This command takes you to the beginning of the database. It is used here to make certain we are not at the end of file. We were not at the end of file when we entered this command block; however, the **display off . . . while** could trip the end-of-file flag, automatically invalidating a decision not to enter a duplicate record. The next command block will always enter a new record if the end-of-file flag is set.

If .not. found( ) .or. upper(OKTOADD) = 'Y'

We enter this block only if we didn't find the record or if we want to enter the record anyway. **Upper( )** is a function that outputs the uppercase of the memory variable. Remember: You can enter one of two cases.

Append blank

This command adds a single blank record to the end of the database and positions the record pointer to that blank record.

Replace NAME with MNAME, . . .

Replace replaces the contents of named fields with the specified items. This command is too long to fit on the printed page. The semicolon allows the command to continue on the next line. Note the expression **str(CONTROLS->CUSTID,6)**. This expression takes the content of the field CUSTID from the database CONTROLS and converts it to a character string so that it can be entered into the character field CUSTID in the customer file. This field in the CONTROLS database always contains the next available customer identification number.

Select CONTROLS
replace CUSTID with CUSTID + 17
select CUSTOMER

You can only make changes in the selected file. This block of commands switches to the CONTROLS database so that we can increment the field CUSTID to the next available customer ID. Then we switch back to the customer file.

Do MENU1S
read

Finally, we bring up the data-entry screen. The **read** command allows us to enter data onto the screen.

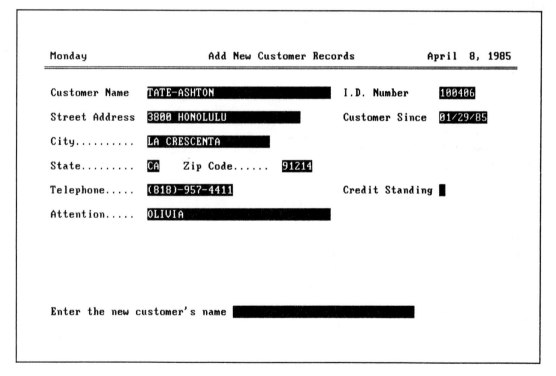

Figure 5–6: CUSTOMER data-entry screen.

```
* MENU1S.PRG

clear
do BANNER with BANNERMSG
                              if deleted()
                                   @ 0,65 say 'DELETED'
                              endif


@  5,50 say 'I.D. Number    ' get CUSTID
@  7,50 say 'Customer Since ' get DATE
clear gets
@  5,2  say 'Customer Name  ' get NAME     picture '@!'

                              if CHOICE = '1'
                                   clear gets
                              endif


@  7,2  say 'Street Address ' get ADDRESS picture '@!'
@  9,2  say 'City.......... ' get CITY    picture '@!'
@ 11,2  say 'State......... ' get STATE   picture '@!'
@ 11,24 say 'Zip Code...... ' get ZIP     picture '99999'
@ 13,2  say 'Telephone..... ' get PHONE   picture '(999)-999-9999'
@ 15,2  say 'Attention..... ' get ATTN    picture '@!'
@ 13,50 say 'Credit Standing' get CREDIT  picture '!'
```

Figure 5–7: Program to produce data-entry screen: MENU1S.PRG.

THE SCREEN-ENTRY PROGRAM: MENU1S.PRG

This program (shown in Figure 5-7) is to be used for four of the menu choices in the customer records system. The program first clears the screen and displays the screen title using the procedure BANNER.

If deleted( )

dBASE III PLUS has one byte of overhead for each record in the database. This byte occurs at the beginning of the record. The byte contains an asterisk if the record has been marked for deletion and a space if it has not been. The **deleted( )** function is true if the record has been marked for deletion. In this case we want to display the legend DELETED at the upper right of the screen.

Clear gets

This prevents any subsequent **read** command from allowing the fields before the **clear gets** to be edited. Note that we are not allowed to edit the customer name field when a record is being added.

Picture

The item in quotes following the word *picture* can be either a *picture* function or a *template* or both. Functions begin with the @ symbol and apply to the entire variable. For example, @! forces the entire variable to uppercase for both entry and display. The zip code provides an example of a template. This template is character by character. In this case we limit the display and entry of each character to the range 0-9. The phone number demonstrates another kind of picture template.

Symbols that have not been designated as template symbols become a part of the picture and cannot be affected by data-entry. The parentheses and the dash are not designated symbols and become a permanent part of each phone number. We could save a few bytes in the phone number field by using the picture function **R**. This function would exclude the parentheses and dash from the data—they would exist only on the screen.

EDITING CUSTOMER RECORDS: MENU12.PRG

When we select option 2 on the customer file menu we select the program shown in Figure 5–8, MENU12.PRG. This program also does more than just provide the ability to edit a record. We want the program to:

- Display the last record edited.
- Accept a customer name for editing.
- Search the database for the customer.
- Display all customers with names beginning with the search name.
- Allow the operator to select among these alternate records.

The ability to conduct a search for customers whose names have a common beginning is particularly important. This is a feature that we will need in other elements of our overall business system. So, we have chosen to isolate the part of the program that does search and selection as a separate procedure that we can use elsewhere. This procedure is FINDCUST.

BANNERMSG = "Edit Customer Records "

Our first step, as in the last program, is to store the screen title to the variable BAN-NERMSG.

```
set index to CUSTID
seek CONTROLS->LASTEDIT
do MENU1S
clear gets
set index to CUSTNAME, CUSTID
```

Next, we want to display the last record edited—whenever that was. In the controls database we keep a field that contains the customer identification number of that record. This field is updated every time a record is edited. To use this field, we first

```
* menu12.prg    Program to Edit Customer Records

BANNERMSG = "Edit Customer Records"
set index to CUSTID
seek CONTROLS->LASTEDIT
do MENU1S
clear gets
set index to CUSTNAME, CUSTID

do while .T.
   MNAME = space(30)
   do FINDCUST with "Enter the Customer's name ",MNAME

                         if MNAME = space(30)
                             return
                         endif
   if .not. eof()
      do MENU1S
      read
      select CONTROLS
      replace LASTEDIT with CUSTOMER->CUSTID
      select CUSTOMER
   endif
enddo
```

Figure 5–8: MENU12.PRG.

change the controlling index from CUSTNAME to CUSTID. Then we position the database to that record with the **seek** command. Next we display the record with the program MENU1S.PRG. We must display the record before we change back to using CUSTNAME as the controlling index. When you switch indexes the **set index** command takes you to the top of the new index order. Finally, we prevent possible editing of this record by clearing **get** commands from MENU1S.

FINDING A CUSTOMER

The procedure FINDCUST (shown in Figure 5–9) must be added to the procedure file MENUPROC.PRG. If the procedure file has been opened, you must use **close procedure** to close the file before you can edit it. It is a good idea to enter your procedures in alphabetical order. Also, use the asterisk to build a table of contents at the beginning of the procedure file.

FINDCUST expects to receive two parameters from the calling program, a legend that will be displayed on line 23, and the variable MNAME. If we don't enter a name, we want to escape. The order of these passed parameters must match the order in which the receiving program or procedure expects them. The **parameters** command assigns names to the parameters in the order they are received.

```
procedure FINDCUST
   parameters LEGEND,MNAME
   do while .T.
      MNAME = space(30)
      @ 23,2  say  LEGEND get MNAME pict '@!'
      read
                       if MNAME = space(30)
                           exit
                       endif
      seek trim(MNAME)
                       if eof()
                           do ERRORMSG with 'No record for '+MNAME, 21, 2
                           loop
                       endif
      @ 21,2
      do DUPECHK
      exit
   enddo
return
```

Figure 5-9: Procedure to find a customer: FINDCUST.

Do while .T.

We want to stay in the procedure until we either enter a valid customer name or escape by choosing not to enter a name. If a name was entered and the search was unsuccessful, we want to inform the user and try again. This is accomplished by displaying a message on line 21, ringing the bell, and looping back to the beginning of the **do** loop.

Exit

The **exit** command takes you to the first executable command outside of the **do** loop. If this procedure had been a regular program, we might have used **return** instead. However, in this case the program would be unable to distinguish between the **return** that terminates the procedure and the use of **return** to escape. Do not use **return** within a procedure.

Do ERRORMSG with

ERRORMSG is a procedure (shown in Figure 5-10) to display an error message and ring a bell. We have made it a procedure because we are going to use it repeatedly. You should identify tasks as procedures whenever possible because it makes your code simpler and more reliable.

```
procedure ERRORMSG
    parameter MESSAGE, ROW, COL
    @ ROW,COL
    @ ROW,COL say MESSAGE
    ?? chr(7)                    && ring the bell
return
```

Figure 5–10: ERRORMSG procedure.

Loop

This command is used to take you back to the beginning of a **do** loop. It should be used only as an escape.

@ 21,2

If the search is successful, we want any error message that might have been displayed to be cleared from the screen. The @ command used in this way will erase the specified screen line from the specified column position to the right edge of the screen.

Do DUPECHK

DUPECHK (Figure 5–11) is another procedure. A procedure can be called from a procedure. DUPECHK tests to see whether there are multiple records beginning with the search name. If there are, the names are displayed with the record numbers. The user is provided with a way to select one of the displayed names. Here is a case where using customer identification numbers that are offset by 17 comes in handy. It is unlikely that an incorrect customer ID will successfully locate a customer.

In this procedure we test for duplicate records. These may not be true duplicates, but merely records beginning with the same character sequence. If duplicates exist, the user is provided with the means to choose between them. At the conclusion of the procedure, the database will either be positioned to a desired record or to the end-of-file.

Skip

Skip moves the record pointer by the argument n. If no argument is specified, n is assumed to be +1. In this procedure we first move the pointer one record, test for duplicate records, and move back to where we started.

DUPERECS = (NAME = trim(MNAME))

The variable DUPERECS stores the result of the test for duplicate records. The test for duplicate records is accomplished by comparing the content of the field NAME with the trimmed variable MNAME. The result will be either true or false.

```
procedure DUPECHK
   skip
   DUPERECS  = (NAME = trim(MNAME))
   MCUSTID = space(6)
   skip -1
   if DUPERECS
      do while NAME = trim(MNAME) .and. readkey() # 12 .and. MCUSTID = space(6)
         clear
         ? 'There are multiple records for '+MNAME
         display off next 15 CUSTID,NAME,ADDRESS while NAME = trim(MNAME)
         ?
         ? 'To select: enter a customer ID number'
         ? 'To abort:  press the Esc Key '
         ? 'otherwise: press the Return Key'
         @ row(), col()+2 get MCUSTID picture '999999'
         read
      enddo
      if MCUSTID = space(6) .and. readkey() # 12    && valid entry
         set order to 2            && customer id index
         seek MCUSTID
         POSITION = recno()        && record number
         set order to 1            && name index
         if .not. found()
                 ?? BELL
                 wait "&MCUSTID is not valid - press Return"
         else
                 go POSITION
         endif
      else
         seek chr(13)              && set end of file
      endif
   endif
return
```

Figure 5–11: Procedure to check for duplicates: DUPECHK.

Do while . . . .and. readkey( ) # 12

Duplicate records are displayed 15 at a time. After each display, the user is presented with three options: to select a customer, to abort, and to view additional "duplicate" records (if any). The **readkey( )** function is used to check for an abort. This function returns the value 12 whenever the **Esc** key is used to terminate a **read**.

Set order to 2
seek MCUSTID

. . .

. . .

set order to 1

Upon leaving the **do loop**, we have either selected a customer or we haven't. If we have, we want to go directly to that customer's record. **Set order to 2** selects the second index, CUSTID, as the controlling index. We use the **seek** command to move to the desired record, and the result of the **seek** is recorded in the **found( )** function. After the **seek** we switch back to using the first index, CUSTNAME.

Seek chr(13)

Under normal conditions a character field does not begin with **chr(13)**, which is a **return**. This means that the seek will be unsuccessful and the database will be positioned to the end-of-file.

DELETING RECORDS WITH MENU OPTION 3

The menu selection for deleting records is satisfied by MENU13.PRG. This program is shown as Figure 5–12. This menu selection lets the user mark (delete) records for future removal. This same selection also removes the deletion mark (recalls) from records. A customer record is selected by means of the procedure FINDCUST that was just discussed.

Once the customer has been selected, the complete customer record is displayed by the screen-entry program, MENU1S. The user is asked whether the record is to be deleted (or undeleted).

Delete

This command places a deletion mark in front of the record.

Recall

This command removes a deletion mark from a record.

Deleted( )

This function is true if the record has a deletion mark.

```
* MENU13.PRG

clear
BANNERMSG = "Delete/Recall Customer Records"
do BANNER with BANNERMSG
DO WHILE .T.
   ANSWER = space(1)
   MNAME  = space(30)
   do FINDCUST with "Customer to be deleted/undeleted", MNAME
                        if MNAME = space(30)
                            return
                        endif
   if .not. eof()
      do MENU1S
      clear gets
      if deleted()
           @ 21,2 say 'Undelete this record (Y/N)? ' get ANSWER
           read
           if ANSWER $ 'Yy'
               recall
           endif
      else
           @ 21,2 say 'Delete this record (Y/N)? ' get ANSWER
           read
           if ANSWER $ 'Yy'
               delete
           endif
      endif
   endif
   if deleted()
      @ 0,65 say 'DELETED'
    else
      @ 0,0
   endif
@ 21,2
enddo
```

Figure 5–12: MENU13.PRG.

REMOVING RECORDS MARKED FOR DELETION

This option (4), MENU14.PRG, is shown as Figure 5–13. It removes any record that is marked for deletion. If the database is large, the removal can be time-consuming. For this reason, it has been decoupled from the deletion operation.

When we enter this process, since it can be time-consuming, a message is displayed to tell the user that we are searching for deleted records. We are searching in the indexed order which can be a lot slower than searching with the indexes off.

```
* MENU14.PRG

clear
do BANNER with 'Remove Deleted Records'
? 'Searching for deleted records'
locate for deleted()
ANSWER  = space(1)
if .not. eof()
  ? 'The following Records are marked for deletion'
  display off next 1000000 NAME,ADDRESS,CITY for deleted()
       if row() > 21
            ?
            ?
       endif
  @ 23,1 say 'Remove these records (Y/N)? ' get ANSWER
  read
  if ANSWER $ 'yY'
       set talk on
       clear
       ? 'Records are being removed - please be patient'
       pack
       set talk off
  endif
else
  ? 'There are no records marked for deletion'
  wait
endif
```

Figure 5–13: MENU14.PRG.

If we don't find any deleted records, we inform the user that there weren't any. If we do, we display selected parts of these records and then verify that the user wants to remove them at this time.

Pack

Records marked for deletion are actually removed by the **pack** command. This process starts at the beginning of the database (record 1). It moves valid records into the space previously occupied by deleted records. When the process is completed, all open index files are automatically updated.

When **talk** is on, the **pack** command displays a counter that indicates the status of the process. We choose to display this counter so that the user remains assured that the computer is still working. When the entire operation is complete, we turn **talk** back off and return to the main program.

```
* MENU15.PRG


clear
BACKWARD   = chr(174)
FORWARD    = chr(175)
BANNERMSG = "View Customer Records"
do BANNER with BANNERMSG
set function  9 to BACKWARD + ";"
set function 10 to FORWARD  + ";"
do while reccount() > 0
   do MENU1S
   clear gets
   MNAME = space(30)
   @ 22,2  say  "Press F9 to Backup  -  F10 to Advance"
   @ 23,2  say  "or enter a Customer's name " get MNAME pict '@!'
   read
   do case
      case MNAME = space(30)
         exit
      case MNAME = BACKWARD .and. .not. bof()
         skip -1
      case MNAME = FORWARD  .and. .not. eof()
         skip
      otherwise
         seek trim(MNAME)
                   if eof()
                       do ERRORMSG with 'No record for '+MNAME,21,2
                   endif
   endcase
enddo
set function  9 to chr(0)
set function 10 to chr(0)
```

Figure 5–14: Program to view customer records: MENU15.PRG.

VIEWING CUSTOMER RECORDS

This menu item allows the user to view the contents of records without the possibility of making an inadvertent change to a record. The program to satisfy menu selection 5, MENU15.PRG, is shown as Figure 5–14.

The idea is to present the user with the option of entering a name or of pressing one of two function keys. One function key causes the system to go back one record, the other causes it to advance one record. All three choices are made via entries into the memory variable MNAME. To make the system sense that the record advance and backup choices are not valid names, we set the function keys to contain symbols from the extended ASCII character set. We have chosen double arrows point-ing forward and backward. These symbols cannot be entered into a field from the keyboard.

An alternative interpretation which might be preferred by many is to use the **readkey** function (see Chapter Thirteen) with the **PgUp**, **PgDn**, and **Esc** keys. However, this program is intended to demonstrate one use of function keys to produce special ef-fects in your programs. A variation of this program, shown as Figure 5–15, uses the direction keys for paging.

```
* MENU15X.PRG

clear
BANNERMSG = "View Customer Records"
do BANNER with BANNERMSG
do while reccount() > 0
   do MENU1S
   clear gets
   MNAME = space(30)
   @ 22,2  say  "Press PgUp to Backup  -  PgDn to Advance  - Esc to Abort'
   @ 23,2  say  "or enter a Customer's name " get MNAME pict '@!'
   read
   do case
      case readkey() = 12                   && esc key
         exit
      case readkey() = 6 .and. .not. bof()  && pgup key
        skip -1
      case readkey() = 7 .and. .not. eof()  && pgdn key
        skip
      case readkey() = 34                   && ctrl pgup
         go top
      case readkey() = 35                   && ctrl pgdn
         go bottom
      case readkey() > 255                   && data entered
         seek trim(MNAME)
             if eof()
                 do ERRORMSG with 'No record for '+MNAME,21,2
             endif
   endcase
enddo
```

Figure 5–15: Alternate program for viewing records: MENU 15X.PRG.

Set function to

Note that we created the variables containing the symbols separately from the **set function** operation. This allows us to make comparisons between the contents of MNAME and the two variables FORWARD and BACKWARD. If the variables con-tained the carriage return (;) or **chr(13)**, it would be filtered by dBASE during the **read** operation. dBASE discards all control characters (characters whose ASCII value is less than 32) when entered via a full-screen operation. Always remember to disable the function keys when finished with a program that uses them.

Do case . . . endcase

These commands mark the boundaries of a series of case statements. A case statement is like an **if**. If the expression following the word **case** is true, the commands between the **case** statement and the next **case** statement (or the **endcase**) will be executed. You can cascade as many **case** statements as you want. Only the first **case** satisfied is executed—even if all are true. This is the principal difference between **do case** and a series of cascaded **if** statements.

CHAPTER SIX
Lists and Labels

Nearly every business that has a mailing list wants to have printed copies in several forms. We've called these *lists* and *labels*. These mailing lists are nearly always name files that are used for the purpose of mailing monthly statements, advertisements, form letters, and for selling to other companies.

The post office has a particular fondness for companies that organize their mailings by zip code. To benefit from this fondness, we need to have one of our mailing lists ordered (alphabetically) by zip code. We have chosen not to maintain an index for this case. Our book dealer needs this arrangement only once a month. We have elected to create this index each time we need it. Each additional index file that you maintain will slow down the operation of your system. For small databases you won't notice it. As the database grows larger, however, the impact of carrying along additional index files becomes noticeable. In this book dealer's system, a customer name index and a customer number index are both needed for operations. Other indexes are needed less frequently—and are created when needed.

The mailing list menu is shown in Figure 6-1. This menu is produced by the program MENU2.PRG, which is shown in Figure 6-2.

FEATURES OF THIS MENU PROGRAM

Relative Addressing: This menu program differs slightly from those shown in the last two chapters. This was done primarily to demonstrate alternate techniques. The screen display itself is done by using the **row( )** function, which allows you to employ relative addressing. This function provides the number for the current screen row. When a line is displayed by means of either @ . . . **say** or @ . . . **get**, the screen row is unchanged unless the line is too long to fit on the screen. In the latter case, the line wraps and enters the next screen row.

To display the line on the next row, use **row( )+1**; to double space, use **row( )+2**; and so on. Relative addressing makes it easy to adjust the position where a display appears on the screen. Move the entire display up and down on the screen by simply changing the row position for menu option 1. Do not attempt to begin a display off-screen.

Menu Selection: The manner in which a menu selection is made has been changed.

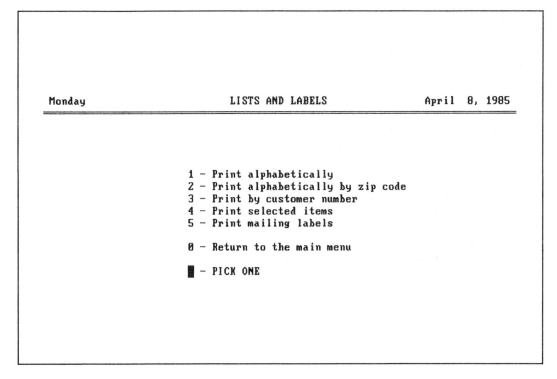

```
Monday                    LISTS AND LABELS            April  8, 1985


                    1 - Print alphabetically
                    2 - Print alphabetically by zip code
                    3 - Print by customer number
                    4 - Print selected items
                    5 - Print mailing labels

                    0 - Return to the main menu

                    ▌ - PICK ONE
```

Figure 6-1: Screen display for mailing list menu.

CHOICE = 0
@ row( ),25 get CHOICE picture '@Z #' range 0,5
read

In this case we have made CHOICE a numeric memory variable. The **get CHOICE** command with the range option is equivalent to the **do** loop in the previous menu examples. The optional range statement allows you to specify the beginning and ending values for the selection range. The term '@Z' was used to suppress the display of the initial 0, and the # sign was used to limit the display to one digit. '@Z' is one of many picture functions that can be used in formatting.

Do case . . . endcase

Case allows you to select one course of action based on a list of possible conditions. In this example, the condition is the number stored in the variable CHOICE. The courses of action are the commands following each case statement.

Set index to . . .

This command closes all index files in the current work area, opens the specified index files, and sets the record pointer to the first record according to the first named index.

```
* MENU2.PRG

select CUSTOMER           && indexes are CUSTNAME and CUSTID
do while .T.
   clear
   do BANNER with  "LISTS AND LABELS"
   @      8,25 say '1 - Print alphabetically'
   @ row()+1,25 say '2 - Print alphabetically by zip code'
   @ row()+1,25 say '3 - Print by customer number'
   @ row()+1,25 say '4 - Print selected items'
   @ row()+1,25 say '5 - Print mailing labels'
   @ row()+2,25 say '0 - Return to the main menu'
   @ row()+2,25 say '  - PICK ONE'

   CHOICE = 0
   @ row(),25   get CHOICE picture '@Z #' range 0,5
   read

   do case
      case CHOICE= 1
         set order to 1              && select CUSTNAME index
         go top
         do MENU2P with 'Alphabetical Customer Listing'
      case CHOICE= 2
         index on ZIP+NAME to ZIP
         do MENU2P with 'Customer Listing by Zip Code'
         set index to CUSTNAME, CUSTID
      case CHOICE= 3
         set order to 2              && select CUSTID index
         go top
         do MENU23 with 'Customer Listing by Customer ID'
      case CHOICE= 4
         set order to 1              && select CUSTNAME index
         go top
         do MENU24
      case CHOICE= 5
         set order to 1              && select CUSTNAME index
         go top
         set console off
         label form MENU25 sample to print
         set console on
      case CHOICE= 0
         return
      endcase
   enddo
```

Figure 6–2: Menu program for mailing lists and labels: MENU2.PRG.

Set order to n

This command selects the *n*th named index as the controlling index without closing and reopening any index files. When the command is issued, the index pointer doesn't point anywhere. You must reposition the database, even by going to the current record. In this example we want to move to the beginning of the index.

Index on ZIP + NAME to ZIP
go top

Here we are building the zip-code index. The **index** command closes any open index files and creates the new index. This index blocks the database by zip code and arranges names alphabetically within each zip-code grouping. When the indexing operation is complete, the database record pointer is positioned to the last record in the database.

THE PRINT PROGRAM: MENU2P

For our list and labels system we have used a single print program. In this book, two versions of this same program are covered. The first version, MENU2P, produces the customer printout in Figure 6–3. The second version, MENU2PX, produces the customer printout shown in Figure 6–5. The print programs MENU2P and MENU2PX are shown as Figures 6–4 and 6–6. The first of these print programs demonstrates the use of the functions **prow( )** and **pcol( )** to format printed output. This particular formatted report could also have been generated by use of the standard display commands and by the **report** command. Preparation of this report is covered in Chapter Fourteen.

The page title is passed to the report by parameter passing from the program MENU2.PRG. The next two lines of this program serve only to remind the user to turn on the printer. Without any message (and the printer off) the user might think that the system has hung and reboot the computer. On some systems you might get a PRN error message from the operating system—convincing you to abort. In either case you run the risk of exiting dBASE III PLUS without properly closing the files, which can be bad news.

Set device to print

@ . . . **say** commands are normally routed to the screen. This command reroutes @ . . . **says** to the printer. They will not appear on the screen. The printer must be on. When you have finished printing, reroute the output to the screen with **set device to screen**. Do not attempt to move the paper back up by using a smaller row number. Such an attempt results in a form feed (that is, the paper is ejected). On some printers you can get back up on a line by using a smaller column number, but don't count on it.

```
        Alphabetical Customer Listing for January 15, 1985


100017 A        52ND STREET BOOK SHOP          (212)-266-4410
                SHIPPING
                126 E. 18TH ST.
                NEW YORK, NY    10003


100068 A        A-1 BOOKS                      (303)-925-1234
                DAVID
                77 E COPPERFIELD
                ASPEN, CO    81611


100051 A        AARDVARK ASSOCIATES            (201)-267-1000
                KAREN
                121 STONE CT.
                NORTHVALE, NJ    07647


100085 A        ABC BOOK SELLERS               (214)-344-3740
                9715 MINERS AVENUE
                DALLAS, TX    75231


100102 A        ABC BOOK SELLERS               (313)-425-7711
                CAROLINE SIMMONS
                12510 FRONTIER
                LIVONIA, MI    48154


100119 A        ACME BOOKS                     (312)-741-3380
                ALBERT LONGMAN
                115 S. WEST ST.
                ELGIN, IL    60120


100153 A        ACRIMONY                       (503)-284-9876
                MORT EASTON
                2512 NE COLUMBIA
                PORTLAND, OR    97232


100034 A        ARTS ARTY BOOKNOOK             (212)-268-4104
                11 E 24TH ST
                NEW YORK, NY    10003


100136 A        ATLANTA BOOKS AND RECORDS      (404)-351-4394
                JAMES B DEWEY
                554 PEACHTREE PLAZA
                ATLANTA, GA    30367
```

Figure 6-3: Printout from program MENU2P.PRG.

Do while prow( ) < 55 .and. .not. eof( )

The **prow( )** function is the printing equivalent to the **row( )** function. It returns the current row that the print head is positioned to. We will use it to let us know when we have finished printing the page. The **eof( )** function is included to terminate the process when the end of file is reached in mid page.

```
* MENU2P.PRG

parameter PAGETITLE
clear
? 'Be sure that the printer is ON'
set device to print
page = 0

do while .not. eof()
   @ 6,10 say PAGETITLE + ' for ' + CDATE
   @ 8,1  say ' '

   do while prow() < 55 .and. .not. eof()
      @ prow()+1,1       say CUSTID
      @ prow(),8         say CREDIT
      @ prow(),15        say NAME
      @ prow(),pcol()+2  say PHONE
                              if ATTN # space(30)
                                   @ prow()+1,15 say ATTN
                              endif
      @ prow()+1,15 say ADDRESS
      @ prow()+1,15 say trim(CITY)+', '+STATE+'   '+ZIP
      skip
   enddo

   PAGE = PAGE + 1
   @ 62,30 say str(PAGE,3)
   eject
enddo

set device to screen
```

Figure 6–4: Program to print out customer listings: MENU2P.PRG.

@ prow( )+1 . . .

The **prow( )** and **pcol( )** functions can be used in relative addressing. Remember that you cannot back the print up on the paper. Don't use negative relative addresses. Using relative column addresses makes it easier to position yourself on the paper.

If ATTN # Space(30)

This provides a simple way of omitting blank fields from the printout. The field is printed only if it contains data.

Eject

This command issues a form feed **chr(12)** that causes the paper to advance to the next page.

PRINTING THE CUSTOMER LIST IN A TWO-COLUMN FORMAT

There is much in favor of printing out your customer list in a two-column format as in Figure 6–5. It's easier to read and takes less paper. The secret to printing with a two-column output is to typeset the page in memory and then print it from memory. The program used is MENU2PX.PRG, shown in Figure 6–6.

Most printers operate at 6 lines per inch. This gives 66 lines on a standard page. We want a top and bottom page margin of one inch with ½ inch between the body of the report and the title. That takes 15 lines. This leaves 51 lines for customer data. Each customer record can require up to 6 lines. So we have to stop "typesetting" when we reach line 45.

Set margin to 5

This **set** command allows you to adjust the left margin. The default margin is the left edge of the paper. While you can effectively specify the left margin by appropriately adjusting your column values, this makes your program more difficult to read. The margin spacing gives a half-inch left margin for most printers (10 cpi).

Do while .not. eof( )

This defines the scope of the **do** loop. When the expression **.not. eof( )** becomes false (all the records have been printed), we want to exit from the **do** loop.

@6,10 Say PAGETITLE + 'for' + CDATE

You can only print one expression with the **say**. However, you can concatenate character items together into a single expression as in this example. Here we pass only the basic title from the main program. We add the standard title boilerplate to the basic title by using concatenation.

```
          Alphabetical Customer Listing for January 15, 1985


    52ND STREET BOOK SHOP               ACME BOOKS
    SHIPPING                            ALBERT LONGMAN
    126 E. 18TH ST.                     115 S. WEST ST.
    NEW YORK, NY    10003               ELGIN, IL    60120
    100017 A    (212)-266-4410          100119 A    (312)-741-3380


    A-1 BOOKS                           ACRIMONY
    DAVID                               MORT EASTON
    77 E COPPERFIELD                    2512 NE COLUMBIA
    ASPEN, CO    81611                  PORTLAND, OR    97232
    100068 A    (303)-925-1234          100153 A    (503)-284-9876


    AARDVARK ASSOCIATES                 ARTS ARTY BOOKNOOK
    KAREN                               11 E 24TH ST
    121 STONE CT.                       NEW YORK, NY    10003
    NORTHVALE, NJ    07647              100034 A    (212)-268-4104
    100051 A    (201)-267-1000

                                        ATLANTA BOOKS AND RECORDS
    ABC BOOK SELLERS                    JAMES B DEWEY
    9715 MINERS AVENUE                  554 PEACHTREE PLAZA
    DALLAS, TX    75231                 ATLANTA, GA    30367
    1000085 A    (214)-344-3740         100136 A    (404)-351-4394
    ABC BOOK SELLERS
                                        BALTHAZARS BOOK BAZAAR
    CAROLINE SIMMONS                    FREDERICK HATHAWAY
    12510 FRONTIER                      11 E 24TH STREET
    LIVONIA, MI    48154                NEW YORK, NY    10003
    100102  A    (313)-425-7711         100134 A    (212)-260-4104
```

Figure 6–5: Two-column mailing list from program MENU2PX.

```
LC = 10
do while LC < = 61
    LC = LC + 1
    MEMVAR = 'L' + str(LC,2)
    &MEMVAR = chr(0)
enddo
```

This loop creates 51 memory variables named L11 through L61. Each of these variables contains an ASCII null **chr(0)**.

The variable LC controls the loop. On each pass through the loop, LC is increased by one. Then, the letter L concatenated with **str(LC,2)** is stored. **Str(LC,2)** represents the number stored in LC as a two-character sequence. The loop begins with LC set to the initial value 10. This is important. Had the loop begun with LC at 0 and the loop control to 51, we would have had to deal with a blank space in MEMVAR after the L when LC was less than 10. This would have made MEMVAR unusable for the following macro operation.

```
* MENU2PX.PRG

parameter PAGETITLE
clear
? 'Be sure that the printer is ON'
set device to print
set print on
set margin to 5
page = 0

do while .not. eof()
   @ 6,10 say PAGETITLE + ' for ' + CDATE
   @ 8,1
   LC = 10
   do while LC <= 61
         LC  = LC+1
         MEMVAR = 'L' + str(LC,2)
         &MEMVAR = chr(0)
   enddo
   LC = 10
      do typeset
   LC = 10
      do typeset
   LC = 10
   do while LC <= 61
         LC  = LC+1
         MEMVAR = 'L' + str(LC,2)
         ? &MEMVAR
   enddo
   PAGE = PAGE + 1
   @ 62, 30 say str(PAGE,3)
   eject

enddo

set device to screen
set margin to 0
set print off
```

Figure 6-6: MENU2PX: Program for printing customer lists in two columns.

This next statement, **&MEMVAR = chr(0)**, actually creates a memory variable with the name stored in MEMVAR. This is why we fussed about the embedded blank; memory variable names may not have embedded blanks. **Chr(0)** stores a null (nothing) to the new variable. We have effectively created an empty variable.

Typesetting is done a record at a time by the procedure TYPESET. The control loop monitors the position on the page. To preserve the bottom margin (and the program

integrity), we stop typesetting if the counter is greater than 55 (45 lines) going into
the next record. Each record can take up to 6 lines to typeset. The detailed command structure for typesetting the record is shown in Figure 6–7.

```
* TYPESET.PRG

   do while LC < 55 .and. .not. eof()
    LC  = LC+1
    MEMVAR = 'L' + str(LC,2)
    &MEMVAR = &MEMVAR + space(5) + NAME
    if .not. ATTN = space(30)
        LC  = LC+1
        MEMVAR = 'L' + str(LC,2)
        &MEMVAR = &MEMVAR + space(5) + ATTN
    endif
    LC  = LC+1
    MEMVAR = 'L' + str(LC,2)
    &MEMVAR = &MEMVAR + space(5) + ADDRESS + space(5)
    LC  = LC+1
    MEMVAR = 'L' + str(LC,2)
    LT  =        space(5) + trim(CITY)+', '+STATE+'  '+ZIP+space(20)
    &MEMVAR = &MEMVAR + substr(LT,1,35)
    LC  = LC+1
    MEMVAR = 'L' + str(LC,2)
    LT  =        space(5) + CUSTID+' '+CREDIT+'  '+PHONE+space(20)
    &MEMVAR = &MEMVAR + substr(LT,1,35)
    LC  = LC+1
    MEMVAR = 'L' + str(LC,2)
    &MEMVAR = &MEMVAR + space(35)
        skip
   enddo
```

Figure 6–7: TYPESET: Program for record layout in MENU2PX.

```
LC = 10
do while LC <= 61
   LC = LC + 1
   MEMVAR = 'L' + str(LC,2)
   ? &MEMVAR
enddo
```

Once typesetting is complete we are ready to begin printing. This loop simply prints
the 51 memory variables L11 through L61. We can use the question mark to print
since we have used the command **set print on** in the program setup. When print
is set on, print output is sent to both the printer and the monitor. To route print
output to the printer only, use **set console off.** Remember to **set console on** when
finished printing.

QUICK PRINTOUT PROGRAM

This program provides a quick printout consisting of only the customer number and the customer name. It is sorted by customer number. The book dealer has only occasional need for the printout in customer order and never for a detailed printout. The program to provide the quick printout for menu option 3 is MENU23.PRG and is shown in Figure 6–8.

```
* MENU23.PRG

parameter PAGETITLE
clear
? 'Be sure that the printer is turned on!'
set device to print
set console off
page = 0
do while .not. eof()
    @ 6,9 say PAGETITLE + ' for ' + CDATE
    @ 8,1 say ' '
    list off next 50 CUSTID, NAME to print
    PAGE = PAGE + 1
    @ 62,30 say PAGE picture '###'
    eject
enddo
set device to screen
set console on
```

Figure 6–8: Program for quick printout of customer data by customer number: MENU23.PRG.

Note that the bulk of the program is similar to the main print program, MENU2P. The difference is that the bulk of the printing is accomplished by the command:

list off next 50 CUSTID, NAME to print

To avoid having all of the data appear on the screen, we used **set console off**.

SELECTING RECORDS FOR PRINTING

Menu option 4 features a program that allows the user to select records or groups of records for printing by simply filling in a screen form. Our form is shown as Figure 6–9. This is a simple *query by example*.

To get a printout of all customers whose names begin with an A, enter an **A** in the screen space for NAME, leaving all other spaces blank. To get a listing of the customers from states beginning with M, enter an **M** in the screen space for STATE, leaving all other spaces blank. To get a printout of all customers on Peachtree Street in ATLANTA, enter **Peachtree** into the space for street and **Atlanta** into the space for

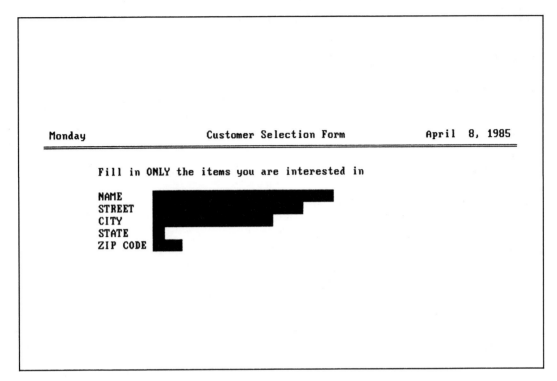

Figure 6–9: Screen display of program MENU24.PRG.

city, leaving all other spaces blank. The combinations are endless. All printouts will be alphabetical by customer since the file is indexed by customer name.

The bush-league artificial intelligence program to accomplish menu option 4 is MENU24.PRG, shown in Figure 6–10. Again, our first step is to set up the memory variables and create the screen. Then we use the contents of these variables to set a *filter* in this work area. A filter is used to hide unwanted records. The process that we are going to go through determines which records we want to hide.

If len(trim(MNAME+MSTREET+MCITY+MSTATE+MZIP)) = 0

This command determines whether we entered any data into any of the variables. We can read the above statement as "if everything is blank." We have concatenated all of the variables so that **trim** will treat them as a single item. If a character (other than a blank space) is contained within the expression being trimmed, the logical length of the expression will be greater than 0.

Having decided that there is data somewhere, we must now find it. The next series of **if** statements is designed to determine which of the five variables contain data. Each variable that contains data will have its content incorporated into the variable COMMAND according to a formula in the program. The formula is slightly different for each field.

```
* MENU24.PRG
clear
do BANNER with "Customer Selection Form"

COMMAND = chr(0)
MCITY   = space(20)
MNAME   = space(30)
MSTATE  = space(2)
MSTREET = space(25)
MZIP    = space(5)

@  5,10 say 'Fill in ONLY the items you are interested in'
@  7,10 say 'NAME    ' get MNAME    picture '@!'
@  8,10 say 'STREET  ' get MSTREET  picture '@!'
@  9,10 say 'CITY    ' get MCITY    picture '@!'
@ 10,10 say 'STATE   ' get MSTATE   picture '@!'
@ 11,10 say 'ZIP CODE' get MZIP     picture '@#'
READ

    if len(trim(MNAME+MSTREET+MCITY+MSTATE+MZIP)) = 0
        return
    endif
    if len(trim(MNAME)) > 0
        COMMAND = COMMAND + 'NAME = trim(MNAME) .and.'
    endif
    if len(trim(MSTREET)) > 0
        COMMAND = COMMAND + 'trim(MSTREET) $ ADDRESS .and.'
    endif
    if len(trim(MCITY)) > 0
        COMMAND = COMMAND + 'CITY = trim(MCITY) .and.'
    endif
    if len(trim(MSTATE)) > 0
        COMMAND = COMMAND + 'STATE = trim(MSTATE) .and.'
    endif
    if len(trim(MZIP)) > 0
        COMMAND = COMMAND + 'ZIP = trim(MZIP) .and.'
    endif

COMMAND = substr(COMMAND,1,len(COMMAND)-5)
set filter to &COMMAND
go top
    if .not. eof()
        do MENU2P with "Special Customer Listing"
    else
        ? 'No Records Meet Your Criteria'
        wait
    endif
set filter to
```

Figure 6–10: MENU24.PRG.

For four out of the five cases, we make use of the fact that the equal sign used to compare character data should be read as *begins with*. The shorter item should be on the right side of the expression. For example, in the following expression, the variable MNAME is the same length as NAME. However, **trim(MNAME)** is the same length or shorter. If we were to reverse the order of these variables, the comparison would be valid only when MNAME and NAME were exactly the same and contained no blanks.

NAME = trim(MNAME)

For the street comparison, we recognize that it is unlikely that we're going to find complete street addresses. We allow the user to enter any part of the address. That part of the address can occur anywhere within the field. Here, however, the order is reversed. The shorter item must be on the left.

Trim(MSTREET) $ ADDRESS

As each item is added to the variable COMMAND, add the logical connector **.and.** to the end. When finished, simply remove the last **.and.** from the sequence—with the **substr** function. This statement determines the length of the variable COMMAND and removes the last five characters.

To set the filter condition built up as the variable COMMAND, use macro substitution into the command string.

Set filter to &COMMAND

When setting the filter, we might have been positioned to a record which was to be hidden. If we issued a **print** or **display** command, the current record would be displayed—even if it was supposed to be "hidden." To make sure you are not on such a record, use the command

go top

This takes us to the first record that is not hidden. If all of the records are hidden, which could be the case, we will be positioned to the end of file. This is very consistent in dBASE III PLUS. If dBASE can't find a record, you should be at the end of the file.

Finally, print the remaining records, the ones that match the search criteria. We have used the detailed program MENU2P. There is no reason that some other printing program cannot be used instead.

PRINTING MAILING LABELS

Labels are printed by using the **label form** command. This command uses information stored in the file MENU25.LBL to print in label format. Up to five labels across can be printed using this command. The word **sample** in the command indicates that a sample row of labels is to be printed so that the operator can align the labels in the printer. When the sample row has been printed, dBASE asks the operator whether another sample is needed. The phrase **to print** indicates that the output is to go to the printer in addition to the screen.

Label forms are created by the command **create label**. They can be changed by the command **modify label**. Both commands are identical. Set up the label form MENU25.LBL from the keyboard with

. create label menu25

This command produces the screen form shown as Figure 6–11, which allows you to define the label format. Horizontal dimensions are in character spaces, while vertical dimensions are in rows. Parameters for five standard labels, as shown below, are built into the form.

> 3 1/2″ by 15/16″ by 1
> 3 1/2″ by 15/16″ by 2
> 3 1/2″ by 15/16″ by 3
> 4″ by 1 7/16″ by 1
> 3 1/5″ by 11/12″ by 3 (Cheshire)

To select a standard label, use the **Up/Down Arrow** keys to highlight the selection *Predefined size*. Press the **Return** key until the desired label parameters are displayed. Each time the key is pressed, a different predefined menu size will be displayed in the selection window. When the desired menu size is displayed, press the **Right Arrow** key to move to the second screen form (Figure 6–12). If your label requirements are not satisfied by one of the five standard values, press the **Up/Down Arrow** keys to highlight the specific parameter values. Press the **Return** key to signal your intent to change the parameter, make the desired change, then press **Return** again to exit.

Figure 6–12 is the screen used to describe what you want printed on the label. All you need to do is fill in the fieldnames to be printed on each line. In this example the ATTN field is printed on line 2. If the field is blank, data from the following lines will be moved up automatically so that a blank line is not printed in the center of the label. The CITY, STATE, and ZIP CODE are printed on line 4. Trailing blank spaces in each field are discarded, and one blank space is printed between each of the fields.

Figure 6–13 shows the exit screen. Use this screen to save or abandon the label. Sample labels from the CUSTOMER file are shown in Figure 6–14.

In this chapter, we have reviewed some of the techniques that you can employ to print the contents of *name* files. We've also shown that you can typeset your printout in memory before sending it to the printer. This trick allows you to make elaborate printed output that isn't usually possible—even if your printer can back up. Finally, the simple query system allows the user to specify which records are to be printed.

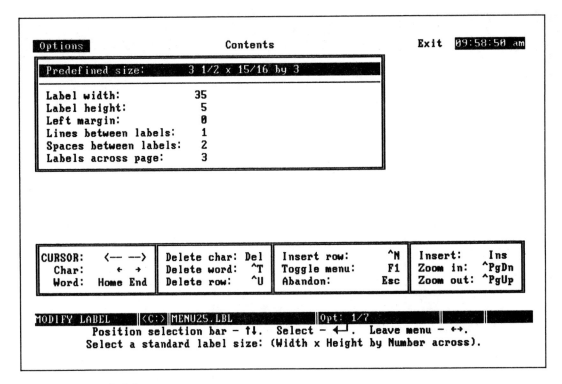

Figure 6–11: Label format screen.

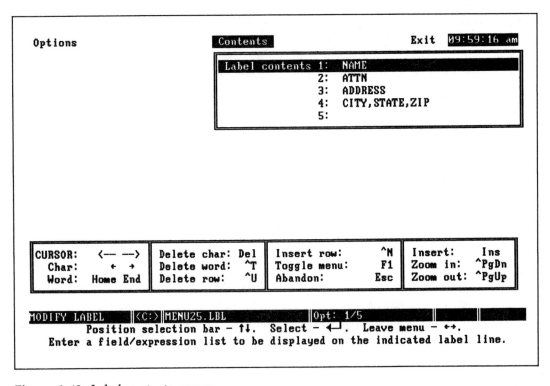

Figure 6–12: Label contents screen.

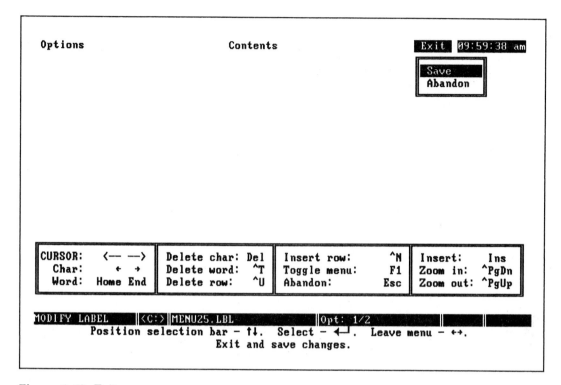

Figure 6–13: Exit screen.

```
************************************    ************************************
************************************    ************************************
************************************    ************************************
************************************    ************************************
************************************    ************************************

52ND STREET BOOK SHOP                   A-1 BOOKS
SHIPPING                                DAVID
126 E. 18TH ST.                         77 E COPPERFIELD
NEW YORK NY 10003                       ASPEN CO 81611


                                        ABC BOOK SELLERS
ABC BOOK SELLERS                        CAROLINE SIMMONS
9715 MINERS AVENUE                      12510 FRONTIER
DALLAS TX 75231                         LIVONIA MI 48154


ACRIMONY                                ACTION BOOKS
MORT EASTON                             ED D. SPORT
2512 NE COLUMBIA                        450 SMALL ROAD
PORTLAND OR 97232                       ACTION MA 01720


ATLANTA BOOKS AND RECORDS               SOFTWORDS, INC
JAMES B DEWEY                           SOFTY
554 PEACHTREE PLAZA                     3301 MILLS AVENUE
ATLANTA GA 30367                        LA CRESCENTA CA 91214
```

Figure 6–14: Sample labels.

CHAPTER SEVEN
The Inventory

This chapter covers programs to help our friendly book dealer better manage the inventory. Specifically included are programs to add, edit, and delete inventory records; automatically issue purchase orders for items that fall below a minimum stock level; and update stock levels when new shipments are received. Although the inventory system in this book is tailored to the special needs of the book distributor, it is easily adapted to most inventory problems.

Inventory management provides our first opportunity to work with a database consisting of several database files. The inventory database for our book distributor consists of three database files.

The Basic Inventory File:	INV
The Supplier File:	PUBLISH
The Books on Order File:	ONORDER

The relationship between these three files is shown in Figure 7-1. The database plans for these files are shown as Figures 7-2, 7-3, and 7-4.

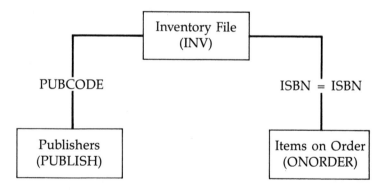

Figure 7-1: Schematic representation of an inventory database.

If we view the database from the supplier's file, each supplier record may connect to many records in the inventory file. This is a *one-to-many* relationship. Conversely, multiple records in the inventory file can point to a single record in the supplier's file. This is a *many-to-one* relationship.

To help keep track of inventory processing, several fields have been added to the CONTROLS database file. The revised plan for CONTROLS is shown in Figure 7-5. The structure of a database is changed by the command **modify structure**. This command is virtually identical to the **create** command used to define the original file.

DESCRIPTION	FIELDNAME	FIELDTYPE	FIELDWIDTH	
ISBN Number	ISBN	Character	13	
Supplier's Code	PUBCODE	Character	7	
Author's Name	AUTHOR	Character	30	
Title of Book	TITLE	Character	30	
Subject Area	SUBJECT	Character	15	
Qty Sold This Year	SOLDTHISYR	Numeric	4	
Qty Sold Last Year	SOLDLASTYR	Numeric	4	
Date of Last Sale	LASTSALE	Date	8	
Qty of Last Shipment	QTYRCVD	Numeric	3	
Date of Last Shipment	LASTRCV	Date	8	
Selling Price	SELLPRICE	Numeric	6	2
Our Cost	COST	Numeric	6	2
Standard Order	ORDERSIZE	Numeric	3	
Min. Stock Level	MINSTOCK	Numeric	3	
Qty in Stock	QTYONHAND	Numeric	3	

RECORD SIZE   ...144 BYTES

FILE TO BE INDEXED ON: ISBN TO ISBN

Figure 7–2: Inventory database plan: INV.DBF.

DESCRIPTION	FIELDNAME	FIELDTYPE	FIELDWIDTH
Supplier's Name	NAME	Character	30
Name of Contact	ATTN	Character	30
Street Address	ADDRESS	Character	25
City	CITY	Character	20
State	STATE	Character	2
Zip Code	ZIP	Character	5
Supplier's Code	PUBCODE	Character	7
Phone Number	PHONE	Character	13

RECORD SIZE   ...133 BYTES

FILE TO BE INDEXED ON: PUBCODE TO \BOOK\DATA\PUBCODE

Figure 7–3: Supplier (publisher) database plan: PUBLISH.DBF.

Modify structure makes a backup copy of the data records in the database being modified. These records are automatically appended to the new structure. The backup copy uses the file extension .BAK.

DESCRIPTION	FIELDNAME	FIELDTYPE	FIELDWIDTH	
ISBN Number	ISBN	Character	13	
Purchase Order No.	PONUMBER	Character	6	
Supplier Code	PUBCODE	Character	7	
Our Cost	COST	Numeric	6	2
Date of Order	ORDERDATE	Date	8	
Qty Ordered	ORDERSIZE	Numeric	3	
Qty Received	QTYRCVD	Numeric	3	

RECORD SIZE ..... 47 BYTES

FILE TO BE INDEXED ON: ISBN TO\BOOK\DATA\ISBN-0

Figure 7–4: Books on order database plan: ONORDER.DBF.

DESCRIPTION	FIELDNAME	FIELDTYPE	FIELDWIDTH
Customer Number	CUSTID	Numeric	6
Last Cust. Edited	LASTEDIT	Character	6
Last Title Edited	INRECORD	Character	13
Update Pgm Cont. Code	UPDATESTEP	Numeric	1
Purchase Order No.	PONUMBER	Numeric	6
Purchase Order Date	PODATE	Date	8

Record Size ..... 41 BYTES

Figure 7–5: CONTROLS.DBF database plan.

The file shown in Figure 7-6, INVUPDAT.DBF, is used in the programs to update inventory quantities when new stock is received.

DESCRIPTION	FIELDNAME	FIELDTYPE	FIELDWIDTH
ISBN Number	ISBN	Character	13
Quantity Received	QTYRCVD	Numeric	3

RECORD SIZE ..... 17 BYTES

Figure 7–6: Update database plan: INVUPDAT.DBF.

The basic inventory database file INV contains the usual information about each inventory item—a description of the item, a part number, a supplier's code, quantity on hand, and so on. Because the database is customized for the book dealer, we use the ISBN number instead of a regular part number. The ISBN number is the book industry's equivalent to a part number. It is a special identifying number that uniquely identifies books published. The ISBN number will be discussed in detail later in this chapter.

The books are supplied by the publishers. Each publisher (supplier) is given a unique identifying code. This code, stored in the field PUBCODE, provides a link between records in the inventory database file and records in the supplier's database PUBLISH. Each record in that database file contains all the relevant information about each supplier: name, point of contact, address, phone number, and so on. The ONORDER file keeps track of each book that is currently on order.

THE INVENTORY MENU

The menu for our inventory system is shown as Figure 7–7. The program used to produce this menu is shown as Figure 7–8. As you might expect, the primary purpose of this program is to display the program choices available and to provide a way for the user to select from among the menu options.

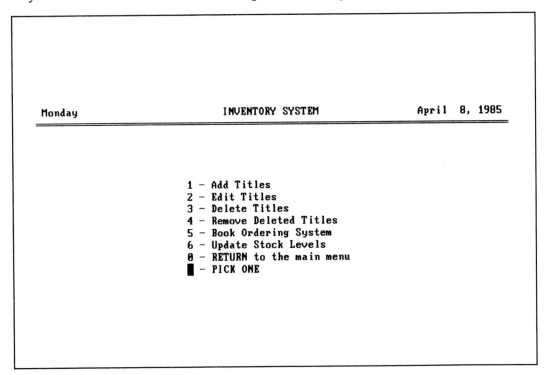

Figure 7–7: Inventory system menu.

When we enter the menu program, our first action is to run program SETUP3. This program, shown as Figure 7–9, sets up the initial conditions for the inventory management system by opening all the inventory database files. An advantage of using these setup files is that it makes it easy to keep track of which files are open.

```
* MENU3.PRG

do SETUP3
do while .T.
   clear
   select INVENTORY
        set relation to PUBCODE into SUPPLIER
        do BANNER with "INVENTORY SYSTEM"
        CHOICES= '01'

        @  8,26 say '1 - Add Titles'
        if reccount() > 0
                @  9,26 say '2 - Edit Titles'
                @ 10,26 say '3 - Delete Titles'
                @ 11,26 say '4 - Remove Deleted Titles'
                @ 12,26 say '5 - Book Ordering System'
                @ 13,26 say '6 - Update Stock Levels'
                CHOICES=CHOICES+'23456'
        endif
   @ row()+1,26 say '0 - RETURN to the main menu '
   @ row()+1,26 say '  - PICK ONE'
   do CHOICE with 26, CHOICES

   do MENU3&CHOICE

enddo
```

Figure 7–8: The inventory menu program—MENU3.PRG.

```
* SETUP3.PRG

clear
? 'Opening Inventory Databases'
select CUSTOMER
                use
select 4
                use PUBLISH index PUBCODE alias SUPPLIER
select 5
                use ONORDER index ISBN-O
select 6
                use INVUPDAT alias UPDATE
```

Figure 7–9: The inventory setup program—SETUP3.PRG.

Remember, you have only 15 files with which to work. When you enter this inventory menu, there are already 11 open files:

MENU.PRG	(the main menu)
MENUPROC.PRG	(the procedure file)
MENU3.PRG	(this menu program)
CONTROLS.DBF	(the controls file)
INV.DBF	(the inventory file)
ISBN.NDX	(the inventory index)
PUBLISH.DBF	(the supplier file)
PUBCODE.NDX	(the supplier index)
ONORDER.DBF	(the onorder file)
ISBN-0.NDX	(the onorder index)
INVUPDAT.DBF	(the update file)

Managing the files is relatively easy when you can use the setup files and menu tree to keep track of where you are. Each file you are using counts as one open file.

One of the first actions in SETUP3 is to close the CUSTOMER file and any associated indexes. Do this with the **use** command without an accompanying filename. These files are not needed in the inventory system. Always close files that aren't needed—but don't do it more often than necessary. Continually opening and closing files makes it difficult to keep track of the files you are using. Upon leaving the inventory menu program—to return to the main menu—we use the program MENU30 (Figure 7–10) to close the inventory files PUBLISH, ONORDER, and INVUPDAT and reopen the CUSTOMER file. Most of the other menu selections expect CUSTOMER to be open.

```
* MENU30.PRG

clear
? 'Closing Inventory Databases'
select 4
                  use
select 5
                  use
select 6
                  use
select 1
                  use CUSTOMER
return to master
```

Figure 7–10: MENU30.PRG.

Returning to the menu program itself, you should notice that the INVENTORY file is selected on each pass through the **do** loop. This step makes sure that a selection is made with the files in a known configuration.

Set relation to PUBCODE into SUPPLIER

The **set relation** command links the file in the selected work area (in this case IN-VENTORY) to the file in the named work area. The key to the linkage is the

INVENTORY field PUBCODE. Each time the INVENTORY file is repositioned, the SUPPLIER index is searched automatically for the content of the INVENTORY field PUBCODE. The fieldnames in the two files need not be the same. Only the contents of the fields must match. The **set relation** command is equivalent to issuing the following command sequence every time INVENTORY is repositioned:

```
select SUPPLIER
seek INVENTORY->PUBCODE
select INVENTORY
```

ADDING TITLES TO THE INVENTORY

New titles are added to the inventory by MENU31.PRG. This program, shown in Figure 7–11, uses two auxiliary programs: MENU3S.PRG and ISBNTEST.

MENU3S.PRG (Figure 7–12) produces the screen for entering data about both books and publishers (Figure 7–13). ISBNTEST is a procedure to validate ISBN numbers and should be added to the procedure file MENUPROC.PRG.

Let's look at the logic of MENU31.PRG. Books are to be added to the inventory by their ISBN numbers. As a convenience to the user, the last record entered is displayed when the user is prompted to enter the next ISBN number.

Note that most of this program consists of tests. Was an ISBN number entered? If not, we want to return to the inventory menu. If one was, we must determine whether it is already in the database. If it is, a beep is sounded and the program **loop**s back to the beginning of the **do** loop.

If the ISBN number is not in the database, we probably want to add it, but first we use the procedure ISBNTEST to verify that the number is valid. ISBNTEST also extracts the publisher's identification code from the ISBN number. If the ISBN number is valid, we add a blank record to the inventory file. If the publisher is not already in the supplier file, we want to SELECT that file and add a blank record.

Note the command **go recno( )**. This translates as "go to where you are." This command is vital. **Append blank** added a blank record to the inventory file. This command repositioned the inventory file to that new blank record. Remember SUPPLIER is related to INVENTORY by the content of the inventory field PUBCODE. SUPPLIER was automatically searched for a matching PUBCODE by that repositioning. Since there is no such record, SUPPLIER is positioned to the blank record at the end of file. The **replace** command does not affect positioning and hence does not trigger another search of SUPPLIER for the now correct PUBCODE. **Go recno( )** is a positioning command and does trigger a search of SUPPLIER, moving its record pointer to the matching record (if there is one).

To find out whether the publisher is already in the SUPPLIER file, we compare the publisher's codes from both INVENTORY and SUPPLIER. If they match, the publisher

```
* MENU31.PRG

clear
do BANNER with "Add Title To Inventory"
if reccount() > 0
   go reccount()
endif
do MENU3S
clear gets
select INVENTORY

do while .T.
   MISBN     = space(13)
   MPUBCODE  = space(7)
   VALIDTEST = .F.
   @ 23,2 say "Enter the ISBN Number" get MISBN
   read
                         if MISBN = space(13)
                             exit
                         endif
   @ 23,40
   seek MISBN
                         if .not. eof()
                             @ 23,40 say MISBN + ' is in the database'
                             ?? BELL
                             loop
                         endif
   do ISBNTEST with MISBN, MPUBCODE, VALIDTEST
                         if .not. VALIDTEST
                             @ 23,40 say MISBN + ' is not valid'
                             ?? BELL
                             loop
                         endif
   append blank
   replace ISBN with MISBN, PUBCODE with MPUBCODE
   go recno()            && force reposition of related file
                         if SUPPLIER->PUBCODE = space(7)
                             select SUPPLIER
                             append blank
                             replace PUBCODE with MPUBCODE
                         endif
   select INVENTORY
   do MENU3S
   read
enddo
? 'Saving New Book Information .... please wait'
use INV index ISBN alias INVENTORY    && open and close to protect data
select SUPPLIER
use PUBLISH index PUBCODE alias SUPPLIER
```

Figure 7–11: MENU31.PRG.

```
* MENU3S.PRG

@ 0,0
if deleted()
   @ 0,65 say 'Deleted'
endif
@  5,2  say 'Title   '           get INVENTORY->TITLE      picture '@!'
@  6,2  say 'Author  '           get INVENTORY->AUTHOR     picture '@!'
@  7,2  say 'Subject '           get INVENTORY->SUBJECT    picture '@!'
@  6,53 say 'Our Cost       '    get INVENTORY->COST
@  7,53 say 'Selling Price  '    get INVENTORY->SELLPRICE
@  8,53 say 'Quantity on hand '  get INVENTORY->QTYONHAND
@  9,53 say 'Min. Stock Level '  get INVENTORY->MINSTOCK
@ 10,53 say 'Std. Order Size  '  get INVENTORY->ORDERSIZE
@  5,53 say 'ISBN Number '   + INVENTORY->ISBN
@  8,28 say 'Last Sale     ' + dtoc(INVENTORY->LASTSALE)
@  9,28 say 'Last Shipment ' + dtoc(INVENTORY->LASTRCV)
@ 10,28 say 'Quantity Rcvd ' + str(INVENTORY->QTYRCVD,3)
@  9,2  say str(INVENTORY->SOLDTHISYR,3)+' sold this year'
@ 10,2  say str(INVENTORY->SOLDLASTYR,3)+' sold last year'
@ 14,1  say BAR
@ 14,30 say "Information on Publisher"


@ 16,3  say 'Publisher   '  get SUPPLIER->NAME      picture '@!'
@ 17,3  say 'Attention   '  get SUPPLIER->ATTN      picture '@!'
@ 18,3  say 'Address     '  get SUPPLIER->ADDRESS   picture '@!'
@ 19,3  say 'City        '  get SUPPLIER->CITY      picture '@!'
@ 20,3  say 'State       '  get SUPPLIER->STATE     picture '@!'
@ 20,50 say 'Zip Code    '  get SUPPLIER->ZIP       picture '99999'
@ 16,50 say 'Phone Number '  get SUPPLIER->PHONE    picture '(999)999-9999'
```

Figure 7–12: MENU3S.PRG.

is already there. If not, we must **select** the supplier file, add a blank record, and return to INVENTORY.

Book information is entered into both the INVENTORY record and the SUPPLIER record by the single program MENU3S.PRG. The data-entry screen produced by this program is shown in Figure 7–13. This screen makes it appear that book and publisher information form a single record. Note that we can enter information into both files from this screen. When entering data into other than the selected file, you must specify the file's alias as well as the fieldname. In earlier versions of dBASE, you weren't permitted to do this.

Note that we used **exit** rather than **return** to escape from the loop. **Exit** takes us to the first command after the **enddo**. In this case we want to close and then reopen both the SUPPLIER and INVENTORY files. By doing this we protect the user from possible data loss caused by an untoward event—such as tripping over the power

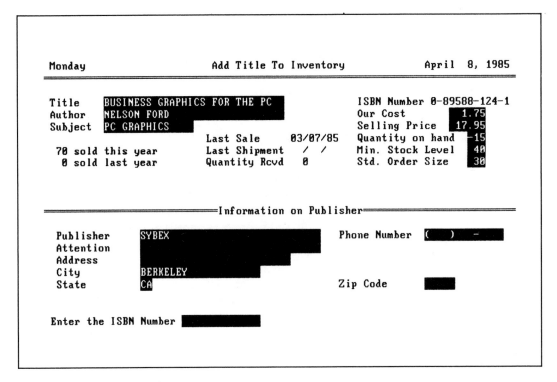

```
Monday                    Add Title To Inventory            April  8, 1985


 Title   BUSINESS GRAPHICS FOR THE PC        ISBN Number 0-89588-124-1
 Author  NELSON FORD                         Our Cost               1.75
 Subject PC GRAPHICS                         Selling Price         17.95
                         Last Sale   03/07/85 Quantity on hand       -15
    70 sold this year    Last Shipment  /  /  Min. Stock Level        40
     0 sold last year    Quantity Rcvd   0    Std. Order Size         30



                   ═══════════Information on Publisher═══════════

    Publisher  SYBEX                    Phone Number  (   )   -
    Attention
    Address
    City       BERKELEY
    State      CA                       Zip Code


    Enter the ISBN Number
```

Figure 7–13: Inventory data-entry screen.

cord. When a file is closed, the record counter in the database file header is updated (the records had been written to disk all along) to match the number of records added to the file. If many records are to be added at a single sitting, it is wise to pull this operation into the loop—opening and closing on each record. Doing so might slow the computer operation (particularly on floppy disks). The trade-off that you must make balances the chance of losing data against the slowdown caused by closing and reopening (in this case, four) files.

THE ISBN NUMBER

The ISBN number is worth a great deal of discussion. For readers who have the option of creating a part-numbering system, it deserves consideration. It provides an excellent example of a numbering system designed for use in a computer, combining supplier identification and part identification.

ISBN stands for International Standard Book Number. The ISBN number itself is normally represented (and used) as a 13-character number. The number is composed of four parts, normally separated by hyphens. There are ten digits in the four groups. Examples of ISBN numbers are:

3-88053-002-5
950-7000-10-X

The size of each of the first three groups can vary, although there are always nine digits total. The last group is always a single digit.

The first group is the group identifier, which is used to identify countries, geographic regions, languages, and so forth. The second group identifies the publisher (a supplier code). The number of digits in this group varies according to the number of titles for a publisher. Large publishers have small publisher identifiers and vice versa. The third group is the book identification number for the publisher. The fourth group, which is always a single digit, is the check digit.

The ISBN number can be verified by a simple calculation. If the result of the following operation is evenly divisible by 11 (that is, the number is modulo 11), the number is a valid ISBN number. This is an example of a number that is designed for use by a computer. The number is unique and can be tested for validity.

```
ISBN                     3 8 8 0 5 3 0 0 2 5
DIGIT MULTIPLIER        10 9 8 7 6 5 4 3 2 1

PRODUCT      30+72+64+0+30+15+0+0+4+5 = 220
```

ISBNTEST

The procedure to validate ISBN numbers is shown in Figure 7-14. The procedure should be added to the procedure file MENUPROC.PRG. The procedure assumes that hyphens are used to separate the four groups in the ISBN number. It extracts the publisher's ID code as well as validating the number.

To separate the number into four groups, we make use of the **at**, **left**, **right**, and **len** functions. **At( )** gives us the position of the first hyphen in the ISBN number. The **left( )** function extracts the characters to the left of the hyphen. The **right( )** function together with the **len( )** function gives us the characters to the right of the hyphen.

The only "group" whose position we can be sure of is the check digit, so our first step is to separate the ISBN number into two pieces—CHECKDIGIT and REM (for remainder). The character before the check digit, which is assumed to be a hyphen, is discarded.

Next, we use the **at( )** function to locate the first hyphen in REM. The **left( )** and **right( )** functions give us the GROUP identifier and a new REM. The operation is repeated to extract the publisher's ID, MPUB, and the book identifier, BOOKID. These three variables are concatenated to form a new variable, ISBNNUMBER, which contains the first nine digits of the ISBN number without the hyphens.

The **do** loop multiplies each digit by the appropriate multiplier for that digit and stores the accumulated result in CHECK. We can perform arithmetic operations on character variables by means of the **val( )** function, which treats the numeric characters

```
procedure ISBNTEST
   parameters MISBN,MPUB,TEST
   private CHECKDIGIT, ISBNNUMBER, REM, DASH, GROUP, BOOKID, ISBNTEST, CHECK
   CHECKDIGIT = right(MISBN,1)
   REM        = left(MISBN,11)
   if '-' $ REM
        DASH     = at('-',REM)
        GROUP    = left(REM,DASH-1)
        REM      = right(REM,len(REM)-DASH)
   endif
   if '-' $ REM
        DASH     = at('-',REM)
        MPUB     = left(REM,DASH-1)
        BOOKID   = right(REM,len(REM)-DASH)
   endif
   ISBNNUMBER = GROUP+MPUB+BOOKID
   if len(ISBNNUMBER) = 9 .and. CHECKDIGIT $ '0123456789X'
        CHECK    = iif(CHECKDIGIT = 'X',10,val(CHECKDIGIT))

        X = 1
        do while X <= 9
           CHECK = CHECK + val(substr(ISBNNUMBER,X,1)) * (11-X)
           X = X+1
        enddo
        if mod(CHECK,11) = 0        && is check evenly divisible by 11
           TEST = .T.
        endif
   endif
return
```

Figure 7–14: Procedure to validate an ISBN number: ISBNTEST.

as if they were numbers. The **val** of any non-numeric character is zero.

If the candidate ISBN number is valid, CHECK will be evenly divisible by 11. We can test for this condition with the **mod( )** function. **Mod( )** has two arguments; a number and a divisor. The output of this function is the remainder after the number is divided by the divisor. If the output is zero, there is no remainder. In our case this means the ISBN number is valid.

EDITING INVENTORY RECORDS

The program MENU32.PRG, to edit inventory records, is shown in Figure 7–15. This program is similar to the program for editing customer records. The user is prompted to enter a key (the ISBN number). The database is searched for that key. When a record is found we go into the edit mode, using the screen created by MENU3S.PRG (Figure 7–13).

```
* MENU32.PRG

clear
do BANNER with "Edit an Inventory Record"
seek CONTROLS->INVRECORD
do MENU3S
clear gets

do while .T.
    select INVENTORY
    MISBN     = space(13)
    do FINDISBN with "Enter the ISBN Number", MISBN
                        if MISBN = space(13)
                            return
                        endif
    do MENU3S
    read
    select INVENTORY
        replace ISBN with ISBN
    select CONTROLS
        replace INVRECORD with INVENTORY->ISBN
enddo
```

Figure 7–15: Program to edit inventory records: MENU32.PRG.

When finished editing each record, we immediately select the INVENTORY file and replace any field with itself. This ensures that any changes made to the inventory data are written to the disk (remember, MENU3S selects the SUPPLIER file). Then the CONTROLS file is selected and the current ISBN number is entered. This record keeps track of the last item edited. The next time this menu item is selected, CONTROLS will remember which record was last edited.

The procedure FINDISBN is used to select records for editing. This procedure is shown in Figure 7-16. FINDISBN receives a screen legend and a blank memory variable MISBN from the calling program. The user is asked to enter an ISBN number. When a number is entered, the index file is searched for that ISBN number. If the search is successful, we return to the calling program. Otherwise, we run the procedure ISBNTEST to validate the ISBN number. We have to pass three parameters to ISBNTEST. But, in this case, we don't care about the publisher's code. Nevertheless, because of the *parameter* statement in FINDISBN, we have to pass a parameter in the correct location. We choose to send the 'BOGIE' character string.

DELETE/UNDELETE TITLES

The program for deleting and undeleting inventory records is shown as Figure 7-17. As when editing, we want to enter an ISBN number and have the program retrieve

```
procedure FINDISBN
    parameters LEGEND, MISBN
    do while .T.
       private all
       VALIDTEST = .F.
       a 23,2 say LEGEND get MISBN picture 'a!'
       read
       a 23,40
                      if MISBN = space(13)
                          exit
                      endif
          seek MISBN
                      if found()
                          exit
                      endif

       do ISBNTEST with MISBN, 'BOGIE', VALIDTEST
       do ERRORMSG with ;
           MISBN+ iif(VALIDTEST,' is not in the database',' is invalid'),23,40
    enddo
return
```

Figure 7–16: Procedure FINDISBN.

and display the record. We used the procedure FINDISBN for the ask and search part of this program.

Once we have a record on screen, we want to verify that this is the correct record and that the action to be taken is correct. A very common procedure is to ask the user a yes/no question. We use the procedure QUERY for the purpose of asking the user such questions. This single procedure (shown in Figure 7–18) saves you much typing. QUERY is exactly the kind of process for which procedures were designed: short programs that can be used over and over.

For QUERY we pass four parameters: a legend, the starting row and the starting column position for the display, and the name of the variable to contain the response. We created ANSWER in the original setup program and declared it to be a public variable. There is no need to re-create this variable in the calling program. It is created in the subroutine to make sure that it is initially blank.

REMOVING INVENTORY RECORDS

Removing records is usually reserved for a separate operation from deleting records. This allows the user to choose when the records are actually removed. The **pack** process can be time-consuming if the database is large. The program for removing inventory records is similar to that for removing customer records. This program, MENU34.PRG, is shown as Figure 7–19.

```
* MENU33.PRG

clear
do BANNER with "Delete/Undelete Titles From Inventory"
do while .T.
   ANSWER   = space(1)
   MISBN    = space(13)
   do FINDISBN with "Enter the ISBN Number ", MISBN

               if MISBN = space(1)
                   return
               endif


   do MENU3S
   clear gets
   do QUERY with iif(deleted(),'Recall','Delete')+' this title (Y/N)? ',;
               23,2,ANSWER

               if ANSWER = 'Y'
                   if .not. deleted()
                       delete
                   else
                       recall
                   endif
                   @ 0,65 say iif(deleted(),'Deleted',space(7))
               endif
enddo
```

Figure 7–17: Program to delete/undelete inventory records: MENU33.PRG.

```
procedure QUERY
     parameters LEGEND, ROW, COL, ANSWER
     ANSWER = ' '
     @ ROW,COL
     do while .not. ANSWER $ 'YN'
         @ ROW,COL say LEGEND get ANSWER picture '!'
         read
     enddo
     @ ROW,COL
return
```

Figure 7–18: Procedure QUERY.

```
* MENU34.PRG

clear
? 'Searching for deleted records'
locate for deleted()
if .not. eof()
    ? 'The following Records are marked for deletion'
    display off next 1000000 ISBN,TITLE for deleted()
                ?
                ?
    do QUERY with 'Remove These Records (Y/N)? ',row(),2,ANSWER

            if ANSWER $ 'yY'
                set talk on
                clear
                ? 'Records are being removed - please be patient'
                pack
                set talk off
            endif
else
    ? 'There are no records marked for deletion'
    wait
endif
```

Figure 7–19: Program to remove deleted records: MENU34.PRG.

ORDERING BOOKS

Menu selection 5 to order books is itself a menu selection to allow the user to order books, reprint purchase orders, and obtain information about books on order. The menu program MENU35.PRG is shown in Figure 7–20. The screen display from this program is shown as Figure 7–21. Programs called from this sub-menu will use all three of the inventory database files, as well as the CONTROLS file.

On each pass through the menu, ONORDER and INVENTORY are selected and relations are set into the INVENTORY and SUPPLIER files. This provides us a single point of initialization—and a single place to look for each program's initial conditions. Remember, although this menu is first entered from the inventory menu, it can (and will) be entered from below as options are selected and completed.

Again, we have hidden most menu selections when the ONORDER file is empty. This is a nice touch, even though no harm would be done if the hidden selections were made when the database file was empty. On a different note, we hide the order-books selection when books have already been ordered the same day.

```
*MENU35.PRG

do while .T.
   CHOICES = '0'
   select INVENTORY
      set relation to PUBCODE into SUPPLIER
   select ONORDER
      set relation to ISBN into INVENTORY
   clear

   do BANNER with "Book Ordering System"
   if year(CONTROLS->PODATE) # 0
      @ 23,3 say 'Last Purchase Order was '+CONTROLS->PONUMBER-1+;
                'dated '+dtoc(CONTROLS->PODATE)
   endif


   if CONTROLS->PODATE # date()
       @ 8.26 say '1 - Order Books'
       CHOICES = '01'
   else
       @ 8,26 say ' '
   endif
   if reccount() > 0
       @ row()+1,26 say '2 - Reprint Book Orders'
       @ row()+1,26 say '3 - Display Books On Order'
       @ row()+1,26 say '4 - Print Books On Order'
       CHOICES = CHOICES + '234'
   endif
       @ row()+1,26 say '0 - RETURN to the main menu '
       @ row()+1,26 say '  - PICK ONE'

   do CHOICE with 26,CHOICES

   do case
      case CHOICE = '0'
           return
      case CHOICE = '2'
           do MENU352 with CHOICE,CDATE,BAR
      otherwise
           do MENU35&CHOICE
   endcase
enddo
```

Figure 7–20: Menu program for ordering books: MENU35.PRG.

```
Monday                    Book Ordering System          April  8, 1985


                          1 - Order Books
                          2 - Reprint Book Orders
                          3 - Display Books On Order
                          4 - Print Books On Order
                          0 - RETURN to the main menu
                          █ - PICK ONE




Last Purchase Order was   100005 dated 01/29/85
```

Figure 7–21: Book ordering menu.

PROGRAM TO ORDER BOOKS

The program to order books is shown as Figure 7–22. What does this program actually do? First it scans the inventory to determine which books (if any) need to be ordered. If any are found, the program enters the book-ordering mode; otherwise, it informs the user that "no books need to be ordered." Books that need to be ordered are those where the quantity on hand plus the quantity already on order still falls below the minimum stock level.

To determine whether any books need to be purchased, we select the INVENTORY file and relate it to the ONORDER file. We must previously turn off the relation from ONORDER to INVENTORY. Not doing so would have created a *cyclic relation* where ONORDER was related to INVENTORY and vice versa. Cyclic relations are not permitted. Once we have established the relation linking ONORDER to INVENTORY we use the command:

set filter to QTYONHAND + ONORDER->ORDERSIZE < MINSTOCK

Set filter hides all the records in the selected database (INVENTORY) that do not meet a specified condition. This condition includes the linked record in ONORDER. This command translates as "Hide all records in INVENTORY where the content of the field QTYONHAND plus the content of ORDERSIZE are not less than the

```
* MENU351.PRG

clear
? 'Searching Inventory for books that need to be ordered '
select ONORDER
   set relation to
select INVENTORY
   set relation to ISBN into ONORDER
   set filter to QTYONHAND + ONORDER->ORDERSIZE < MINSTOCK
   go top
               if eof()
                  ? 'No books need to be ordered'
                  wait
               else
                  ? 'Processing Book Orders'
               endif
MPONUMBER = CONTROLS->PONUMBER
do while .not. eof()
     MPUBCODE = PUBCODE
     do while INVENTORY->PUBCODE = MPUBCODE .and. .not. eof()
        select ONORDER
        sum ORDERSIZE while INVENTORY->ISBN = ISBN to QTYONORDER
        if QTYONORDER + INVENTORY->QTYONHAND < INVENTORY->MINSTOCK
           append blank
           replace ISBN      with INVENTORY->ISBN,;
                   ORDERDATE with date(),;
                   ORDERSIZE with INVENTORY->ORDERSIZE
           replace COST      with INVENTORY->COST,;
                   PONUMBER  with str(CONTROLS ->PONUMBER,6);
                   PUBCODE   with INVENTORY->PUBCODE
           do while QTYONORDER + ORDERSIZE < INVENTORY->MINSTOCK
              replace ORDERSIZE with ORDERSIZE+INVENTORY->ORDERSIZE
           enddo
        endif
        select INVENTORY
        skip
     enddo
        select  CONTROLS
        replace PONUMBER  with PONUMBER +1,PODATE with date()
        select INVENTORY
enddo
set filter to
set relation to PUBCODE into SUPPLIER
select ONORDER
set relation to ISBN into INVENTORY
if MPONUMBER # CONTROLS->PONUMBER
   do MENU352 with '1',CDATE,BAR
endif
```

Figure 7–22: Program to order books: MENU351.PRG.

minimum stock level." When this condition is set, you are positioned to an INVEN-TORY record. At this point you are at that same record—whether the filter condition is true or not. We want to be at the first record meeting the condition (the first book to be ordered). We accomplish this by **go top**. If there are no records to be ordered, **go top** takes you to the end of the file—setting the EOF flag. The **do** loop to order books is only activated if the record pointer is not at the end of file when the **do while** command is encountered. The variable MPONUMBER is used as a flag to control printing of purchase orders if any were issued.

If we think that books are to be ordered, we want to order all the books from a particular publisher in a group. Owing to the nature of the ISBN number—which begins with a group ID followed by a publisher's ID, books from a publisher are naturally grouped together in the inventory. We use the inner **do** loop to process potential orders from a particular publisher. The control on this loop is set by the variable MPUBCODE, which contains the inventory publisher's code when the loop is entered. We stay in this loop until we encounter a different publisher code.

The first step within this loop is to select the ONORDER file and add up the quantity of books on order for the particular ISBN number. Why? There can be several orders already placed for a particular item. The relation picks up only the first of multiple orders. We must be selected to ONORDER to have access to any multiple records. The **sum** command picks up the total quantity already on order for an ISBN number. That quantity may be less than the minimum stock level. If it is, we want to add a blank record to the ONORDER file and automatically enter all the relevant information for the order with **replace**. The **replace** commands could be written as a single command:

```
replace ISBN with INVENTORY->ISBN, ORDERDATE with date( ),;
ORDERSIZE with INVENTORY->ORDERSIZE, COST with INVENTORY->COST,;
PONUMBER with str(CONTROLS->PONUMBER,6),;
PUBCODE with INVENTORY->PUBCODE
```

The command as shown in the program is formatted to be more readable, although it will work as shown. There is a compromise between making the program readable and making it efficient. Readable programs are more maintainable. But, as in this case, they can be slightly less efficient. Two replace commands were used because dBASE limits commands to 254 characters. When a command is continued on multiple lines, use the semicolon to indicate continuity.

A word of caution: The dBASE III PLUS **modify command** editor wraps at 66 characters. When you get this automatic line wrap do *not* use the semicolon.

The innermost **do** loop is used to handle the case where the standard order is not large enough to bring the inventory up to the minimum stock level.

When the book has been entered into the ONORDER file, we go back to the INVENTORY file and advance to the next record that meets the filter criteria. If that record does *not* have the publisher code stored in the variable MPUBCODE or if we've hit the end of the database, we have finished with this purchase order. We automatically exit from the loop, select the CONTROLS file and increment the purchase order number.

If we haven't yet reached the end of file, we store the new publisher's code to the variable MPUBCODE and start the next purchase order. If we have, we exit from the **do** loop and "turn off" the filter with **set filter to**.

Next, we return to the standard file conditions of the menu system and (provided that purchase orders were issued) enter the print routine. How do we know that purchase orders were issued? Before we entered the **do** loop, we stored the last purchase order number to MPONUMBER. If the current purchase order is different from that variable, we must have issued at least one purchase order.

The print routine used here is the same one that can be called from the menu. To distinguish between the two, we pass the parameter '1' to indicate the source of the program called.

PRINTING PURCHASE ORDERS

The program to print purchase orders is shown as Figure 7–23. You should always provide a way to print duplicates of any paperwork. There is always the possibility that the original will get shredded in the printer or destroyed in some other way.

This program is automatically called by the ordering program. It can also be selected from the menu. When it is called by the ordering program, we want to print only those orders just entered into the file ONORDER. When it is called from the menu, we might want to print a single purchase order or all of the orders issued on a particular day. To tell the program how it was called, we pass a parameter. If the program was called from the menu, we pass the menu selection CHOICE.

Declaring all variables private hides any higher-level variables with the same name from this and the subroutine MENU35P.PRG, which prints the invoices. This program merely prepares the system. If the program is called from the menu, SELECTION ='2' is true. We display the variables MPONUMBER and MDATE together with descriptive text and let the user select what is to be printed. The **text** command will display the text between the command and the command **endtext**. **Text** tells dBASE III PLUS to stop interpreting—until an **endtext** is encountered.

If the variable PONUMBER is greater than 100000, which it can be only if the selection is '2,' we set the filter to that purchase order number. Otherwise we set the filter to a date. All records that don't meet the filter condition are hidden until the filter is turned off or changed.

THE PURCHASE ORDER PRINT PROGRAM

The program that actually prints the selected purchase orders is shown in Figure 7–24. A sample purchase order printed by this program is shown in Figure 7–25. This

```
* MENU352.PRG

parameter SELECTION,CDATE,BAR
private all
clear
do BANNER with "Print Purchase Orders"
    MDATE     = CONTROLS->PODATE
    MPONUMBER = space(6)
    MTOTAL = 0

if SELECTION = "2"
    @ 6,3 say "Purchase Order Number" get MPONUMBER
    @ 8,3 say "Date " get MDATE
       text
       To print a single purchase order - enter the P.O. Number

       To print all purchase orders on a date - enter the date
       endtext
    read
endif

if VAL(MPONUMBER) >= 100000
    set filter to PONUMBER = MPONUMBER
else
    set filter to MDATE = ORDERDATE
endif

go top
read
? 'Be sure that your printer is turned on!'
set device to print
do MENU35P
set device   to screen
set filter to
```

Figure 7–23: Program to reprint purchase orders: MENU352.PRG.

program consists of two **do** loops, one inside the other. The outer loop is used to set up the conditions for the inner loop, to print the page heading and the purchase order totals, and to eject each page as it is finished. This print program automatically prints items from three database files: ONORDER, INVENTORY, and SUPPLIER. For the information of those readers interested in relational operations, the program performs a virtual, natural **join**.

```
* MENU35P.PRG

do while .not. eof()
    MPONUMBER = PONUMBER
    ODATE  = cmonth(ORDERDATE) + str(day(ORDERDATE),3) + ;
              ','+str(year(ORDERDATE),5)

    @ 3,1  say 'Purchase Order: '+PONUMBER
    @ 3,(69-len(ODATE)) say ODATE
    @ 5,1  say 'TO: '
    @ 5,10 say SUPPLIER->NAME
    @ 6,10 say SUPPLIER->ADDRESS
    @ 7,10 say trim(SUPPLIER->CITY)+', '+SUPPLIER->STATE+'  '+SUPPLIER->ZIP
    if SUPPLIER->ATTN # space(30)
        @ 8,10 say 'ATTN: '+SUPPLIER->ATTN
    endif
    @ 10,1  say 'FROM:'
    @ 10,10 say "BOB'S BETTER BOOKS"
    @ 10,57 say '213-204-5570'
    @ 11,10 say '3800 Honolulu Avenue'
    @ 12,10 say 'La Crescenta, California   91214'
    @ 13,1  say replicate('-',68)
    @ 14,1  say 'ISBN Number    Title'
    @ 14,41 say '   QTY    COST        TOTAL'
    @ 15,1  say replicate('-',68)

    do while MPONUMBER = PONUMBER .and. prow() < 55 .and. .not. eof()
        MTOTAL = MTOTAL + (COST * ORDERSIZE)
        @ prow()+2,1      say ISBN
        @ prow(),16       say INVENTORY->TITLE
        @ prow(),45       say ORDERSIZE     picture "###"
        @ prow(),50       say COST          picture "###.##"
        @ prow(),59       say COST*ORDERSIZE picture "###,###.##"
        skip
    enddo
    if MPONUMBER # PONUMBER .or. eof()
        @ prow()+2,44 say '* Total *'
        @ prow(),56   say MTOTAL picture '##,###,###.##'
        MTOTAL = 0
    endif
    eject
enddo
```

Figure 7–24: Print program: MENU35P.PRG.

```
Purchase Order:   100001                    January 29, 1986

TO:       ROBERT J. BRADY CO.
          1776 INDEPENDENCE CIRCLE
          ANNAPOLIS, MD  20715
          ATTN: DAVID CULVERWELL

FROM:     BOB'S BETTER BOOKS                      213-204-5570
          3800 Honolulu Avenue
          La Crescenta, California   91214
-----------------------------------------------------------------
ISBN Number     Title                       QTY    COST      TOTAL
-----------------------------------------------------------------

0-89303-241-7   IBM PC ASSEMBLY LANGUAGE    101    1.00     101.00

                                        * Total *           101.00
```

Figure 7-25: Sample purchase order.

Each purchase order has a header, a body, and a footer. The header consists of the purchase order number, the date, to and from, and column titles. The body of the purchase order (P.O.) consists of information about each book being ordered. The footer consists of just the total. A purchase order may take more than one page.

The header and footer are printed by the outer **do** loop. The body of the report is created by the inner **do** loop. Note that the inner loop has several conditions attached to it. It continues only as long as the ONORDER records are for the same purchase order. If there are too many records for a single page, the loop is terminated when the print position on the page reaches line 55 **(prow( ) < 55)**. In addition, the loop is terminated by the end-of-file condition.

The records are in the proper order (by PONUMBER) even though they are indexed by the ISBN number because records from other dates (or purchase orders) are hidden by the filter. The ORDER program is prevented from running more than once on the same date by the ORDER menu. So we cannot have two purchase orders for the same item on a given date.

Note that the total is printed only when the purchase order number does not match that stored in the variable MPONUMBER. At this time, we reset the variable MTOTAL to zero. This variable was originally set in the calling program.

DISPLAY PURCHASE ORDERS ON THE SCREEN

To get information about purchase orders, we have provided the program MENU353.PRG, which is shown in Figure 7-26. This program produces a screen display similar to that shown in Figure 7-27. This program is used to demonstrate the use of the **list** command to display data. By using **list** in this way we have avoided using another **do** loop.

```
* MENU353.PRG

go top
do while .T.
   clear
   do BANNER with "Books Currently On Order"
   do while row() < 17 .and. .not. eof()
     MPUBCODE = PUBCODE
     ?
     ? SUPPLIER->NAME
     ?
     list off ISBN, INVENTORY->TITLE, ORDERDATE, ORDERSIZE, PONUMBER  ;
             while row() <= 20 .and. MPUBCODE = PUBCODE
   enddo
   a 23,3 say "Press Esc to abort"
   KEYCODES = ' 27'
   if .not. bof()
      ?? ', PgUp to Backup'
      KEYCODES = KEYCODES + ' 18'
   endif
   if .not. eof()
      ?? ', PgUp to Advance'
      KEYCODES = KEYCODES + '  3'
   endif
   do INKEY with KEYCODES
   do case
        case INKEY = 27      && escape
            exit
        case INKEY = 18      && PgUp key
            skip -40
        case INKEY =  3      && PgDn key
            skip
     endcase
enddo
```

Figure 7-26: Program to display open orders: MENU353.PRG.

This program displays information about each book on order. The books are grouped by the publisher. The inner loop continues until text is displayed on at least line 16. Note that the command list can continue until line 20. The loop shuts off to prevent displaying a publisher's name without any books.

User options are displayed at the bottom of the screen. The options: *backup, forward,* and *abort* depend on position. If the **bof** flag is set, the backup option is excluded, while the forward option is prevented when the end of file is reached.

Selection and control are accomplished by the procedure INKEY (shown in Figure 7-28), which makes use of the **inkey( )** function. INKEY pauses the program until an

```
Monday                    Books Currently On Order              April  8, 1985
================================================================================

MACMILLAN PUBLISHING CO., INC.

   ISBN            INVENTORY->TITLE                 ORDERDATE ORDERSIZE PONUMBER
   0-02-501980-5 HOW TO SAVE ON YOUR INCOME TAX 02/21/85        105 100005
   0-02-501980-5 HOW TO SAVE ON YOUR INCOME TAX 02/21/85        107 100007
   0-02-501980-5 HOW TO SAVE ON YOUR INCOME TAX 02/21/85        113 100013

ASHTON-TATE

   ISBN            INVENTORY->TITLE                 ORDERDATE ORDERSIZE PONUMBER
   0-8359-1246-9 DBASE II FOR EVERY BUSINESS     02/21/85        114 100014

ROBERT J. BRADY CO.

   ISBN            INVENTORY->TITLE                 ORDERDATE ORDERSIZE PONUMBER
   0-89303-241-7 IBM PC ASSEMBLY LANGUAGE        01/29/85        101 100001



   Press B to Backup, Space Bar to move forward, A to abort
```

Figure 7–27: Screen display of open orders.

allowed key is pressed. The allowed keys are stored in the variable KEYCODES. Each key has a numeric code. For example, 27 is the code for the **Esc** key.

```
procedure INKEY
   parameter KEYCODES
   INKEY = 500              && impossible value
   do while .not. str(INKEY,3) $ KEYCODES
      INKEY = inkey()
   enddo
return
```

Figure 7–28: INKEY procedure.

The allowed keycodes are passed to INKEY as a single character variable. This is because dBASE requires us to know how many parameters are being passed, and the number of allowed keys will change depending on the situation, just as in this program. We get around the problem by converting each numeric value to a three-digit character string and concatenating the allowed codes into the single variable KEYCODES. INKEY is a public variable.

PRINTING BOOKS ON ORDER

The last item on the sub-menu lets the user get a printout of books on order by supplier. The program is shown as Figure 7–29. The program is basically the same as the program for displaying orders on screen.

```
* MENU354.PRG

clear
do BANNER with "Print Books On Order"
read
? 'Be sure that your printer is turned on!'
go top
PAGE     = 0
LINEFEED = chr(10)
set console off
set print on
do while .not. eof()
   PAGE = PAGE+1
   ? LINEFEED,LINEFEED,LINEFEED,LINEFEED
   ? 'BOOKS ON ORDER AS OF '+CDATE
   ? 'Page Number',ltrim(str(PAGE,3)),LINEFEED,LINEFEED
   do while prow() < 52 .and. .not. eof()
     MPUBCODE = PUBCODE
     ?
     ? SUPPLIER->NAME
     ?
     list off ISBN, INVENTORY->TITLE, ORDERDATE, ORDERSIZE, PONUMBER ;
             while prow() <= 55 .and. MPUBCODE = PUBCODE
   enddo
   eject
enddo
set print off
set console on
```

Figure 7–29: Program to print open orders: MENU354.PRG.

As with most print and display programs, this one uses an inner and an outer **do** loop. The inner loop is used to print one page of the final report. The outer loop is used to print the heading, set up the inner loop, and eject the page when the inner loop runs its course.

The heading is adjusted on the page by means of the memory variable LINEFEED. This variable contains the control character **chr(10)**, which advances the printer (or the screen) one line. The line is advanced at the current position of the printhead (or the cursor). The line containing four LINEFEEDs produces the same result as using four additional lines with a single ?. You might wonder why **chr(13)**, the carriage return, was *not* used. The carriage return moves the carriage to the left edge of the paper. It does *not* respect dBASE III PLUS margins. The object of this example was to show how to obtain vertical spacing by means of **chr(10)**. You can use this idea in conjunction with the **replicate( )** function to write a procedure to do vertical positioning. This procedure, LINEFEED, is shown in Figure 7–30.

```
procedure LINEFEED
   parameter LFS
   ? replicate(chr(10),LFS)
return
```

Figure 7–30: LINEFEED procedure.

Set console off prohibits normal output to the screen. The **list** and **?** commands usually direct their output to the screen. With **set print on**, the output goes to both the screen and the printer. By setting the console off, the console display is controlled and the output to the printer is unaffected. You cannot **set console off** from the keyboard—only during command operation.

UPDATING STOCK LEVELS

Menu selection 6 provides the capability to update stock levels in response to the receipt of new merchandise or in response to an actual inventory of stock on hand. It provides the opportunity to explore a new design problem: error recovery. For many data-entry situations, a computer failure, such as disconnecting the power cord by accident, may result in some lost data. It is often relatively easy to determine which data has been lost and, even though it's irritating, to reenter the data.

Certain kinds of data entry can provide a different problem. When the data is not being changed directly, we may have a problem determining what hasn't been changed properly. In the following menu system, when stock is received, the quantity received and the ISBN number are entered into a transaction file. Once all of the data has been entered, the transaction file is used to update stock levels in the inventory file and close out open orders in the ONORDER file. If the system were to crash during this update, what are the correct stock levels and what is the correct status of the ONORDER file?

In this menu system, we use the CONTROLS file to keep track of where we are in the process. The sample programs use a relatively small number of checkpoints to monitor the updating process. These programs would benefit by increasing the number of check points.

The Update Menu

The menu program for the Update System is shown as Figure 7–31. There are only three items on the menu: to update stock levels, to reprint the *last* update, and to return to the inventory menu.

```
* MENU36.PRG

do while .T.
    select INVENTORY
    clear
    do banner with "Inventory Update System"
    @  8,26 say '1 - Update Stock Levels'
    @  9,26 say '2 - Reprint Last Update'
    @ 10,26 say '0 - Return To Inventory Menu'
    @ 12,26 say '  - Pick One'

    do CHOICE with 26,'012'

    if CHOICE = '0'
        return
    endif
    do MENU36&CHOICE
enddo
```

Figure 7–31: Update menu program: MENU36.PRG.

Updating Inventory Quantities

The program to manage the updating process is shown as Figure 7–32. The process has been broken into four steps, labeled 0 through 3. As each step is completed, the content of the field UPDATESTEP in the CONTROLS file is incremented. The update program, MENU361.PRG, automatically begins at the proper step level if some problem has previously interrupted updating.

The four basic steps that we are considering are data entry, inventory file update, ONORDER file update, and update summary printout. The user enters all of the updating information, the ISBN number, and the quantity received into the transaction file UPDATE. The content of the transaction file is used to automatically update the content of the QTYONHAND and QTYRCVD fields in the INVENTORY. The same transaction file then updates the ONORDER file by removing filled orders from the file. Once these processes have run to completion, the transactions are printed out—providing a permanent record of the transactions.

ENTERING DATA

The data-entry program for the update system is shown as Figure 7–33. The screen display used by the program is shown as Figure 7–34. This program is entered only when the CONTROLS field UPDATESTEP is set to zero. The first activity upon entering the program is to empty the database file UPDATE.

```
* MENU361.PRG


* ----------------- MENU361A - Enter ISBN numbers and quantity received
* ----------------- MENU361B - Update Inventory File
* ----------------- MENU361C - Update Onorder Files
* ----------------- MENU362  - Prints the update information

if CONTROLS->UPDATESTEP = 0
    do MENU361A
    select UPDATE
                if reccount() > 0
                    return
                endif
    go top
    select CONTROLS
    replace UPDATESTEP with 1
endif


if CONTROLS->UPDATESTEP = 1
  do MENU361B
endif


if CONTROLS->UPDATESTEP = 2
  do MENU361C
endif


if CONTROLS->UPDATESTEP>=3
    do MENU362
    select CONTROLS
    replace UPDATESTEP with 0
    select INVENTORY
endif
```

Figure 7–32: Inventory update program: MENU361.PRG.

Zap

The **zap** command erases all records in a database file—instantly. With **set safety off**, as in this case, the database is cleared without a warning message. The command has the same effect as **delete all** followed by **pack**.

The screen becomes a form that is to be filled in—partly by the user, partly by the computer. The procedure FINDISBN is used to locate the inventory record for each ISBN number entered. This procedure verifies that such a number is actually in the inventory. When the record is found, information is placed on the screen at the screen row controlled by the variable ROW. After the record is found in the inventory file, the update file is searched for the same record. The **locate** command is used because the UPDATE file is not indexed. It was judged that this file would be small enough

```
* MENU361A.PRG

clear
select UPDATE
zap
@ 1,1 SAY 'ISBN Number    Qty     Title'
ROW = 2
do while .T.
    select INVENTORY
    MISBN    = space(13)
    do FINDISBN with "ISBN Number", MISBN
                    if MISBN = space(13)
                            exit
                    endif
    @ 23,2
    select UPDATE
    locate for ISBN = MISBN
                if .not. found()
                    append blank
                    replace ISBN with MISBN
                endif
    @ ROW,1  say ISBN
    @ ROW,20 say INVENTORY->TITLE
    @ ROW,16 get QTYRCVD
    read
    do ROWCHECK with ROW
enddo
select UPDATE
use INVUPDAT alias UPDATE
```

Figure 7–33: Data-entry program:MENU361A.PRG.

that it could be searched sequentially without an apparent time lag. If a record is not present, a blank record is added to the update file, and the ISBN field is replaced by the memory variable MISBN. In either event, the field QTYRCVD is edited. This last feature allows the user to edit the UPDATE file by reentering an ISBN number.

If enough books are entered, the data begins to overwrite line 23, the line used for data entry. Even if this were to be permitted, dBASE III PLUS protests if you attempt to write to a nonexistent screen position (row 25). To guard against this, we use the procedure ROWCHECK, which uses the **?** command to push the screen up one row when the value of ROW reaches 22. See Figure 8–11 in Chapter Eight.

When data entry is complete, we return to MENU361 and set the value of UPDATESTEP to 1. This lets us proceed to the next step. Note that the UPDATE file was saved by issuing the **use** command.

Figure 7–34: Data-entry screen.

UPDATING THE INVENTORY

The program to update the inventory, MENU361B.PRG, is shown as Figure 7–35. The first step is to close the INVENTORY index. **Close index** is used to close all index files in a work area. Then we back up the current value of QTYONHAND to a backup file that has been imaginatively named INVBKUP. Each record in the backup file matches the physical record in the INVENTORY file. Note that we're only backing up the single field. It's not important to back up the other fields, and it's significantly faster to copy only part of the database. Once the backup has been made, we turn the index back on.

Update on ISBN . . .

The **update** command uses data from one file (the source) to make changes in another (the target). Both target and source files must be open. In this program the target file is INVENTORY and the source file is UPDATE.

The target and source file must have a common field that is used to *link* the files together for the updating process. In this example, this common *key* field is ISBN. The mandatory phrase **on ISBN** specifies the linking field, which must have the same fieldname in both files.

```
* MENU361B.PRG

select INVENTORY
close index
if file('INVBKUP.DBF')
    select UPDATE
    use INVBKUP alias BACKUP
    select INVENTORY
    set relation to recno() into BACKUP
    replace all QTYONHAND with BACKUP->QTYONHAND
    select BACKUP
    use INVUPDAT alias UPDATE
    select INVENTORY
else
    copy all fields QTYONHAND to INVBKUP
endif
set index to ISBN
update on ISBN replace QTYONHAND with QTYONHAND + UPDATE->QTYRCVD,;
           QTYRCVD with UPDATE -> QTYRCVD, LASTRCV with date();
           from UPDATE random
erase INVBKUP.DBF
select CONTROLS
replace UPDATESTEP with 2
```

Figure 7–35: Inventory update program: MENU361B.PRG.

The term **random** is added because the source file UPDATE is neither sorted or indexed by the ISBN number (the key field). The target file, in this case, *must* be **index**ed by the key field. The command will step through the source file, and the target file's index is searched for a record matching the content of the key source field. The appropriate changes are made in the target and the source file is advanced one record.

If the term random is omitted, both the source and target files *must* be either **sort**ed or **index**ed by the key field. The command then works its way through the two files. The command operation is then equivalent to the command sequence:

```
select UPDATE
go top
do while .not. eof( )
   select INVENTORY
   seek UPDATE->ISBN
   replace . . .
   select UPDATE
   skip
enddo
```

When the update is completed, the backup file is erased. This provides a clue as to where we were when the lights went out. Note that when we enter the program, we test for the existence of the backup file with **if file**.

```
if file('INVBKUP.DBF')
```

The **file** function is true if the filename in the parentheses exists and false if it doesn't. If the file exists, the lights went out somewhere between the time that the program was originally entered and the point at which the checkpoint was logged. If this is the case, we want to restore the INVENTORY file to its original condition and try again. Each record in the BACKUP file contains the QTYONHAND for the matching record number from the INVENTORY file.

Set relation to recno( ) into BACKUP links the two files together by record number. This allows us to use the **replace** command to restore the INVENTORY file. We closed the UPDATE file during this time. We're out of disk files—15 are open. When the restoration was completed, we closed the backup file and reopened the UPDATE file.

UPDATING AN ONORDER FILE

When we enter this program (shown in Figure 7-36), we are either entering from a routine updating operation or in response to some computer failure. The backup ONORDER file is called ONORDBUP.

If this file already exists, we assume that something has gone wrong and **zap** the current contents of the ONORDER file. The **append from** command copies the contents of the backup file into the ONORDER file. The source file cannot be (and is not) open when using **append from**. Next we redo the ISBN index for ONORDER because it too may have been affected.

If the backup file does not exist, we create it by copying the entire ONORDER file to ONORDBUP. The entire file is backed up in this case because a part of this update process involves removing entire records from the ONORDER file. The file is assumed to be reasonably small—and hence, the copy operation should be reasonably quick. To backup a large file, close the file and use the **copy file** command. **Copy file** cannot be used with an open file. The revised code would look like

```
select ONORDER
if .not. . . .
   use
   copy file ONORDER.DBF to ONORDBUP.DBF
   use ONORDER index ISBN-0
else
   zap
   append from . . .
   reindex
endif
```

```
* MENU361C.PRG

select ONORDER
close index
if .not. file('ONORDBUP.DBF')
     copy all to ONORDBUP
     set index to ISBN-O
else
     zap
     append from ONORDBUP
     index on ISBN to ISBN-O
endif


select UPDATE
go top
set deleted on
do while .not. eof()
    select ONORDER
    QTY = UPDATE->QTYRCVD
    seek UPDATE->ISBN
    do while ISBN = UPDATE->ISBN .and. QTY > 0 .and. .not. eof()
        replace QTYRCVD with QTYRCVD + QTY
        QTY = QTYRCVD - ORDERSIZE
            if QTYRCVD >= ORDERSIZE
                    delete
            endif
        skip
    enddo
    select UPDATE
    skip
enddo
set deleted off

select ONORDER
pack
erase ONORDBUP.DBF
select CONTROLS
replace UPDATESTEP with 3
```

Figure 7-36: ONORDER update program: MENU361C.PRG.

In the ONORDER file we must deal with a couple of problems that the **update** command is not equipped to handle. There may be more than one record with the same ISBN number. The quantity received may be adequate to "close out" more than one order record. We also have to take into account the case where orders are partially filled.

```
* MENU362.PRG

select UPDATE
go top
set relation to ISBN into INVENTORY
clear
? 'Be sure that your printer is turned on!'
set device to print
do while .not. eof()

    @ 5,10 say 'INVENTORY UPDATE FOR ' + cdate
    @ 7,1  say 'ISBN Number'
    @ 7,15 say 'Quantity'
    @ 7,25 say 'Title'

    do while .not. eof() .and. prow() <= 55
        @ prow()+1,1  say ISBN
        @ prow(),15   say QTYRCVD
        @ prow(),25   say INVENTORY->TITLE
        skip
    enddo
    eject

enddo
set device to screen
set relation to
```

Figure 7–37: ONORDER print program: MENU362.PRG.

For each record in the UPDATE file, we search for the first matching record (if any) in the ONORDER file. We have a memory variable QTY that contains the quantity received. We will change this memory variable—the data remains intact. As long as the variable is greater than zero and the ISBN number matches the controlling ISBN number in the UPDATE file, we increment the quantity received field by the value of the variable QTY. Next we store the excess (if any) back to the variable. If the order is completely filled, the record is marked for deletion and we move to the next record and try again. **Set deleted on** was used to hide all deleted records.

When this process is complete, we select the ONORDER file and clear out all filled records by **pack**ing.

THE PRINT PROGRAM

The print program is shown as Figure 7-37. This program produces the printout shown as Figure 7-38. The program called from the updating process is the same program that can be called from the menu. The print program ought to provide the ability

```
          INVENTORY UPDATE FOR April  8, 1985

ISBN Number     Quantity    Title
0-89303-241-7 100           IBM PC ASSEMBLY LANGUAGE
0-8359-1246-9  60           DBASE II FOR EVERY BUSINESS
0-02-501980-5  10           HOW TO SAVE ON YOUR INCOME TAX
0-02-501980-5   0           HOW TO SAVE ON YOUR INCOME TAX
0-8359-1246-9   0           DBASE II FOR EVERY BUSINESS
0-89303-241-7   0           IBM PC ASSEMBLY LANGUAGE
0-89588-124-1   0           BUSINESS GRAPHICS FOR THE PC
0-912677-01-5 105           ENCYLOPEDIA FOR THE IBM PC
0-912677-14-7 104           UP AND RUNNING
0-912677-04-X 106           DATA MANAGEMENT FOR PROFESSION
0-912677-08-2 107           DBASE II FOR THE 1ST TIME USER
0-912677-18-X 108           VISUAL GUIDE TO ORGANIZATION
0-912677-10-4 109           ILLUSTRATED GUIDE TO DBASE II
0-912677-12-0 110           SYSTEM DESIGN GUIDE
```

Figure 7-38: Sample printout.

to reprint most printed items on demand. Printed copy can be lost, damaged, or destroyed; therefore, you should be able to recreate it for some reasonable period.

CHAPTER EIGHT
Sales Order Entry

Sales order entry is the process of entering new orders for goods into the computer so that these orders can be filled. Once filled, they become invoices and are used by accounts receivable to prepare billings. Sales orders are prepared with the help of information stored in the CUSTOMER and INVENTORY files. A record of each sales order is stored in a SALES ORDER database. Each sales order record consists of several pieces of information, including:

- *who* the order is for
- *what titles* were ordered
- *how many* of each title were ordered
- *when* the order was entered

Each sales order record varies in length according to how many titles are ordered. This chapter focuses on the difference between business records and dBASE III PLUS records. In the sales order database we could use a separate database file record for each title ordered—just as in the purchase order file (ONORDER) of the last chapter. However, we want to keep our sales order records on-line for at least a year. The overhead associated with keeping direct track of who, when, and so forth for each title will become very large.

To keep the sales order file manageable, we have split it into two files: SALES and SALESDET. The plans for these two files as well as a file to keep track of open sales orders are shown as Figure 8–1. A schematic of the overall database system is shown as Figure 8–2.

The SALES file is a master listing of all orders that have been entered into the system, whether they have been filled or not. The SALESDET file contains sales details on each order. The file OPENORD is a listing of orders that have not yet been filled. The three database files, SALES, SALESDET, and OPENORD, are linked to each other by the sales order number SONUMBER. The sales record is linked to the customer file by means of the CUSTID, and the titles are linked to the inventory by the ISBN number. Splitting the sales order system into two files can save an enormous amount of disk space. Suppose that our business gets an average of 20 orders per day, and the average order is for 10 titles. There are 200 business days in a year. If we hold the records on-line for one year, the SALES file will have 4000 records and SALESDET will have 40,000.

If we multiply the number of records in each file by the record size (the data size plus one byte for overhead), we find that the two-file version of the sales order database uses just under 1.3 million bytes of disk space. If we combine the files into a single file, each of the 40,000 records uses 52 bytes (data plus overhead). Combin-

| Database file: SALES.DBF | | | |
DESCRIPTION	FIELDNAME	FIELDTYPE	WIDTH
Sales Order Number	SONUMBER	Character	6
Customer ID Code	CUSTID	Character	6
Date Order Was Entered	DATE	Date	8
Customer's P.O. Number	PONUMBER	Character	8
S.O. Canceled?	VOID	Logical	1
	DATA SIZE	. . . . . 30 BYTES	

| Database file: SALESDET.DBF | | | | |
DESCRIPTION	FIELDNAME	FIELDTYPE	WIDTH	DECIMALS
Sales Order Number	SONUMBER	Character	6	
Book ISBN Number	ISBN	Character	13	
Quantity Ordered	QTY	Numeric	3	
Price to Customer	PRICE	Numeric	6	2
	DATA SIZE	. . . . . 29 BYTES		

| Database file: OPENORD.DBF | | | |
DESCRIPTION	FIELDNAME	FIELDTYPE	WIDTH
Sales Order Number	SONUMBER	Character	6

Figure 8–1: Database plans for sales order files.

ing the files takes a total of over 2 million bytes of disk space. By splitting the files we have saved about 800,000 bytes of disk space (40 percent of the combined file) that would have consisted of duplicate information.

We have saved disk space at the cost of making the software more complex. This is the trade-off that you have to make. You could make enormous simplifications in the sales order software by spending the 800K. Normally, if your file is small—as was the case in the ONORDER file—you should "waste" the disk space. If the file is large, break it up into pieces and spend the time to write software to relate the pieces. You should contrast the software in this chapter with that required to manage the ONORDER file in the last chapter.

You should notice that the sales order files are *not* indexed. In this chapter we will show you how you can take advantage of the *natural order* of certain classes of data to make your job easier. Sales orders are representative of this kind of *naturally ordered* data. Sales orders are entered as they are received, and sales order numbers are assigned sequentially. They are naturally sorted by sales order number and by entry date. Don't assign indexes to naturally sorted data unless you frequently need direct

SALES DATABASE			
Sales Order Number	Customer ID Code	Date	Customer's PO Number
100411	071254	04/08/85	A76382
100412	200461	04/08/85	B-2761
100413	598326	04/09/85	T3477
100414	553929	04/10/85	X-63-85
100415	072453	04/10/85	Z777234
100416	110762	04/10/85	C-2345-X
100417	112162	04/11/85	B762091
100418	042056	04/11/85	R-3056

SALES DETAIL DATABASE			
Sales Order Number	ISBN Number	Qty	Price
100411	0-912677-03-1	21	19.95
100411	0-912677-42-2	14	29.95
100411	0-912677-16-3	7	18.95
100414	0-912677-26-0	23	17.95
100415	0-912677-06-6	64	28.95
100416	0-912677-47-3	101	29.95
100417	0-912677-56-2	39	14.95
100418	0-912677-29-5	32	18.95

OPEN ORDER
Sales Order Number
100411
100412
100413
100414
100415

Figure 8–2: Schematic diagram of sales order system.

access to *any* record. As you will see, there are other ways to gain rapid access to a data record.

Another characteristic of this kind of business system is that we are usually interested in the most recently entered records. This is a class of record that is referred to as

LIFO—last in, first out. In many LIFO systems, such as sales order entry and your personal checkbook, we are only rarely interested in the "older" records; it's the most recent that are used for day-to-day business. We will be making use of this characteristic in the search strategies that we will develop for locating particular sales order records.

The menu program for sales-order entry is shown as Figure 8–3. The screen produced by this menu program is shown as Figure 8–4. The particular features of sales order entry to be addressed are illustrated by the selections on this menu. The special file selection required is shown as Figure 8–5. You might note that we have kept this setup as a separate program even though it is short and simple. This setup could easily be incorporated directly into the menu program. Keeping it separate, however, lets us know when file setup is required for a particular system.

```
* MENU4.PRG

do SETUP4
do while .T.
   select SALES
   CHOICES = '01'
   clear
   do BANNER with "SALES ORDER SYSTEM"
   @  8,26 say '1 - Enter a Sales Order'
   if reccount() > 0
      @ row()+1,26 say '2 - Edit a Sales Order'
      @ row()+1,26 say '3 - Void a Sales Order'
      @ row()+1,26 say '4 - Print Sales Orders'
      @ row()+1,26 say '5 - Prepare Sales Report'
      @ row()+1,26 say '6 - Outstanding Orders'
      @ row()+1,26 say '7 - Delete Orders More than 1 Year Old'
      CHOICES = CHOICES + '234567'
   endif
   @ row()+1,26 say '0 - GO BACK TO THE MAIN MENU'
   @ row()+1,26 say '  - Pick One'

   do CHOICE with 26,CHOICES

   if CHOICE = '0'
      return
   endif

   do MENU4&CHOICE
enddo
```

Figure 8–3: Sales order entry menu program: MENU4.PRG.

```
  Monday                      SALES ORDER SYSTEM              April  8, 1985




                     1 - Enter a Sales Order
                     2 - Edit a Sales Order
                     3 - Void a Sales Order
                     4 - Print Sales Orders
                     5 - Prepare Sales Report
                     6 - Outstanding Orders
                     7 - Delete Orders More than 1 Year Old
                     0 - GO BACK TO THE MAIN MENU
                     ▌ - Pick One
```

Figure 8-4: Sales order entry menu.


```
* SETUP4.PRG

clear
? 'Opening Sales Order Databases'
select CUSTOMER
                    close index
select 4
                    use SALES
select 5
                    use SALESDET
select 6
                    use OPENORD
```

Figure 8-5: Sales order entry setup program: SETUP4.PRG.

ENTERING A SALES ORDER

The program to add sales orders to the system is shown as Figure 8–6. A logic diagram for this program is shown in Figure 8–7. On each pass through the program, summary information on the last ten sales orders is displayed. The user is prompted to enter a customer's name. The customer's record is retrieved and displayed. The user is asked to verify that the program has retrieved the correct customer. If so, we proceed to enter the remaining sales order information—the ISBN number and quantity for each title ordered. The program fills in the remainder of the data items in SALES and SALESDET.

Before we enter the **do** loop, we need to set up two memory variables: NEXTSO and BANNERMSG. NEXTSO initially contains the first sales order number ever assigned to a sales order. This feature is important only when we haven't yet issued the first sales order. We get the next sales order number by the simple process of finding the last one and adding 17 to it. The last sales order is at the bottom of the file. Incrementing the sales orders by 17 helps to reduce typographical errors. BANNERMSG contains the legend to be displayed at the top of the screen by the procedure BANNER.

Our first step is to select the CUSTOMER file and set the index to CUSTID. Then we can select the SALES file and *relate* it to the customer file by means of the customer ID number. We don't actually care what the ID number is; it simply allows us to link the files together so that we can display information, including the customer's name, from the last few sales orders. Displaying *placeholder* information is an aid to the data-entry worker; keep in mind that the program is supposed to improve the productivity of those who use it. Never leave them guessing to save a line or two of code—that's lazy programming. Note that we went to the bottom of the sales file and then "backed up" ten records. When we display records, we begin with the current record. **List next 10** would not get us back to the record we started with—next 10 includes the current record. You need to be careful when skipping back and forth.

Once these records have been displayed, reselect the CUSTOMER file and switch the controlling index from CUSTID to CUSTNAME. This puts the program in the proper configuration to search for a customer name. FINDCUST, as you may recall, was developed in Chapter Five to search for customers by name. We've used the same procedure here. Practically speaking, procedures are broken out separately when we recognize that we've done this function before. When a function—such as locating a customer record—is common to two or more programs, it should be made into a separate program or procedure. This is one of the basic ideas of structured programming. These procedures then become a sort of "super command."

Once the customer has been found, we can use the data-entry screen of MENU1S to display information about the customer. This is another program that was originally developed for customer file maintenance. We've used it here to help with sales order entry; there's no value in developing a separate screen for sales order entry. Also, by using one program for all full-screen displays of customer data, we can more easily incorporate changes in the structure of the customer file into our business program. Most changes to that file (such as adding and deleting fields, for example) affect only this one program.

```
* MENU41.PRG

BANNERMSG = 'SALES ORDER ENTRY'
NEXTSO    = 100000
do while .T.
   MNAME     = space(30)
   MPONUMBER = space(8)
   clear
   do BANNER with BANNERMSG
   select CUSTOMER
   set index to CUSTID
   select SALES
   go bottom
   if reccount() > 0
       NEXTSO    = val(SONUMBER)+17
       skip -10
       set relation to CUSTID into CUSTOMER
       list off next 11 SONUMBER, CUSTOMER->NAME,PONUMBER,DATE
   endif
   select CUSTOMER
   set index to CUSTNAME
   MNAME = space(30)

   do FINDCUST with "Enter Customer Name", MNAME
                              if eof() .or. MNAME = space(30)
                                   return
                              endif
   do MENU1S
   clear gets
   do QUERY with 'Is this the correct customer (Y/N)? ',23,2,ANSWER
   if ANSWER = 'Y'
       a 23,2
       a 23,2 say "Customer's Purchase Order Number " get MPONUMBER;
             picture '@!'
       read
       do MENU41A
       if SONUMBER = str(NEXTSO,6)
          select OPENORD
          append blank
          replace SONUMBER with str(NEXTSO,6)
          select SALES
          set relation to
          append blank
          replace SONUMBER with str(NEXTSO,6),DATE with date(),;
                CUSTID with CUSTOMER->CUSTID, PONUMBER with MPONUMBER
          do MENU4P with SALES->SONUMBER
       endif
   endif
enddo
```

Figure 8–6: Sales order entry program: MENU41.PRG.

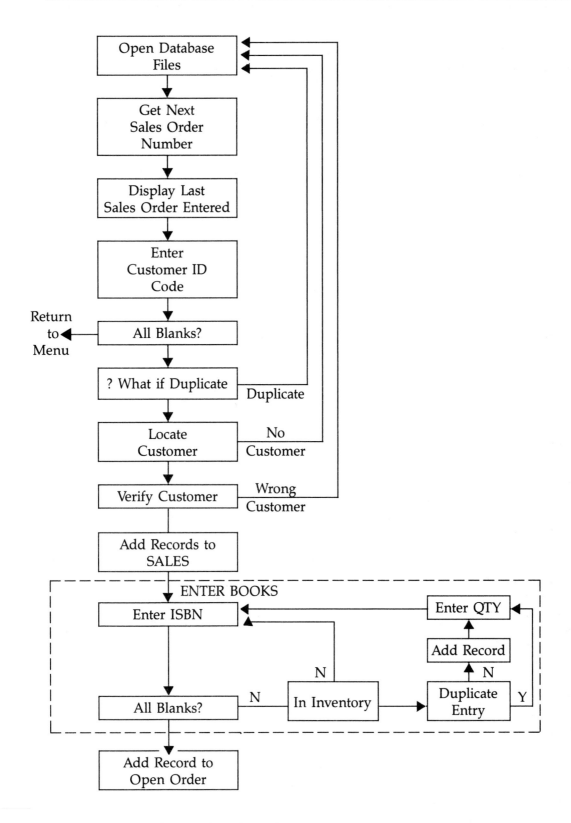

Figure 8–7: Logic diagram for sales order entry.

The program MENU41A shown in Figure 8–8 performs the bulk of the manual entry of titles and quantities into the detail file SALESDET. If a valid ISBN number is entered, the last record in SALESDET has a sales order number that matches the variable NEXTSO. That is our clue as to whether or not to add the sales order to the SALES and OPENORD files. Note that only one of the data items entered into the SALES file was entered directly by the user. By choosing to add records to files in this particular order, we are always certain that there is at least one record in the SALESDET file for every sales order number in the SALES and OPENORD files.

```
* MENU41A.PRG

select SALESDET
copy structure to TEMPFILE
use TEMPFILE
clear
@ 1,1  say 'ISBN Number   QTY     Title                  Price'
@ 2,1  say BAR
do SALESDET with 3
delete for QTY = 0
pack
use SALESDET
append from TEMPFILE
erase TEMPFILE.DBF
```

Figure 8–8: MENU41A.PRG.

Note that when SALES was selected the relation in effect was switched off. This was done to keep the CUSTOMER file from being repositioned with **append blank**. It was important to keep the customer file at the correct record because it is the source of the customer ID number, CUSTID.

The actual entry of the detailed sales order information (ISBN numbers and quantities) is handled by the program MENU41A. When we exit from that program, we are positioned to the last record in the file SALESDET. If any books were actually entered into the file, the content of the field SONUMBER will match the content of the sales order memory variable NEXTSO. If this is true, we add that sales order number to the open orders file OPENORD and to the master sales file SALES.

THE SALES DETAIL FILE

This program, shown in Figure 8–8, is used to set up the system for using data entry SALESDET. Data is to be entered into a temporary file—named TEMPFILE, which is created for each sales order by the **copy structure** command. **Copy structure** creates an empty file with the same structure as the active file. When we open TEMPFILE, the active file SALESDET is closed and TEMPFILE resides in the work area previously occupied by SALESDET.

Books are actually entered into the temporary file TEMPFILE by means of SALESDET, which is also used to edit sales records in the next menu selection. Upon returning from data entry to MENU41A, we are still using the temporary file. We clear out all records (if any) where the quantity ordered (QTY) is zero—by deleting and packing. We can expect this file to be reasonably small so the **delete** and **pack** operation is very quick.

Next we reopen the SALESDET file—thereby closing TEMPFILE. We have never left the work area, so we are exactly where we were when we entered this program. Records are moved from TEMPFILE to SALESDET by **append from** TEMPFILE. To use **append from**, the source file (TEMPFILE) must not be open. Next we erase TEMP-FILE; strictly speaking, this command is not needed. The **copy structure** operation overwrites TEMPFILE if it already exists.

Entering Titles Into the Sales Order—SALESDET

Books are entered into the sales order file by using the ISBN number. This is the most expeditious way of ordering books. SALESDET (shown as Figure 8–9) prompts the clerk to enter an ISBN number. The inventory file is searched for that ISBN number

```
* SALESDET.PRG

parameter ROW
do while .T.
        select INVENTORY
        MISBN = space(13)
        do FINDISBN with "ISBN Number", MISBN
                              if MISBN = space(13)
                                      exit
                              endif
        @ 23,2
        select TEMPFILE
        locate for ISBN = MISBN
            if eof()
               append blank
               replace ISBN with MISBN, SONUMBER with str(NEXTSO,6),;
                       PRICE with INVENTORY->SELLPRICE
            endif
        @ ROW,1  say ISBN
        @ ROW,20 say INVENTORY->TITLE
        @ ROW,col()+1 say PRICE
        @ ROW,16 get QTY picture '@Z ' range 0,999
        read
        do ROWCHECK with ROW
    enddo
select TEMPFILE
```

Figure 8–9: SALESDET.PRG procedure.

using the procedure FINDISBN, which was developed for the inventory system. When the inventory record has been located, TEMPFILE is searched to see whether the record already exists. If it doesn't, a blank record is added to the temporary file and all information except for the quantity ordered is automatically added to the record. The book information is displayed and the clerk is prompted to enter the quantity. A representative screen display created by this program is shown as Figure 8–10.

The quantity is displayed with the help of the picture function **@Z**. This function prevents a zero from being displayed on-screen. The range 0,999 represents the minimum and maximum values that can be entered into the field QTY.

ROWCHECK (Figure 8–11) is the procedure used to prevent our attempting to use an off-screen address (line 25, for example) with an @ . . . **say** command (see Chapter Seven).

EDITING A SALES ORDER

We might reasonably expect sales orders to be edited only rarely. But people *do* make mistakes and the clerk at Bob's Better Books is a poor typist. The importance of this particular program is that it demonstrates one way to edit this kind of business record.

```
Monday                    SALES ORDER ENTRY           April  8, 1985

SONUMBER CUSTOMER->NAME              PONUMBER DATE
100017   SOFTWORDS, INC              ZZZ999XX 02/01/85
100034   A-1 BOOKS                   0-02-501 02/01/85
100051   SOFTWORDS, INC              a-12345  02/02/85
100068   TATE-ASHTON                          02/02/85
100085   TATE-ASHTON                 A-223344 02/02/85




        Enter Customer Name  ████████████████████████
```

Figure 8–10: Screen display for sales order entry.

```
procedure ROWCHECK
    parameter ROW
    clear gets
      if ROW >= 22
        ?
        ?
      else
        ROW = ROW+1
      endif
return
```

Figure 8–11: ROWCHECK procedure.

Remember, the sales detail file contains one record for each title ordered. Editing the business record means adding to and deleting from the sales detail file as well as simply changing existing records in that file.

The program to edit sales orders is shown as Figure 8–12. We only permit sales orders to be edited if they have not, as yet, been filled. Sales orders that haven't been filled are entries in the OPENORD (open orders) file. Our first step is to search OPENORD for the sales order number. If we find the record, we proceed to search the master SALES file for the sales order number. Here is where we first make use of the LIFO nature of the sales order system. If the sales order is open, we expect that it is somewhere near the bottom of the database file. To search for it, we can go to the bottom and then skip toward the top of the database file, one record at a time.

```
* MENU42.PRG

clear
BANNERMSG = 'EDIT SALES ORDER RECORD'
select CUSTOMER
set index to CUSTID
select SALES
set relation to CUSTID into CUSTOMER
go bottom
do while .T.
    MSONUMBER = space(6)
    select OPENORD
    do BANNER with BANNERMSG
    @ 23,2 say 'Sales Order to be Edited' get MSONUMBER picture '999999'
    read
                        if MSONUMBER = space(6)
                            return
                        endif
    @ 22,2
    locate for SONUMBER = MSONUMBER
        if eof()
          if MSONUMBER <= SALES->SONUMBER
              do ERRORMSG with MSONUMBER + ' has been filled',22,2
          else
              do ERRORMSG with MSONUMBER + ' is not valid',22,2
          endif
          loop
        endif
    select SALES
    go bottom
    do while SONUMBER > MSONUMBER .and. .not. bof()
        skip -1
    enddo
    if SONUMBER = MSONUMBER
        @ 6,2  say CUSTID+'      '+CUSTOMER->NAME
        select SALES
        @ 8,2  say "Customer Purchase Order " get PONUMBER
        read
        select SALESDET
        do SEARCH with MSONUMBER,"SONUMBER"
        if .not. eof()
            do MENU42A
        endif
        clear
    endif
enddo
```

Figure 8–12: Program for editing sales orders: MENU42.PRG.

SKIP n

Skip repositions the database by *n* records from the current record. The argument *n* can be either positive or negative. Records that are "hidden" by means of the **set deleted** or the **set filter** commands are not counted in the **skip**. **Skip** will not take you beyond the end (or the beginning) of the database file. However, if an end-of-file flag has been set, an attempt to skip toward that end of the file produces an error message—even with **set talk off**. Skipping long distances is slow. Each record must be examined to determine whether it is to be counted in the **skip**—because "hidden" records are to be ignored.

Once we have located the proper sales order record in the SALES file, we need to find the first matching record in the SALESDET file. This second search is done using the SEARCH procedure shown in Figure 8–13. The SEARCH procedure is a generally useful program for locating records in naturally-ordered files. We could have used the program to position within the SALES file. However, we expect the sales record to be near the end of the file—so skipping backward is reasonably efficient.

```
procedure SEARCH                      && for ordered, UNindexed database
   parameters SEARCHVAR, SEARCHFLD
   Private all
   JUMPSIZE = reccount()
do while JUMPSIZE > 1
   if SEARCHVAR = &SEARCHFLD
     exit
   endif
   if SEARCHVAR < &SEARCHFLD .and. recno() > JUMPSIZE
     go recno() - JUMPSIZE
   endif
   if SEARCHVAR > &SEARCHFLD .and. recno() + JUMPSIZE <= reccount()
     go recno() + JUMPSIZE
   endif
   JUMPSIZE = int(round(JUMPSIZE/2,0))
enddo
do while .not. bof()
    skip -1
        if &SEARCHFLD < SEARCHVAR
            exit
        endif
enddo
locate rest for &SEARCHFLD >= SEARCHVAR
if .not. &SEARCHFLD = SEARCHVAR
   do GOEOF
endif
return
```

Figure 8–13: The SEARCH procedure.

Once we have positioned SALESDET to the first record belonging to the sales order, we go into the edit setup program MENU42A.PRG. This program is shown as Figure 8–14. You should notice that we have considered what to do if either the SALES or SALESDET records were not found. In this particular case we have contrived to know that sales order records are there. This may not always be the case. Always have the program contain instructions about what to do if an alternative is encountered.

```
* MENU42A.PRG

FIRSTREC = recno()
NEXTSO   = val(SONUMBER)
copy to TEMPFILE while SONUMBER = SALES -> SONUMBER
select 9
use TEMPFILE
clear
set relation to ISBN into INVENTORY
do BANNER with "Edit Sales Order Record"
display off all ISBN, QTY, INVENTORY->TITLE,PRICE
set relation to
ROW = row()
do ROWCHECK with ROW
do SALESDET with ROW
set relation to recno()+FIRSTREC -1 into SALESDET
go top
do while .not. eof()
     select SALESDET
     if SONUMBER # TEMPFILE->SONUMBER
         insert blank before
     endif
     replace QTY with TEMPFILE->QTY, ISBN WITH TEMPFILE -> ISBN,;
             PRICE with TEMPFILE->PRICE, SONUMBER with TEMPFILE->SONUMBER
     select TEMPFILE
     skip
enddo
use
```

Figure 8–14: MENU42A.PRG.

SETUP SYSTEM FOR EDITING

Records are edited using SALESDET. This procedure is the same as that used to enter and edit records in menu selection 1. We make a temporary copy of all sales detail records for the particular sales order number and then edit the copy. The temporary file TEMPFILE is created by

copy to TEMPFILE while SONUMBER = SALES -> SONUMBER

Before we copy these records to the temporary file, we want to store the record number of the first record to the variable FIRSTREC. We will use this variable, after editing, to link TEMPFILE to SALESDET by the offset record number.

Unlike the last menu selection, we need to use the sales detail file with TEMPFILE. In this case we open TEMPFILE in another work area. Next, before editing, we want to display information about the sales order. To display the title, we link the inventory file to TEMPFILE by the ISBN number in TEMPFILE. As soon as the display is complete, we disconnect from the relation. The procedure SALESDET, used to edit the sales records, does not make use of a relationship.

The current row position on the screen, **row( )**, is stored to the variable ROW to let SALESDET pick up the display at the right point. Then we perform the actual editing with SALESDET as in menu selection 1. When we return from editing TEMP-FILE, we need to transfer the information from TEMPFILE back into SALESDET.

The records in SALESDET are linked to TEMPFILE by record number. Each time we reposition TEMPFILE the record pointer in SALESDET is moved to a record that has the record number offset from the TEMPFILE record number by (FIRSTREC-1). Positioning TEMPFILE with **go top** adjusts both files to the first record for the sales order being edited.

For each record in TEMPFILE, we replace all of the data fields in the matching SALESDET record with the contents of the TEMPFILE record. If there is no matching record in SALESDET, we create one with the **insert** command. **Insert blank before** is used to add records into the database at the current record position. Each use of **insert** adds a single record to the file and positions the file to the new record. When we run out of records in the temporary file, we close it with the **use** command. This also "turns off" the relation to SALESDET.

The Search Procedure

The procedure SEARCH (Figure 8-13) is designed to find the first occurrence of a particular record in a file that contains records that are ordered either alphabetically, chronologically, or numerically. In the sales order system, records are naturally ordered by both date and sales order number. This particular search routine allows you to specify the field to be searched and what to search for by passing these items as parameters.

This procedure is a *binary* search. We go to the end of the file. If the record isn't there, we go to the beginning. If that's not it, we go to the middle. If the content of the middle record is larger than the search value, we go halfway to the beginning. Otherwise, we jump halfway to the end. Each successive jump is one half as far as the last jump. This process allows you to "home in" on the desired record. You can search a file of a million records in just 15 jumps. This is not as fast as using indexes—but it can be faster than using a sequential search command such as **locate**. A diagram of the search path is shown in Figure 8-15. The variable RECCOUNT stores the number of records in the file. The **reccount** procedure provides a routine for determining the number of records in the file.

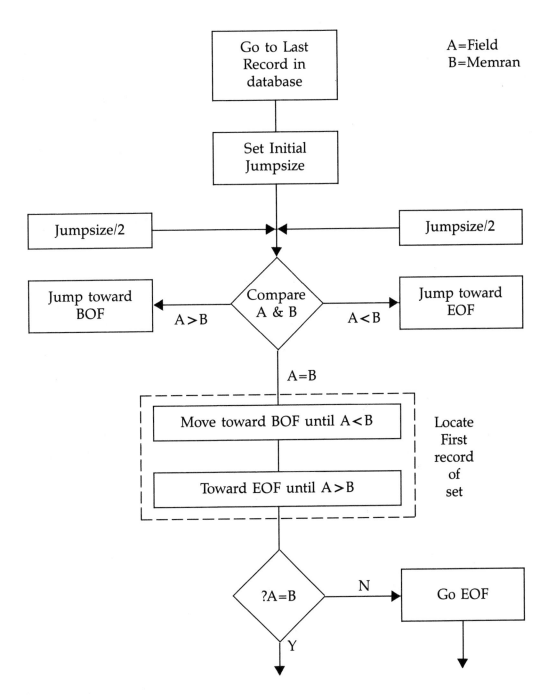

Figure 8–15: A search algorithm.

The **do** loop is used to make the jumps during the search. On each pass through this loop, we jump to a desired record and set up the jump size for the next pass. Note that we have to protect against the case where the jump would take us past either end of the file. An important point demonstrated by this **do** loop is that you cannot use macro substitution in a **do while** condition. That made it necessary to compare SEARCHVAR with &SEARCHFLD using an **if** statement inside of the loop.

When the **do** loop has run its course we will be close—but not necessarily on the desired record. If we've overshot the record we are positioned in front of the desired record. If we've undershot the record (that is, the desired record has a lower record number) or we've landed on one of the "duplicate" entries, the second **do** loop will take us to the record just prior to the desired record. Remember, we're close to the desired record when entering this loop.

At this point we are either positioned in front of the desired record or at the first occurrence of the record (if it happens to be record 1). The **locate** command takes us to the first record meeting the search criteria—even if we're already there. The term **rest** in the command is read as "from here on." It is "safer" to use **next 1000000**.

When we exit from the **locate** command, we will be positioned at the first occurrence of a desired value, at the first occurrence of a greater value, or at the end of file. If the record was not found, we force an end-of-file condition.

VOIDING A SALES ORDER

Selection 3 will "cancel" a sales order. We don't remove it from the physical database, although we do close out the "open order." The other two databases are large, and immediate removal is too time-consuming. The removal process then consists of marking the main sales record as "void" and setting the quantity ordered in the detail records to zero. This menu selection, MENU43.PRG, is shown as Figure 8–16.

PRINTING SALES ORDERS

Selection 4 prints either individually-selected sales orders or all sales numbers on a given date. There is no restriction that the sales orders be current. This means that the selected sales orders are not necessarily near the end of the file. This selection, MENU44.PRG, shown in Figure 8–17, opens by offering the user three choices. The selection is made by means of the procedure CHOICE.

```
* MENU43.PRG

clear
select CUSTOMER
set index to CUSTID
select SALES
set relation to CUSTID into CUSTOMER
go bottom
do while .T.
    do BANNER with "Void A Sales Order"
    MSONUMBER = space(6)
    select OPENORD
    a 23,2 say 'Sales Order to be Voided' get MSONUMBER picture '999999'
    read
                    if MSONUMBER = space(6)
                        return
                    endif
    locate for SONUMBER = MSONUMBER
        if eof()
           if MSONUMBER <= SALES->SONUMBER
               do ERRORMSG with MSONUMBER + ' has been filled',22,2
           else
               do ERRORMSG with MSONUMBER + ' is not valid',22,2
           endif
           loop
        endif
    a 22,2
    select SALES
    go bottom
    do while SONUMBER > MSONUMBER .and. .not. bof()
        skip -1
    enddo
    if SONUMBER = MSONUMBER
      a 22,2
      a  6,2  say CUSTID+'       '+CUSTOMER->NAME
      a  8,2  say "Customer Purchase Order "+ PONUMBER
      do QUERY with "Void this Sales Order (Y/N)?",23,2,ANSWER
      if ANSWER = 'Y'
         replace VOID with .T.
         select SALESDET
         do SEARCH with MSONUMBER,"SONUMBER"
         replace QTY with 0 while SONUMBER = MSONUMBER
         select OPENORD
         delete for SONUMBER = MSONUMBER
         pack
      endif
    endif
clear
enddo
```

Figure 8–16: MENU43.PRG.

```
* MENU44.PRG

clear
do BANNER with "Print Sales Orders"
@  8,26 say "1 - Print Individual Sales Orders"
@  9,26 say "2 - Print Sales Orders For Date"
@ 10,26 say "0 - Exit"
@ 13,26 say "    Pick One"
do CHOICE with 26,"012"
do while CHOICE = '1'
    select SALES
    MSONUMBER = space(6)
    do GETREC with "Sales Order Number",MSONUMBER,"SONUMBER"
                    if MSONUMBER = space(6)
                          return
                    endif
    do MENU4P with MSONUMBER
enddo
if CHOICE = '2'
    select SALES
    go TOP
    MDATE1 = DATE
    go bottom
    MDATE = DATE
    @ 23,2 say "Enter Date to be Printed" get MDATE ;
            range MDATE1,MDATE
    read
    do SEARCH with MDATE,"DATE"
    do while DATE = MDATE .and. .not. eof()
       do MENU4P with SALES->SONUMBER
       select SALES
       skip
    enddo
endif
```

Figure 8–17: MENU44.PRG.

If the choice is to print individual sales orders, we enter the loop **do while CHOICE = '1'**. This loop makes use of the procedure GETREC (Figure 8–18) to enter and locate a sales order from the SALES file. If no sales order is entered, we return to the sales order menu. If a valid sales order is entered, we print the order using the sales order printing program MENU4P.PRG, shown in Figure 8–19. A sample sales order is shown as Figure 8–20.

```
procedure GETREC
parameters LEGEND, MEMVAR, FIELDNAME
private all

do while .T.
    MEMVAR    = space(6)
    @ 23,2 say LEGEND get MEMVAR picture "999999"
    read
                    if MEMVAR = space(6)
                        exit
                    endif

                    if .not.  mod(val(MEMVAR)-100000,17)=0
                        do ERRORMSG with MEMVAR + ' is invalid',22,2
                        loop
                    endif
    @ 22,2
    go bottom
    OFFSET  = (val(&FIELDNAME) - val(MEMVAR))/17
    if recno() - OFFSET > 0
       go recno() -  OFFSET
    else
       go top
    endif
    locate rest for &FIELDNAME >= MEMVAR
                    if &FIELDNAME = MEMVAR
                          exit
                    endif
    do ERRORMSG with MEMVAR + ' not found',22,2
enddo
return
```

Figure 8–18: GETREC procedure.

If the choice is to print the sales orders for a given date, we first go to the top of the database and store the date of the oldest record to the variable MDATE. Then we jump to the bottom and store the date for the most recent sales order to MDATE. Next we prompt the user to enter the date to be printed into the variable MDATE. The range of possible entries is restricted to dates between the two variables. Note that the variable is used as its own upper range. This is okay. The range limit is the value of the variable when the command was called.

Once a valid date is entered, we use the SEARCH procedure to hunt for the date. We can do this since SEARCH is a general procedure *and* because the dates are naturally in chronological order. If the entered date is in the database, we enter the printing loop and print all the sales orders for that date.

```
* MENU4P.PRG

parameter MSONUMBER
clear
select SALESDET
do SEARCH with MSONUMBER,"SONUMBER"
set relation to ISBN into INVENTORY
set device to print
PAGE = 1
do while SONUMBER = MSONUMBER .and. .not. eof()
   @ 6,1   say 'SALES ORDER '+SONUMBER+'   DATED: '+dtoc(SALES->DATE)
   @ 7,1   say 'Page Number '+str(PAGE,2)
   @ 9,1   say CUSTOMER->name
   @ 9,40  say 'CUSTOMER P.O. '+SALES->PONUMBER
   if .not. CUSTOMER->ATTN = space(30)
      @ 10,1  say CUSTOMER->ATTN
   endif
   @ prow()+1,1  say CUSTOMER->ADDRESS
   @ prow()+1,1  say trim(CUSTOMER->CITY)+', '+CUSTOMER->STATE+'  '+;
                 CUSTOMER->ZIP
   @ prow()+2,1  say 'ISBN NUMBER    QTY     PRICE     TITLE'
   @ prow()+1,1  say ' '

      do while SONUMBER = MSONUMBER .and. .not. eof() .and. prow() < 55
             @ prow()+1,1  say ISBN
             @ prow(),17    say QTY
             @ prow(),25    say PRICE
             @ prow(),35    say INVENTORY->TITLE
             skip
      enddo
      eject
enddo
set device    to screen
set relation to
```

Figure 8-19: MENU4P.PRG.

GETREC—The Procedure to Get a Record

This procedure can be used to position to a particular sales order record in the main
sales file. It makes use of the natural order of sales order records and the structure
of sales order numbers to position the database. The parameters transferred from
the calling program are a legend to be displayed, a memory variable used to determine whether or not to return to the menu, and the fieldname to be searched.

When a sales order number is entered, we evaluate whether or not the number is
valid. We have constructed these sales order numbers (as well as most other numbers
that we use) so that, after subtracting an offset (100000), the remainder is divisible

```
SALES ORDER 100051    DATED: 02/02/85
Page Number   1

TATE-ASHTON                           CUSTOMER P.O. a-12345
OLIVIA
3800 HONOLULU
LA CRESCENTA, CA  91214

ISBN NUMBER        QTY      PRICE      TITLE

0-02-501980-5      75       16.95      HOW TO SAVE ON YOUR INCOME TAX
0-8359-1246-9      76       19.95      DBASE II FOR EVERY BUSINESS
0-89588-124-1      77       17.95      BUSINESS GRAPHICS FOR THE PC
```

Figure 8–20: Sample printout.

by 17. Test for this condition with the **mod( )** function, which has two arguments—a number and a divisor. The output of the **mod( )** function is the remainder. If the output is zero, the number is evenly divisible by the divisor.

Here we make use of the natural order of the database. Go to the last record and subtract the desired sales order number from that stored in the last database record. Divide the result by 17. This produces a number which is the relative position of the desired record with respect to the last record in the file. If this number is positive and smaller than the current record number, we can go directly to the desired record. The program considers the possibility that a sales order number is "missing," which means that we could overshoot. If all is perfect, we land directly on the desired record. Otherwise, the sales order is found by locating from the current position.

Printing the Sales Order

Each sales order is printed by means of the program MENU4P.PRG, shown in Figure 8–19. A printout prepared by this program is shown as Figure 8–20. This procedure uses the search command to position the SALESDET file to the first occurrence of a sales order number. Then we link to the INVENTORY file. Note that the linkage can be either before or after the search. However, the search will be slower if the linkage preceded the search—because the inventory file would have been repositioned for every repositioning statement in SEARCH.

THE DAILY SALES REPORT

Menu selection 5 generates the daily report, and the program is shown in Figure 8–21. The first step is to determine the number of sales orders processed during the day and to position the master sales file to the first sales record of the day. To do this, we select the file SALES and go to the last record. Once positioned to the last record, we store the content of the date field to the variable SALESDAY and set the initial value of the variable SALES to 0.

```
* MENU45.PRG

clear
select SALES
go bottom
SALES      = 0
SALESDAY   = DATE

do while DATE = SALESDAY .and. .not. bof()
   skip -1
   if .not. VOID
      SALES = SALES + 1
   endif
enddo
locate rest for DATE = SALESDAY       && move back to beginning of sales day
select SALESDET
do SEARCH with SALES->SONUMBER,"SONUMBER"
sum rest QTY,QTY*PRICE,1 to SOLD,WORTH,ENTRIES for QTY > 0

set device to print

@  6,1  say 'Sales Report for '+dtoc(SALESDAY)
@  9,1  say 'Sales Orders Processed'
@  9,30 say SALES                       picture '###,###,###'
@ 11,1  say 'Number of books sold '
@ 11,30 say SOLD                        picture '###,###,###'
@ 13,1  say 'Avg Books Per Sales Order '
@ 13,30 say round(SOLD/SALES,1)         picture '###,###,###.#'
@ 15,1  say 'Avg Value Per Sales Order '
@ 15,30 say round(WORTH/SALES,1)        picture '###,###,###.#'
@ 17,1  say 'Number of Titles Per S/O '
@ 17,30 say ENTRIES/SALES               picture '###,###,###.#'
@ 19,1  say 'Total value of sales orders '
@ 19,30 say WORTH                       picture '###,###,###.##'
eject
set device to screen
```

Figure 8–21: Daily sales report program: MENU45.PRG.

Next we skip backward, a record at a time, until we encounter either a different date from that stored in SALESDAY or the beginning of the file. On each pass through this loop, we increment the value of SALES by one—provided that the sales order is not void. When we complete the loop, SALES contains the number of valid sales orders processed, and we are positioned to either the last record of the preceding sales day or record 1 (if this is the first day of sales). To make sure that we are at the first record for the day, we use **locate rest**.

The SEARCH procedure positions SALESDET to the first record of the day. We can acquire all the information needed to make the calculations by using the **sum** command. The last item summed is the constant 1, which causes the variable ENTRIES to be incremented by 1 each time a record is included in the command operation. The remainder of this program simply formats the report for printing. The printed output is shown as Figure 8–22.

```
Sales Report for 02/02/85

Sales Orders Processed              2

Number of books sold             243

Avg Books Per Sales Order        121.5

Avg Value Per Sales Order       2159.4

Number of Titles Per S/O          2.0

Total value of sales orders     4318.85
```

Figure 8–22: Sample sales report printout.

OPEN SALES ORDERS

The file OPENORD is the list of sales orders that have not as yet been filled (menu selection 6). This is the controlling file for all processes that use the sales order records. Since sales order numbers are removed from this file when they are filled, we know that this file is never very large. From time to time, we want to know the status of this file: which orders have not been filled and to whom they belong. MENU46.PRG, shown in Figure 8–23, is intended to provide a video copy of open orders with an option for a printed copy.

Three files are used in preparing this report: OPENORD, SALES, and CUSTOMER. An example of a report prepared by this program is shown as Figure 8–24. Items to be displayed are the sales order number, the date of the order, the customer's purchase order number, and the customer's name.

Our first step is to set up the three files. First we go to the beginning of OPENORD. If the file is empty, we inform the user and return to the menu program. If there are records in the file, we select the CUSTOMER file and set its index to CUSTID so that it can be linked to SALES. Next we select SALES and position this file to just before the first open sales order. Then we set the relation that links the customer file to the sales file.

The command **@ 4, 0 clear** erases the portion of the screen below and to the right of the coordinates and places the cursor at the specified screen coordinates. Once we enter the **do** loop, the bulk of the program consists of display controls related to whether the report is to be printed or not. For a program of this size and complex-

```
* MENU46.PRG
clear
select OPENORD
   if reccount() = 0
      wait 'There are no open sales orders - press any key'
      return
   endif
   go top
select CUSTOMER
   set index to CUSTID
select SALES
   go bottom
   do while SONUMBER > OPENORD->SONUMBER .and. .not. bof()
        skip -1
   enddo
   set relation to CUSTID into CUSTOMER
select OPENORD
do BANNER with "Open Sales Orders"
do QUERY with "Do you want a printed copy?",23,2,ANSWER
a  4,0 clear
do while .not. eof()
    if ANSWER = 'Y'
       set print on
       set device to print
       a  6,1  SAY 'Open Sales Orders as of '+dtoc(DATE())
       ?
    endif
    ? 'Sales                 Purchase '
    ? 'Order       Dated      Order         Customer Name'
    ?
    do while prow() < 55 .and. .not. eof()
        select SALES
        locate rest for SONUMBER = OPENORD->SONUMBER
        ? SONUMBER,'   ',DATE,'   ', PONUMBER,'    ', CUSTOMER->NAME
        select OPENORD
        skip
        if eof() .or. (ANSWER = 'N' .and. row() = 23)
           wait
           a 4,0 clear
        endif
    enddo
    if ANSWER = 'Y'
       eject
    endif
enddo
select SALES
set print off
set device to screen
set relation to
```

Figure 8–23: MENU46.PRG.

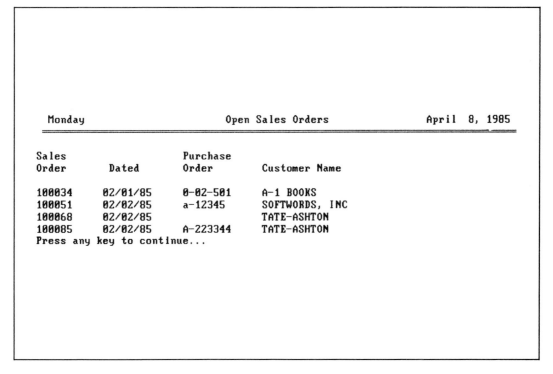

```
Monday                      Open Sales Orders              April  8, 1985


Sales                    Purchase
Order         Dated      Order         Customer Name

100034       02/01/85    0-02-501      A-1 BOOKS
100051       02/02/85    a-12345       SOFTWORDS, INC
100068       02/02/85                  TATE-ASHTON
100085       02/02/85    A-223344      TATE-ASHTON
Press any key to continue...
```

Figure 8–24: Sample report.

ity, you would probably be better served by completely separating print and screen-display code. The simplification and ease of understanding that will be gained easily justify the extra lines of code.

In this program we again make use of the natural ordering of the two files. In the process of preparing the report, we skip through the file OPENORD one record at a time. For each record in this file, we select SALES and locate the next record using the command:

locate rest for SONUMBER = OPENORD->SONUMBER

Remember, we have made sure that the sales order number can *only* exist in the OPENORD file if it has been entered into the SALES file. Therefore, we need not be concerned about the consequences of not finding the sales order.

Note that the control for the inner loop is the **prow( )** function. This function will never be true when directing output to the screen. Paging for the inner loop is controlled by the enclosed **if** statement. The page **eject** command is also enclosed within an **if** statement. **Eject** issues a form feed to the printer regardless of whether or not print is set on.

DELETING OLD SALES ORDER RECORDS

To get rid of records that are more than one year old, use MENU47.PRG (menu selection 7). This program is shown in Figure 8–25. This program is reasonably simple and substantially faster than it would be if either file were indexed.

* MENU47.PRG

```
clear
do BANNER with "Clearing Out Records Over 1 Year Old"
select SALES
go top
delete while DATE <= date() - 365
if recno() > 1
    set talk on
    pack
    set talk off
    go top
    select SALESDET
    go top
    delete while SONUMBER < SALES->SONUMBER
    if recno() > 1
        set talk on
        pack
        set talk off
    endif
endif
```

Figure 8–25: MENU47.PRG.

The records to be removed occur in blocks at the very beginning of both files. First we delete old records from SALES. This file contains the date field we need to identify which records are to be deleted. Dates can be used in arithmetic. A date plus a number is a date. A date minus a number is a date. The number is considered to be a number of days. There are 365 days in a year; to delete all records more than a year old, we:

delete while DATE < = date( ) – 365

Even though deleting and packing is faster with unindexed files than with indexed files, these operations are still time-consuming when the files are large. So, we perform the **pack** operation to remove the records only if they have been marked for deletion.

Once the packing operation has been completed, we reposition to the beginning of the SALES file. The first record in this file is the control for removing records from its subsidiary SALESDET file. In this file we want to delete all records where the sales order number is less than the first sales order in the SALES file. To be sure that we start at the beginning, we need to issue the **go top** command to both files.

Failing to rewind the SALES file would erase all the records in the detail file. To delete the desired records, use

delete while SONUMBER < SALES -> SONUMBER

Why is packing so slow? When the database is packed, records are physically moved from one place on the disk to another. If the first 100 records have been marked for deletion, the first unmarked record is record 101. When we **pack**, record 101 is moved to the disk location previously occupied by record 1. Record 102 is moved to where record 2 was, and so on. Record 201 goes to where 101 was, and so forth. It involves a great deal of motion for the disk head.

For slow operations of this type, it is considerate of the programmer to keep the user informed about what is going on. Use **set talk on** as an easy way to entertain the user. This produces a counter that increments as each record is moved. When finished with the packing operation, **set talk off** again so that your program functions normally.

CHAPTER NINE
Order Fulfillment

The order fulfillment system is diagrammed in Figure 9-1. Once a sales order has been entered into the computer, the next step is filling the order and preparing an invoice. The invoice is printed for the customer and stored to the invoices file for use by Accounts Receivable in the monthly billing.

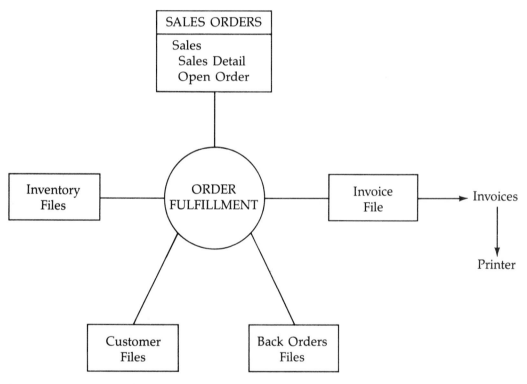

Figure 9–1: Diagram of the order fulfillment system.

Another task of order fulfillment is to set up a system for back-ordering books. If a customer order exceeds books in stock, we need to create a record of owing the customer so many copies of a particular book at the original order price. When the books come in, we ship them to the customer and prepare a billing invoice.

The *order-fulfillment* menu is shown as Figure 9–2. The menu program to produce this menu, MENU5.PRG, is shown as Figure 9–3. The particular features of order fulfillment and invoicing to be addressed in this chapter are illustrated by the selections on the menu.

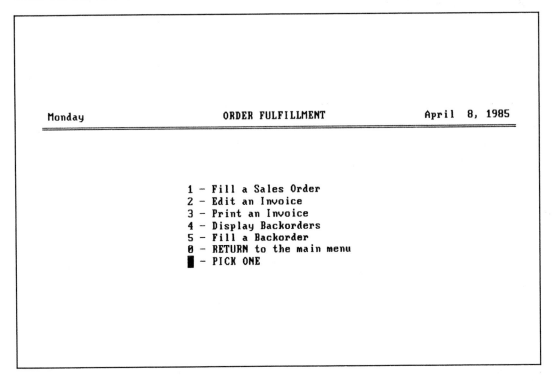

Figure 9–2: Order fulfillment menu.

Invoice records are kept *on-line* for only 30 days by our bookseller. This allows us to combine book invoicing information into a single file, providing some simplification in the programs, as well as holding down the total number of open files. An alternative implementation would be to keep the invoice information on-line for a year and to shorten the time that sales orders are saved.

The ORDER FULFILLMENT database consists of the CUSTOMER file, the INVENTORY file, the three SALES ORDER files, an INVOICES file, and a BACK-ORDERS file. These files are opened by the setup program shown in Figure 9–4. The database plans for the invoices and back-orders files are shown as Figure 9–5. The relationships between these files are shown by Figure 9–6. Note that the structure of BACKORD is identical to that of INVOICES.

```
* MENU5.PRG

do SETUP5
do while .T.
   select INVOICES
   CHOICES = '01'
   clear
   do BANNER with "ORDER FULFILLMENT"

   @ 8,25 say '1 - Fill a Sales Order'
   if reccount() > 0
       @ row()+1,25 say '2 - Edit an Invoice'
       @ row()+1,25 say '3 - Print an Invoice'
       @ row()+1,25 say '4 - Display Backorders'
       @ row()+1,25 say '5 - Fill a Backorder'
       CHOICES = CHOICES + '2345'
   endif
       @ row()+1,25 say '0 - RETURN to the main menu '
       @ row()+1,25 say '  - PICK ONE'

   do CHOICE with 25,CHOICES
   do MENU5&CHOICE
enddo
```

Figure 9–3: MENU5.PRG program.

```
* SETUP5.PRG

clear
? 'Opening Order Fulfillment Databases'
select CUSTOMER
               set index to CUSTID
select 4
               use SALES
select 5
               use SALESDET
select 6
               use OPENORD
select 7
               use INVOICES
select 8
               use BACKORD
```

Figure 9–4: The setup program: SETUP5.PRG.

Database Plan for: INVOICES.DBF

DESCRIPTION	FIELDNAME	FIELDTYPE	WIDTH	DECIMALS
Invoice Number	INVOICE	Character	6	
Sales Order No.	SONUMBER	Character	6	
Customer ID Code	CUSTID	Character	6	
Date of Invoice	DATE	Date	8	
Customer P.O. No.	PONUMBER	Character	8	
ISBN Number	ISBN	Character	13	
Quantity Ordered	QTY	Numeric	3	
Quantity Shipped	QTYDEL	Numeric	3	
Price to Customer	PRICE	Numeric	6	2
		Data Size	.....59 BYTES	

Database Plan for: BACKORD.DBF

DESCRIPTION	FIELDNAME	FIELDTYPE	WIDTH	DECIMALS
Invoice Number	INVOICE	Character	6	
Sales Order No.	SONUMBER	Character	6	
Customer ID Code	CUSTID	Character	6	
Date of Invoice	DATE	Date	8	
Customer P.O. No.	PONUMBER	Character	8	
ISBN Number	ISBN	Character	13	
Quantity Ordered	QTY	Numeric	3	
Quantity Shipped	QTYDEL	Numeric	3	
Price to Customer	PRICE	Numeric	6	2
		Data Size	.....59 BYTES	

Figure 9–5: Database plans.

A major design consideration for this menu selection is managing the open files. As soon as we enter the menu program, we are already using 13 files as listed below. This leaves only two more files that can be opened.

MENU.PRG
  MENUPROC.PRG
  MENU5.PRG
  CUSTOMER.DBF index CUSTID
  INV.DBF index ISBN
  CONTROLS.DBF

SALES.DBF
  SALESDET.DBF
  OPENORD.DBF
  INVOICES.DBF
  BACKORD.DBF

A difference between this order fulfillment menu program and previous menus is the way that we handle returning to the main menu. Since we have so many open files, we don't want to handicap other menu selections by using valuable file space. The return to the main menu is handled by MENU50.PRG (in Figure 9–7).

CUSTOMER

Customer ID Code	Name	Attn
071254	Cave Books	Mr. Clarinet
598326	Costello Enterprises	Mso. Rentzel

SALES

Sales Order Number	Customer ID Code	Date	Customer's PO Number
100411	071254	04/08/85	A76382
100412	200461	04/08/85	B-2761
100413	598326	04/09/85	T3477

SALES DETAIL

Sales Order Number	ISBN Number	QTY	Price
100411	0-912677-03-1	21	19.95
100412	0-912677-42-2	14	29.95
100413	0-912677-16-3	7	18.85
100414	0-912677-26-0	23	17.95

INVOICES

Invoice #	Customer ID #	Date of PO	Amount
141612	071254	04/08/85	289.95
141613	200461	04/08/85	47.95
141614	598326	04/09/85	411.95

INVENTORY

ISBN #	Supplier	Qty in stock	Qty on order
0-912677-03-1	912677	23	5
0-912677-42-2	912677	47	15
0-912677-16-3	912677	48	27
0-912677-26-0	912677	101	14

BACK ORDERS

Invoice #	Sales Order #	ISBN	QTY	Price	Qty Del
141612	100414	0-912677-16-3	10	8.95	5

Figure 9–6: Order fulfillment.

```
* MENU50.PRG

clear
? 'Closing Invoice Databases'
select 2
                use CONTROLS
select 4
            use
select 5
            use
select 6
            use
select 7
            use
select 8
            use
select 9
            use
return to master
```

Figure 9–7: MENU50.PRG.

RETURNING TO THE MAIN MENU

Before we return to the main menu program (menu selection 0), we make certain that we return to an acceptable set of conditions. This requires that we close all of the open files except for CUSTOMER, CONTROLS, and INVENTORY, by stepping through work areas 4 through 9 and issuing the **use** command.

To return to the main menu from the subroutine (MENU50), we use a variation of the **return** command: **return to master**. This command takes you directly to the highest calling program.

SALES ORDER FULFILLMENT

In our dynamic book distributor's operation, a copy of the sales order is printed for the warehouse to use when filling the order. After the order is filled, the copy of the sales order is returned to the computer clerk. If the warehouse cannot ship the requested number of books for a given title, the actual number shipped is written on the sales order form.

We could adjust the inventory *quantity on hand* for each title at the time the sales order is issued—before it is sent to the warehouse. We choose not to do so for the following reason: Computers normally process orders first in – first out (FIFO), but warehouse workers tend to process orders last in – first out (LIFO). Most orders go into an in basket with the last order on top. A warehouse worker who picks up one of the top orders in the basket might not realize that available stock has been assigned to a previous order. The worker sees only that the book has been back ordered and assumes that the computer has made a mistake.

Later in the day, the worker reaches the earlier sales order to which the computer had assigned the stock. Now, however, there is not enough stock. The worker thinks that the computer has been wrong twice in one day. All records on these orders must then be corrected at the office to adjust the computer to the reality of the warehouse. It is simpler to let the warehouse control the inventory in the first place. Adjusting stock quantities after the order is filled gives us a better match with the realities of our inventory. It also makes for simpler software.

The program to transform a sales order into an invoice (menu selection 1) is shown as Figure 9–8: MENU51.PRG. This program mainly consists of a series of simple operations on each of several database files. The sequence of activities in this program is:

1. Enter the sales order number that has been filled.
2. Verify that the number was still open by checking the open orders file.
3. Locate the sales order in the master sales file.
4. Use the customer ID code from the master sales file to retrieve the customer record. Display that record and verify that we have the correct customer and sales order.
5. Increment the invoice number.
6. Locate the first detailed record for that sales order in the detail file SALESDET.
7. Move data from the SALESDET file to the INVOICES file.
8. Check for back-ordered items.
9. Update inventory quantities.
10. Close out the entry in the open-orders file.

The program begins by selecting OPENORD. OPENORD contains only the sales order numbers of orders that have not been filled. When an order is filled (by this program), the order number is deleted from OPENORD. The open-orders file is not going to be very large. At least not at 20 orders per day with only seven bytes required for each *open* sales order. Even though it's overkill, we use the procedure GETREC to search this tiny file for the sales order number—because there is a series of tests that the procedure applies: Did we enter a number? Is the number valid? Is the number in the file? This is just routine. We have to do it, and, if we were to include these tests in the main program, the program appears much larger and more complex.

Once we've found a number in the open-orders file, we search the sales file for that same sales order number. The search is backward from the end of the file because we expect the open sales order to be near the end. The sales order record provides access to the customer record by means of the field CUSTID.

```
* MENU51.PRG

BANNERMSG  = "Order Fulfillment"
do while .T.
    clear
    do BANNER with BANNERMSG
    select OPENORD
        MSONUMBER = space(6)
        do GETREC with "Sales Order Number ", MSONUMBER, "SONUMBER"
                            if MSONUMBER = space(6)
                                return
                            endif
    select SALES
        go bottom
        do while .not. SONUMBER = MSONUMBER
            skip -1
        enddo
    select CUSTOMER
        seek SALES->CUSTID
        do MENU1S
        @ 23,2 say 'Processing Sales Order '+ MSONUMBER
    select CONTROLS
        replace INVOICE with str(val(INVOICE)+17,6)
    select SALESDET
        do SEARCH with MSONUMBER,"SONUMBER"
        set relation to ISBN into INVENTORY
        do while MSONUMBER = SONUMBER .and. .not. eof()
            select INVOICES
            append blank
            replace INVOICE with CONTROLS->INVOICE, SONUMBER with MSONUMBER,;
                    DATE with date(), PONUMBER with SALES->PONUMBER,;
                    CUSTID with SALES->CUSTID
            replace QTY with SALESDET->QTY, ISBN with SALESDET->ISBN,;
                    QTYDEL with QTY, PRICE with SALESDET->PRICE
            select INVENTORY
            replace QTYONHAND with QTYONHAND-INVOICES->QTYDEL,;
                    SOLDTHISYR with SOLDTHISYR+INVOICES->QTYDEL,;
                    LASTSALE with date()
            select SALESDET
            skip
        enddo
    select INVOICES
        do SEARCH with INVOICES->INVOICE,"INVOICE"
        FIRSTREC = recno()
        do QTYEDIT with INVOICES->INVOICE,FIRSTREC
        go FIRSTREC
        copy to WORKFILE while INVOICE = CONTROLS->INVOICE
    select BACKORD
        append from WORKFILE for QTYDEL < QTY
    select OPENORD
        delete
        pack
enddo
```

Figure 9–8: Invoicing program: MENU51.

To display customer information, we select the customer file and **seek** the record containing the customer ID code stored in the SALES record.

The CONTROLS file contains the last invoice number assigned. The number to be assigned to this invoice will be 17 greater than that number. We are still using this modulo 17 concept; it provides some safeguards against human errors.

The next task is to create a set of records in the INVOICES file. There will be one record in the INVOICES file for each book title in the sales order. To do this, we find the first record in SALESDET and use a **do** loop to create an invoice record for each title. The information for these records is pulled from the other files by the **replace** command as each invoice record is created. We can take advantage of this operation to update inventory quantities. This is done by relating the sales order detail file SALESDET to the INVENTORY. Then, while we are in the process of creating and entering data into the INVOICES file, we simply select the INVENTORY and adjust the QTYONHAND by the QTYDEL. We may alter this value later on when editing the invoice records for QTYDEL.

Next, we want to adjust the QTYDEL in the invoice file for those items that were not completely filled. The procedure QTYEDIT allows us to change the quantity shipped (QTYDEL). When the invoice record was created, we stored the quantity ordered to both QTY and QTYDEL. QTYEDIT is shown in Figure 9–9. This procedure provides for full-screen editing in a manner similar to that for the command **browse**. It is unfortunate that the full-screen editing commands such as **append**, **browse**, **change**, and **edit** are not particularly useful for programming. The problem with these commands is that they offer the user too many uncontrolled options.

When we have finished editing the quantity delivered, we want to create a back-order record for each item where the QTYDEL field is less than the QTY field. To post records to the back-orders file, we first reposition the INVOICES file to the first record of the new invoice. Then we make a copy of the invoice by using the **copy** command. Once we have this copy, we select the back-orders file and add records that haven't been completely filled with the **append from** command. **Append from** allows you to add records from another file. The two files must have common fieldnames. Only data from the fields with common names will be transferred. The source file must not be open.

The sales order is closed by reselecting the open orders file, deleting, and packing the sales order number. Remember, this file is positioned to the correct record by the procedure GETREC and has not been repositioned.

Procedure QTYEDIT—Edit Quantity Shipped

This procedure, shown as Figure 9–9, is used to edit the quantity shipped field (QTYDEL) for an invoice. The program receives the invoice number and the starting record number from the calling program. These items become the memory variables MVAR and FIRSTREC. The variables FIRSTREC, START, and X are declared private. This step hides any variables with the same names that might already exist from

```
procedure QTYEDIT
parameter MVAR, FIRSTREC
private FIRSTREC,START,LASTREC,X
set relation to ISBN into INVENTORY
ANSWER  = "Y"
START   = FIRSTREC
do while ANSWER = "Y"
   clear
   do BANNER with "Editing Invoice " + MVAR
   ? ' ISBN Number      Title '
   a row(),col()+28 say 'Ordered  Shipped   Price'
   ? ' '+BAR
   go START
   X = 10
      do while INVOICE = MVAR .and. X < 27 .and. .not. eof()
         MEMVAR = 'M'+str(X,2)
         store QTYDEL to &MEMVAR
         X = X+1
         ? ' '+ISBN+'   ',INVENTORY->TITLE,str(QTY,8),str(PRICE,18,2)
         a row(),63 get &MEMVAR picture '###' range 0,QTY
         skip
      enddo
   read
   x=10
   go START
      do while INVOICE = MVAR .and. x < 27 .and. .not. eof()
         MEMVAR = 'M'+str(x,2)
         if &MEMVAR # QTYDEL
            select INVENTORY
            replace QTYONHAND with QTYONHAND - (&MEMVAR - INVOICES->QTYDEL),;
                    SOLDTHISYR with SOLDTHISYR+(&MEMVAR - INVOICES->QTYDEL)
            select INVOICES
            replace QTYDEL with &MEMVAR
         endif
         X = X+1
         skip
      enddo
      if INVOICE # MVAR .or. eof()
          do QUERY with "Do you want to re-edit",23,2,ANSWER
          a 23,2
          START = FIRSTREC
      else
          START = recno()
      endif
enddo
set relation to
go FIRSTREC
return
```

Figure 9–9: QTYEDIT procedure.

this program. We didn't use **private all** because we do want to use some of the variables from the higher programs—in particular, the public variables used in BANNER and the variable BAR.

The active file is related to the INVENTORY file by the ISBN number, which allows us to display the book title for each inventory record directly. It also conveniently positions the INVENTORY to the correct record for updating the QTYONHAND.

The variables FIRSTREC and START keep track of our position in the active database file. When we enter this procedure, we are already positioned to the first record in the active file.

The variable ANSWER is used to control the operation of the loop. As long as this variable remains a "Y", the loop continues to operate.

The first five command lines inside of the loop are used to display the screen heading and the column titles. Note that the display commands are mixed between the **?** and @ . . . **say**.

START is the controlling position within the loop. FIRSTREC is used to remember which is the first record for the invoice. The inner loop uses both the value of the counter X and the INVOICE as controls rather than just the invoice number. This inner loop can display up to 17 records on the screen. The field QTYDEL for each record is stored in a separate memory variable named M10 to M26. The variable names begin with M10, given that they must begin with a letter and they cannot contain embedded blank spaces. It is somewhat of a bother to discriminate between one-digit and two-digit character strings.

The first command creates a memory variable MEMVAR and stores an M plus two digits to the variable (for example, M14). The second command stores the content of QTYDEL to the variable name stored in MVAR. For example, if the MVAR contains the character string M14, dBASE III PLUS "reads" this command as **store QTYDEL to M14**.

The bulk of each record is displayed by the **?** command. The two numeric fields are "spaced" by adjusting their size with the **str** function. This allows us to place the QTYDEL between QTY and PRICE. The range of data that can be entered for each variable is zero and the quantity ordered QTY. This QTY is the content of the field QTY in use when the command is issued.

When the data from the first 17 records for the invoice is displayed on-screen, we issue the **read** command. This allows us to change the QTYDEL for any of the displayed records by using the arrow keys to move the cursor to the desired record and type in the correct value. To skip all the items and move on to the next "page," press **Ctrl-PgDn**.

When finished with the **read**, we reset the counter (X) to 10 and reposition the database to the record number stored in the variable START. If the quantity in a record is different from the quantity stored in the equivalent memory variable, we select INVENTORY and adjust the content of QTYONHAND by the difference between the value stored in the QTYDEL field and the value of the equivalent memory variable. Then we reselect INVOICES and replace the QTYDEL by the content of the equivalent memory variable.

When we emerge from the second loop, we compare the content of the field INVOICE with the controlling memory variable MVAR. If these two match, we store the current record number to START and edit the next batch of invoice records. Otherwise, we ask the user whether or not to continue.

When we emerge from the loop, we reset to the original conditions by turning off the relationship with INVENTORY and repositioning the file to its original record position.

This procedure is much more complex than those used to update the INVENTORY file or to edit the SALESDET file. Those procedures could have been used for this function. However, fewer keystrokes are required to edit records using this procedure than when using earlier equivalent procedures. Although more complex for the programmer, it is easier for the user—and that is exactly why we write programs. Given the choice, always opt for the user.

INVOICE RECORDS

Invoice records are edited when we discover that we have entered the wrong quantity delivered for an item on a sales order/invoice. The program for editing invoices (menu selection 2) is MENU52.PRG (Figure 9–10). This program accepts an invoice number from the keyboard. The INVOICES file is searched for the invoice number by the procedure FINDREC. If it is found, the database is positioned to the first record for the invoice. Otherwise, it is positioned to the end of file.

The procedure QTYEDIT, which was just discussed, is used to edit the QTYDEL field within the invoices file. Once the invoice has been edited, we need to readjust the backorder records. We may have more back-order records, fewer records, or just changes in the quantity to be back ordered.

The "best" strategy to use for processing back orders will depend on how many items are back ordered and what the average time to fill a back order is. In short, how big is the back-order file. For our favorite bookseller we have assumed that about ten percent of the items need to be back ordered. In addition, it takes an average of ten working days to fill each back order. Each back-order record requires 60 bytes of disk space. The average size of the back-order file is about 24,000 bytes. Even on a floppy disk, we can search this file in about 6 seconds using the **locate** command. Note that back-order records are in invoice-record order.

The approach that we've taken to adjust the back-order file uses a middle ground. The INVOICES file is positioned to the first record for the invoice. All records for the invoice are copied to the temporary file WORKFILE, just as when transferring the sales order to the invoice file. This time, however, we want to work with the data in the WORKFILE. We open this file in the work area previously occupied by INVOICES. This step closes INVOICES and renames the work area to WORKFILE.

```
* MENU52.PRG

clear
do BANNER with "Edit Invoice Quantity Delivered"
select INVOICES
     do FINDREC with "Invoice Number", "INVOICE"
                              if eof()
                                   return
                              endif
     FIRSTREC = recno()
     MINVOICE = INVOICE
     do QTYEDIT with MINVOICE,recno()
     @ 23,2 say "Processing For " + MINVOICE
     go FIRSTREC
     copy to WORKFILE while INVOICE = MINVOICE
     use WORKFILE
     delete for QTYDEL >= QTY
     pack
select BACKORD
     do SEARCH with MINVOICE, "INVOICE"
     if eof()
          locate for INVOICE > MINVOICE
     endif
     PLACEMARK = recno()
     set relation to recno()-(PLACEMARK-1) into WORKFILE
     do while WORKFILE->INVOICE = MINVOICE
          if INVOICE # MINVOICE
               insert blank before
          endif
          replace SONUMBER with WORKFILE->SONUMBER, INVOICE with MINVOICE,;
                  DATE with WORKFILE->DATE, ISBN with WORKFILE->ISBN,;
                  QTYDEL with WORKFILE->QTYDEL, QTY with WORKFILE->QTY
          replace PONUMBER with WORKFILE->PONUMBER,;
                  CUSTID with WORKFILE->CUSTID,PRICE with WORKFILE->PRICE
          skip
     enddo
     delete while INVOICE = MINVOICE
select WORKFILE
     use INVOICES
```

Figure 9–10: MENU52.PRG.

The last action in the program restores the initial conditions by reopening INVOICES in this same work area.

Now that the WORKFILE is open, we can remove all unwanted records with **delete** and **pack**. The unwanted records are those records that are filled (that is, the quantity ordered equals the quantity delivered). Next we select the back-order file and search for the invoice in the back-order records. If it is not found, we search for the nearest larger record with the **locate** command. **Search** should be faster than **locate**. So we only use the slower command when the fastest option doesn't work. Next we relate the BACKORD file to the WORKFILE by the offset record number.

The **do** loop is entered only if there are records in the WORKFILE (MINVOICE = WORKFILE->INVOICE). As soon as we run out of WORKFILE records, we reach the blank record at the end of WORKFILE (the **eof** record). Then, the two variables will no longer match. Immediately inside the loop we encounter the comparison between MINVOICE and the field INVOICE. If these are not equal, we want to add a record to the back-order file. Regardless of the current value of the remaining fields, we replace all the items with the data from the workfile record. Then we advance to the next record. If we've run out of WORKFILE records, we exit from the loop and delete all remaining back-order records where the INVOICE number matches the control variable MINVOICE.

SEARCHING FOR AN INVOICE NUMBER

This procedure, shown in Figure 9–11, prompts the user to enter a number. The parameters passed from the calling program are the prompt string and the name of the field to be searched. We've assumed that the number to be searched will conform to our construct for number codes; that is, it is divisible by 17 after subtracting a constant.

This procedure is similar to many others that we have constructed for the purpose of searching for a control value. In this case, however, when we deliberately exit from the loop, we force an end-of-file condition by using the procedure GOEOF, which is contained in MENUPROC.PRG. The end-of-file condition is used to tell the program calling FINDREC to terminate.

PRINTING INVOICES

This program, MENU53.PRG, is shown in Figure 9–12. The program, upon entry, displays the last 15 invoices on the screen. This feature is a convenience to the user, who may need to be reminded of a recent invoice number. The screen row position is used to control the processing. On each pass through the loop, we first display the invoice number, the sales order number, and the customer name. Then we initialize the variable MTOTAL. The inner loop accumulates the value of the invoice. When the loop is complete, the database is repositioned to the last record of the previous invoice. The **??** command displays the value of MTOTAL at the current position of the cursor. This command is similar to the **?** command but does not issue a beginning carriage return and line feed.

```
procedure FINDREC
   parameters LEGEND,  FIELDNAME
   private all
   do while .T.
       VALIDTEST = .F.
       MEMVAR    = space(6)
       a 23,2 say LEGEND get MEMVAR picture "999999"
       read
                          if MEMVAR = space(6)
                              if .not. eof()
                                do GOEOF
                              endif
                              exit
                          endif
       * validate number stored in MEMVAR
                          if .not.  mod(val(MEMVAR)-100000,17)=0
                              do ERRORMSG with MEMVAR + ' is invalid',22,2
                              loop
                          endif
       a 22,2
       do SEARCH with MEMVAR, "&FIELDNAME"
                          if eof()
                              do ERRORMSG with MEMVAR + ' not found',22,2
                              loop
                          endif
       exit
   enddo
return
```

Figure 9-11: Procedure to find an invoice number: FINDREC.

The invoice to be printed is found with the help of the procedure FINDREC. This procedure returns either at the end of file—or to the desired record position (the first record of the invoice). At this point we are positioned to the first invoice record and the customer record matching the content of the field CUSTID. We link individual records in the invoice to their inventory titles by relating the file to INVENTORY.

We initialize the two accumulators, PAGE and MTOTAL, by storing a zero to both variables. Use the **STORE** command whenever two or more variables will contain the same value.

The printed invoice, shown in Figure 9-13, is produced by the **do** loop. The program, MENU53A.PRG (in Figure 9-14), prints the page heading. The value of PAGE is incremented by 1 for each page of the printed invoice.

```
* MENU53.PRG

do while .T.
   select INVOICES
     clear
     do BANNER with  'Print Invoices'
     set relation to CUSTID into CUSTOMER
     go bottom
     ? 'Invoice  Sales Order   Customer Name                       Total'
     do while row() < 20 .and. .not. bof()
        MTOTAL = 0
        ? INVOICE,'   ', SONUMBER,'   ', CUSTOMER->NAME
        MINVOICE = INVOICE
        do while INVOICE = MINVOICE .and. .not. bof()
           MTOTAL = (QTYDEL * PRICE) + MTOTAL
           skip -1
        enddo
        ?? MTOTAL
     enddo
     do FINDREC with "Invoice Number ", "INVOICE"
                           if eof()
                                exit
                           endif
     MINVOICE = INVOICE
     set relation to ISBN into INVENTORY
     @ 23,2 say  'Be sure that your printer is turned on!'
     set device to print
     store 0 to MTOTAL, PAGE
     do while INVOICE = MINVOICE .and. .not. eof()
        do MENU53A
        do while INVOICE = MINVOICE .and. prow() < 55 .and. .not. eof()
           MTOTAL = MTOTAL + (PRICE * QTYDEL)
           @ prow()+2,1       say INVENTORY->TITLE
           @ prow(),35        say QTYDEL        picture "###"
           @ prow(),40        say QTY-QTYDEL    picture "@Z ###"
           @ prow(),45        say PRICE         picture "###.##"
           @ prow(),55        say PRICE * QTYDEL picture "###,###.##"
           @ prow()+1,5       say ISBN
           skip
        enddo
        if MINVOICE # INVOICE .or. eof()
           @ prow()+2,39 say '* Total *'
           @ prow(),52   say MTOTAL picture '##,###,###.##'
           MTOTAL = 0
        endif
        eject
     enddo
   set device to screen
enddo
set relation to
```

Figure 9–12: MENU53.PRG.

```
Invoice: 100170    Page:  1                        April  8, 1985

TO:        SOFTWORDS, INC                   Your Purchase Order
           3301 MILLS AVENUE                      a-12345
           LA CRESCENTA, CA   91214
           ATTN: SOFTY

FROM:      BOB'S BETTER BOOKS
           3800 Honolulu Avenue
           La Crescenta, California   91214         (213)204-5570
-----------------------------------------------------------------
Title/ISBN Number                QTY  B/O   PRICE         TOTAL
-----------------------------------------------------------------

HOW  TO SAVE ON YOUR INCOME TAX   25   50   16.95        423.75
     0-02-501980-5

DBASE II FOR EVERY BUSINESS       25   45   19.95        498.75
     0-8359-1246-9

BUSINESS GRAPHICS FOR THE PC      25   45   17.95        448.75
     0-89588-124-1

                                  * Total *           1,371.25
```

Figure 9–13: The printed invoice.

```
* MENU53A.PRG

PAGE = PAGE+1
@ 3,1  say 'Invoice: '+ MINVOICE+'   Page: '+str(PAGE,2)
@ 3,(65-len(CDATE)) say CDATE
@ 5,1  say 'TO: '
@ 5,10 say CUSTOMER->NAME+space(6)+'Your Purchase Order'
@ 6,10 say CUSTOMER->ADDRESS
@ 6,54 say PONUMBER
@ 7,10 say trim(CUSTOMER->CITY)+', '+CUSTOMER->STATE+'  '+CUSTOMER->ZIP
if CUSTOMER->ATTN # space(30)
    @ 8,10 say 'ATTN: '+CUSTOMER->ATTN
endif
@ 10,1  say 'FROM:'
@ 10,10 say "BOB'S BETTER BOOKS"
@ 11,10 say '865 Tahoe Boulevard'
@ 12,10 say 'Incline Village, Nevada    89450'
@ 12,52 say '(213)204-5570'
@ 13,1  say replicate('-',64)
@ 14,1  say 'Title/ISBN Number'
@ 14,35 say 'QTY  B/O   PRICE         TOTAL'
@ 15,1  say replicate('-',64)
```

Figure 9–14: MENU53A.PRG.

On each pass through the inner loop, we print one record from the invoice. The invoice total (stored in MTOTAL) is updated on each pass through this loop. The format of each of the numeric items is controlled by its **picture**. The printed format controls the size and form of the display. **Picture "###"** limits the field display to three spaces—but will display the value 0. **Picture "@Z ###"** also limits the field display to three spaces, but inhibits display of zero values.

We exit from the inner loop when one of three conditions occurs: the end of file is reached, the invoice number no longer matches the control variable, or we've reached the bottom of the page. If either of the first two conditions occurs, we want to print the invoice total. In any event, we need to eject the paper.

DISPLAYING BACK-ORDER DATA

Menu selection 4 shows an alternative method for directing program output to either the screen or the printer. Menu selection 4 is produced by the program MENU54.PRG. This program is shown in Figure 9–15. A typical output screen is shown in Figure 9–16.

Set heading determines whether or not the standard column titles that dBASE usually employs for displays are displayed. **Set heading off** turns the title display off, while **set heading on** turns the title display on.

This program uses only **set print on** to direct the output to the printer. This set command routes all screen display except for that created by @ . . . **say** commands to the printer.

Note that, upon entering the **do** loop, we use two **set relation** commands in succession. Each use of **set relation** repositions the related file to the first matching record. This is done for each pass through the loop because you can only relate the active file to one other file at a time.

Most of this program consists of tests to determine the action to take, depending on whether or not the output is to be printed. This program should be contrasted with the program to print open sales orders of the last chapter. Again, the LINEFEED procedure reduces the number of lines in the program.

FILLING A BACK ORDER

Filling a back order is similar in most respects to filling a sales order. The major difference is that we use the back-order file rather than the sales files as the source to create invoice records. The program for filling back orders is MENU55.PRG and is shown in Figure 9–17.

```
* MENU54.PRG

clear
do BANNER with "Display Backorder Data"
do QUERY with "do you want a printed copy?",23,2,ANSWER
                    if ANSWER = 'Y'
                        ROW      = "prow()"
                        PAGESIZE = 55
                        set print on
                        set console off
                    else
                        ROW      = "row()"
                        PAGESIZE = 20
                    endif
select BACKORD
go top
set heading off
do while .not. eof()
   set relation to CUSTID into CUSTOMER
   set relation to ISBN   into INVENTORY
   if ANSWER = 'Y' .and. &ROW <= 1
       do LINEFEED with 4                      && printer line feeds
       ? 'BACKORDER STATUS AS OF: '+CDATE
   endif
   ?
   ? CUSTOMER->NAME
   ? '  S/O #: '+SONUMBER+'  Invoice: '+INVOICE+'  Dated: '+dtoc(DATE)
   ?
   MCUSTID   = CUSTID
   list off space(10),INVENTORY->TITLE,ISBN,str(QTY,5),str(QTYDEL,5);
           while &ROW < PAGESIZE .and. MCUSTID = CUSTID

   if eof() .or.  &ROW >= PAGESIZE
       if ANSWER = 'Y'
          eject
       else
          wait
          @ 4,0 clear
       endif
   endif
enddo
set print off
set console on
set relation to
set heading on
```

Figure 9–15: MENU54.PRG.

```
   Monday                   Display Backorder Data              April  8, 1985


A-1 BOOKS
   S/O #: 100034  Invoice: 100068  Dated: 02/25/85

              SYSTEM DESIGN GUIDE                0-912677-12-0   111   100

SOFTWORDS, INC
   S/O #: 100051  Invoice: 100187  Dated: 03/07/85

              HOW TO SAVE ON YOUR INCOME TAX 0-02-501980-5    50     0








   Press any key to continue...
```

Figure 9–16: Screen from MENU54.PRG.

To fill a back order, we must supply the original invoice number for the back-ordered records. This data is always available from menu selection 4 (see above). The invoice number is found in the back-order file using the procedure FINDREC. If the invoice is not found, the procedure sets the end-of-file flag and terminates the program. Otherwise, the procedure FINDREC positions the back-order file to the proper record: the first back-order record for the specified invoice number.

Once the invoice has been located in the back-order file, we have access to the customer record via the CUSTID field in the back-order file. Customer information is displayed on-screen by means of the screen display program MENU1S. This program was developed for data entry and display of customer data.

The back-ordered items are assigned a new invoice number when shipped. This invoice is treated exactly as a new order except that the source of the records is the back-order file. The invoice number stored in the CONTROLS file must be incremented for this new invoice.

Next we reselect the back-order file and relate its records to the inventory file by the ISBN number.

The **do** loop creates a record in the invoices file for each back-ordered item to be closed out. For each back-order record, we **append** a blank record to the invoices file. The new blank record is filled in by using the **replace** command. In this case,

```
* MENU55.PRG

BANNERMSG  = "Fill A Backorder"
do while .T.
    clear
    do BANNER with BANNERMSG
    select BACKORD
        do FINDREC with "Invoice Number ", "INVOICE"
                        if eof()
                            return
                        endif
    FIRSTBO  = recno()
    MINVOICE = INVOICE
    select CUSTOMER
        seek SALES->CUSTID
        do MENU1S
        @ 23,2 say 'Processing Sales Order '+ MINVOICE
    select CONTROLS
        replace INVOICE with str(val(INVOICE)+17,6)
    select BACKORD
        set relation to ISBN into INVENTORY
        do while INVOICE = MINVOICE .and. .not. eof()
            select INVOICES
            append blank
            replace INVOICE with CONTROLS->INVOICE,;
                    SONUMBER with BACKORD->SONUMBER,;
                    DATE with date(), PONUMBER with BACKORD->PONUMBER
            replace CUSTID with BACKORD->CUSTID, ISBN with BACKORD->ISBN,;
                    QTY with BACKORD->QTY - BACKORD->QTYDEL,;
                    QTYDEL with QTY, PRICE with BACKORD->PRICE
            select INVENTORY
                    Replace QTYONHAND with QTYONHAND-INVOICES->QTYDEL,;
                            SOLDTHISYR with SOLDTHISYR+INVOICES->QTYDEL,;
                            LASTSALE with date()
            select BACKORD
            delete
            skip
        enddo
    select INVOICES
        do SEARCH with INVOICES->INVOICE,"INVOICE"
        FIRSTREC = recno()
        do QTYEDIT with INVOICES->INVOICE,FIRSTREC
        go FIRSTREC
        copy to WORKFILE while INVOICE = CONTROLS->INVOICE
    select BACKORD
        append from WORKFILE for QTYDEL < QTY
        pack
enddo
```

Figure 9–17: MENU55.PRG

the QTY filled in is the difference between the QTY originally ordered and the QTYDEL.

Then we select the inventory file and use the content of QTYDEL to adjust the values in QTYONHAND and SOLDTHISYR.

Once the update has been completed we reselect the back-order file. Before we advance to the next record, we delete this back-order record.

Next, select the invoices file and locate the first record for this new record using the search procedure. Store the record number to the variable FIRSTREC. We edit the quantity delivered field with the procedure QTYEDIT just in case one or more of the back-ordered items should still be back ordered.

CHAPTER TEN
Customer Payments

Our bookseller, like most businesses, receives payments from customers. These payments must be entered into a payments file. At the end of the month, all the payments received during the month are transferred to another payments file, which is used for billing purposes. The monthly payments file is cleared out, and the process starts over again for the next month's activity.

Three principal types of entries are entered into the monthly payments file: payments received, credit memos, and debit memos. Credit and debit memos are used to record credits and debits to the account that are separate from payments received. For example, a credit memo is issued when a customer receives credit for merchandise returned. A debit memo is issued when a customer's check has "bounced."

THE PAYMENTS DATABASE PLAN

The database plan for the database file PAYMENTS is shown in Figure 10–1. The PAYMENTS file is to be linked to the CUSTOMER file by the content of CUSTID. To do so, we must index PAYMENTS on the field CUSTID. The comments field is used to enter standard comments such as *credit memo*.

Database Plan for: PAYMENTS.DBF				
DESCRIPTION	FIELDNAME	FIELDTYPE	WIDTH	DECIMALS
Customer ID Code	CUSTID	Character	6	
Kind of Payment	COMMENTS	Character	20	
Date Payment Posted	DATE	Date	8	
Amount of Payment	AMOUNT	Numeric	9	2
		Data Size	. . . . . 44 Bytes	
File to be Indexed on: CUSTID		to PAYMENTS		

Figure 10–1: Payments database plan.

THE PAYMENTS MENU PROGRAM

The payments menu selects from among three menu options: entering customer payments, printing a payments summary, and returning to the main menu. The payments menu is shown in Figure 10–2. The menu program, MENU6.PRG, to produce this screen display is shown in Figure 10–3.

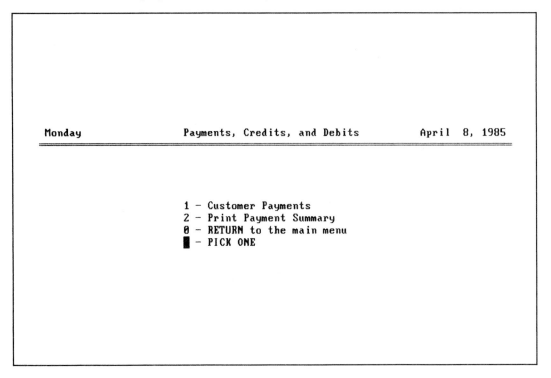

```
Monday                    Payments, Credits, and Debits          April  8, 1985
================================================================================


                          1 - Customer Payments
                          2 - Print Payment Summary
                          0 - RETURN to the main menu
                          ▉ - PICK ONE
```

Figure 10–2: Payments menu.

At the beginning of the month, when no payments have been entered, only two menu selections are displayed. The print option disappears when there is nothing to print.

The only setup required for this program selection is to open the PAYMENTS database file with its associated index file. This selection is opened in work area 4 to make sure that the file will not contribute to the open-file management problem. Any menu selection that needs a number of open files uses this work area and automatically closes the payments files.

ENTERING CUSTOMER PAYMENTS

The program for entering customer payments is MENU61.PRG. This program is shown in Figure 10–4. A typical data-entry screen from this menu selection is shown in Figure 10–5. When we choose this selection, we want to see the last payment entered. This entry will be the last physical record in the payments file. To position to this record, we use the **reccount( )** function.

```
* MENU6.PRG

select 4
   use PAYMENTS index PAYMENTS
do while .T.
   clear
   do BANNER with "Payments, Credits, and Debits"
   CHOICES = '01'

       @ 8,25        say '1 - Customer Payments'
       if reccount() > 0
           @ row()+1,25 say '2 - Print Payment Summary'
           CHOICES = CHOICES + '2'
       endif
       @ row()+1,25 say '0 - RETURN to the main menu '
       @ row()+1,25 say ' - PICK ONE'

   do CHOICE with 25,CHOICES

   if CHOICE = '0'
      return
   endif

   do MENU6&CHOICE
enddo
```

Figure 10–3: MENU6.PRG.

After the proper record has been located, we select the customer file and set its index to CUSTID. This allows us to find the customer record for the particular payment record. Once the customer record has been located, we display the customer's name, address, and phone number in the upper right-hand corner of the screen with the display program, MENU6S.PRG. Next, reselect the payments file to display payments information with the payments display program, MENU6B.PRG.

When the display is complete, we again select the customer file and set the index to CUSTNAME. This step repositions the customer file, but we already have the screen reminder we want. From now on, we want to access customer records by a customer's name.

The **do** loop forms the body of this program. Once inside the loop, we select the customer file. The procedure FINDCUST locates a customer record by means of the customer name. This procedure was discussed in Chapter Five. FINDCUST prompts the user to enter a customer name, and then searches the customer file for matching names.

When a customer name is found, we display customer information with MENU6S.PRG. In this program system, we elect not to use the normal customer

```
* MENU61.PRG

BANNERMSG = 'Customer Payments'
PAYMENTS  = 0
select PAYMENTS
   if reccount() > 0
      go reccount()
   endif
select CUSTOMER
   set index to CUSTID
   seek PAYMENTS->CUSTID
   do MENU6S
select PAYMENTS
   do MENU6B with 'NOREAD'
select CUSTOMER
   set INDEX to CUSTNAME
do while .T.
   select CUSTOMER
   MNAME = space(30)
   do FINDCUST with "Enter the Customer's name ",MNAME

                        if MNAME = space(30)
                            return
                        endif
   if .not. eof()
      do MENU6S
      clear gets
      select PAYMENTS
      do MENU6B with 'NOREAD'
      do MENU6A
   endif
enddo
```

Figure 10–4: MENU61.PRG.

display MENU1S.PRG because we want room on screen to display (and enter) customer payments. With a little more foresight, we could have designed the data-entry screen, MENU1S.PRG, so that it could also have been used in this application.

After the customer data has been displayed, we again select the payments file and display payment data. The "no-read" parameter informs the display program MENU6B.PRG that this use is for display only. The program MENU6A.PRG provides access to the displayed records via the menu displayed in the lower right-hand corner of the screen. Data is entered—or changed—via this menu. To exit from this customer record, we must select the option 0—Next Customer.

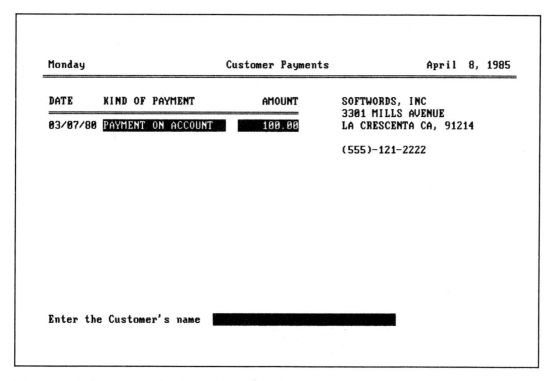

Figure 10–5: Screen display from MENU61.PRG.

DATA-ENTRY SCREEN FOR PAYMENTS

The data-entry screen is produced by three separate programs: MENU6S.PRG, MENU6B. PRG, and MENU6A.PRG. These programs are shown in Figures 10–6, 10–7, and 10–8.

```
* MENU6S.PRG

clear
do BANNER with BANNERMSG
@  5,50 say NAME    picture '@!'
@  6,50 say ADDRESS picture '@!'
@  7,50 say trim(CITY)+' '+STATE+', '+ZIP
@  9,50 say PHONE
```

Figure 10–6: MENU6S.PRG.

This menu selection produces the secondary menu shown in Figure 10–5. It is used to select data entry into the customer payment record displayed on the same screen.

```
* MENU6B.PRG

parameter CONTROL
seek CUSTOMER->CUSTID
X = 10
a 5,2 say "DATE     KIND OF PAYMENT          AMOUNT"
a 6,2 say left(BAR,41)
do while CUSTID = CUSTOMER->CUSTID .and. .not. eof()
    MEMVAR1 = 'MC'+str(X,2)
    MEMVAR2 = 'MA'+str(X,2)
    &MEMVAR1 = COMMENTS
    &MEMVAR2 = AMOUNT
    a row()+1,2  say dtoc(DATE) get &MEMVAR1 picture 'a!'
    a row(),col()+2 get &MEMVAR2 picture "aR( ###,###.##"
    X = X+1
    skip
enddo
PAYMENTS = X-10
if CONTROL = "READ"
   read
   X = 10
   seek CUSTOMER->CUSTID
   do while CUSTID = CUSTOMER->CUSTID .and. .not. eof()
      MEMVAR1 = 'MC'+str(X,2)
      MEMVAR2 = 'MA'+str(X,2)
      if COMMENTS # &MEMVAR1 .or. AMOUNT # &MEMVAR2
          replace COMMENTS with &MEMVAR1, AMOUNT with &MEMVAR2
          if AMOUNT > 0 .and. COMMENTS = 'DEBIT'
              replace AMOUNT with (-1) * AMOUNT
          endif
          if AMOUNT < 0 .and. COMMENTS # 'DEBIT'
              replace AMOUNT with abs(AMOUNT)
          endif
      endif
      X = X+1
      skip
   enddo
endif
```

Figure 10–7: MENU6B.PRG.

We set the function keys **F2**, **F4**, and **F6** to the values shown in the program. The key setup begins with **chr(25)**; this is a **Ctrl-Y** and is used to "clear" the comments field. The semicolon is an "enter" (or **Return**) and automatically takes us out of the comments field. The function key contents are displayed at the bottom of the screen. Function keys are disabled when we exit the program.

```
* MENU6A.PRG

do while .T.
   set function 2 to chr(25)+"PAYMENT ON ACCOUNT;"
   set function 4 to chr(25)+"CREDIT MEMO;"
   set function 6 to chr(25)+"DEBIT MEMO;"
   CHOICES = '01'
   @ 23,2  say "F2 = PAYMENT ON ACCOUNT     F4 = CREDIT MEMO     "+;
              "F6 = DEBIT MEMO"
   @ 14,48 to  19,77 double
   @ 15,50 say '0 - Next Customer      '
   @ 16,50 say '1 - Enter New Payment  '
   if PAYMENTS > 0
       @ 17,50 say '2 - Change Payment Data '
       CHOICES = '012'
   endif
   @ 18,50 say '  - Pick One'
   do CHOICE with 50, CHOICES
   do case
      case CHOICE = '0'
         exit
      case CHOICE = '1'
         append blank
         replace CUSTID with CUSTOMER->CUSTID, DATE with date()
         PAYMENTS = PAYMENTS + 1
         @ 6+PAYMENTS,2  say DATE
         @ row(),col()+1 get COMMENTS picture '@!'
         @ row(),col()+2 get AMOUNT   picture "@R ###,###.##"
         read
         if AMOUNT > 0 .and. COMMENTS = 'DEBIT'
            replace AMOUNT with (-1) * AMOUNT
         endif
         if AMOUNT < 0 .and. COMMENTS # 'DEBIT'
            replace AMOUNT with abs(AMOUNT)
         endif
      case choice = '2'
         do MENU6B with 'READ'
   endcase
enddo
set function 2 to chr(0)
set function 4 to chr(0)
set function 6 to chr(0)
@ 23,2
@ 14,48 clear to 19,77
```

Figure 10–8: MENU6A.PRG.

The small menu at the lower right of the screen is adaptable. The edit selection is enabled (and displayed) only if there is at least one payment displayed for the selected customer.

The decision about what to do when a choice is made is done with the help of **do case**. In this case we want to do only one of three options: exit, add, or edit.

Adding a Payment Record

When adding a record to the payments file (selection 1), we **append** a blank record and automatically store the date and the customer ID code to the appropriate fields. The memory variable PAYMENTS is used to let us know the screen location of the new record. When we first enter the program MENU61.PRG, the variable is created. This step makes PAYMENTS a public variable for all programs called from MENU61.PRG. From that point on, MENU6B.PRG establishes the value. The screen position of the new record is determined by adding 1 to PAYMENTS and then off-setting payments by 6—the screen position of the bar separating the payment data from the column titles. Data entry here is a simple matter of displaying the blank fields at the correct screen location and issuing a **read** command.

Editing a Payment Record

To edit a payment we use the payment display program MENU6B.PRG with the **read** parameter. This program, which is shown in Figure 10-7, displays all payment records for a given customer. As the display is generated, the contents of the fields COM-MENTS and AMOUNT are stored to memory variables. These memory variables are displayed with **get**s. If the parameter passed to the program is "read," the cursor is placed in the first displayed record. The user is free to move the cursor to any displayed comment or amount and make the appropriate changes. One entry check is made. If the entry is for *debit memo*, the program forces the amount to a minus number. The **seek** command at the beginning of the program makes sure that the display begins with the first payment record for the selected customer. The second **seek** repositions the payments file to the first payment record to replace the content of the fields with the corresponding memory variables. The replacement is done only if the memory variable content is different from the field content. **Replace** is a comparatively slow command. As in previous full-screen editing systems of this type (QTYEDIT), the memory variables are created and used by means of macro ex-pansion. To do this, we create a memory variable containing the name of the desired variable. Then we create the variable by using the first variable with an ampersand (&).

PRINT PAYMENT SUMMARY

The print payment summary is produced by menu selection 2. The program called by this menu selection is MENU62.PRG, which is shown in Figure 10-9. A representa-tive printout from this selection is shown in Figure 10-10.

```
* MENU62.PRG

select CUSTOMER
   set index to CUSTID
select PAYMENTS
go top
set relation to CUSTID into CUSTOMER
set heading off
set print on
PAGE = 1
do while .not. eof()
     do linefeed with 4                    && linefeeds
     ? 'Page:'+ltrim(str(PAGE,3)),space(10)+'PAYMENTS RECEIVED AS OF ';
             +CDATE+chr(10)
     do while .not. eof() .and. prow() <= 53
         ?
         ?  CUSTOMER->NAME, CUSTID,chr(10)
         MCUSTID = CUSTID
         list off space(20),DATE, COMMENTS, AMOUNT;
                 while CUSTID = MCUSTID .and. prow() <= 55
     enddo
     eject
enddo
set heading on
set relation to
set print off
```

Figure 10–9: MENU62.PRG.

```
Page:   1                 PAYMENTS RECEIVED AS OF April  8, 1985


SOFTWORDS, INC                     100389

                       03/07/80 PAYMENT ON ACCOUNT        100.00
```
Figure 10–10: Sample printout.

For this selection we want to print out the contents of the payments file in the order of the customer ID code CUSTID. To display the customer names, it is most convenient to link the customer file to the payments file by CUSTID. We must first select the customer file and set its index. Next we reselect the payments file and set the relation into the customer file. At the end of the program, we turn the relation off.

The standard dBASE heading produced for the **list** command is obtrusive in this report. To eliminate these standard headings, we **set heading off**. At the end of this program we set the heading back on.

The outer **do** loop continues until the end of file is reached. The inner loop continues until either the end of file is reached or the page position reaches line 53. Once inside of the inner loop, we issue one blank line, and then display the customer's name and identification code at the left-hand margin. The **list** command is used to display all payments for the customer.

CHAPTER ELEVEN

Accounts Receivable

Even though our business sends out an invoice with every shipment, the actual billing is done once a month—at the first of the month. This chapter discusses the programs that are involved with monthly billing. As usual, each of the billing programs is "called" from a menu program. The menu program shown in Figure 11-1 is MENU7.PRG. This program produces the screen menu shown in Figure 11-2.

```
* MENU7.PRG

do SETUP7
do while .T.
   select CUSTOMER
   set order to 1
   go top
   clear
   do BANNER with 'Customer Billing Menu'
   @  8,25 say '1 - Monthly Activity Summary'
   @  9,25 say '2 - Prepare Customer Statements'
   @ 10,25 say '3 - Prepare Single Customer Statement'
   @ 11,25 say '4 - Prepare Ageing Report'
   @ 12,25 say '0 - Return to the main menu'
   @ 14,25 say '  - Pick one'

   do CHOICE with 25,'01234'
      if CHOICE = '0'
          select 4
              use
          select 5
              use
          select 3
              use INV index ISBN alias INVENTORY
          return
      endif
   DO MENU7&CHOICE
enddo
```

Figure 11–1: MENU7.PRG.

What do we want these programs to do? We want a summary of the month's activities. This summary is produced by menu selection 1. We want to prepare customer statements. Statements are prepared by menu selections 2 and 3. We want an ageing

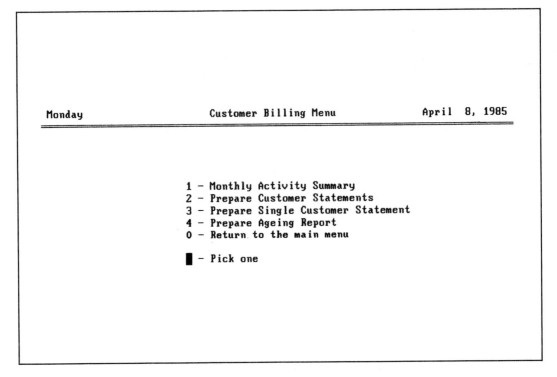

Figure 11-2: MENU7.PRG screen.

report, which shows the recent payment history for each customer. This report is prepared by menu selection 4. We also want the system to initiate the billing process automatically on the first working day of each month. This feature requires that the software monitor when the bills were last issued and then compare that date to the current date. When a month has passed, the billing process needs to be triggered.

During the month, payments are posted to a payments file and invoices to an invoices file. When the billing process is initiated, we transfer these payment and invoice records to files used for billing and clear out the monthly files so that new payments and invoices can be entered. This provides a clean separation of the billing data from the day-to-day logging of payments and invoices.

THE DATABASE PLANS

Four database files are used to prepare customer billings: the CUSTOMER file, an invoices file called INVOICED, a PAYMENTS file called PAID, and the CONTROLS file. Fields to keep track of each customer's payments and charges history have been added to the CUSTOMER file. These fields could make up a separate database. However, because they are to match the customer records one-for-one, it is more efficient to include this data directly in each customer record. The database plan for the revised customer file is shown in Figure 11-3. Asterisks are used to identify those fields that are to be added. Two fields have been added to the CONTROLS file: BILLDATE and LASTBILL. The plan for the revised CONTROLS file is shown in Figure 11-4.

The fields M1CHG through M6CHG contain invoice totals for the past five months. M1CHG contains the most recent data. M1PAY through M6PAY contain payment totals for the past five months. M1PAY contains the most recent payment data. HISTORY is the sum of payments and invoices for all previous months. Each month, the information stored in the M1 fields is shifted by one month and new data is entered into M1PAY and M1CHG. BILLDATE is the date of the last billing. BALANCE is the amount due from the customer as of that date.

All the information needed to prepare an ageing report is now stored directly in the customer record. It is reasonable to display all information regarding a customer each time the customer record is displayed. Even though we haven't done so in this book, the customer menu programs could (and perhaps should) be modified to display the customer's complete financial status each time the customer record is displayed from the customer menu programs. Indeed, it should not be possible to delete a customer record if the customer has outstanding charges or payments in the current month's invoices or payments and transactions files.

The payments file PAID contains the payments that were received during the previous month. This file is indexed on the customer ID code CUSTID. The database plan for PAID is shown in Figure 11-5.

The invoices file INVOICED contains invoices that were posted during the previous month. This file is also indexed on the customer ID code CUSTID. The database plan for INVOICED is shown in Figure 11-6.

AUTOMATIC BILLING

Automatic operations are easy to set up. We want the program to know when it's time for the monthly billing and to remind us to send out the bills. The best way to do this is to put a sensor in the SETUP.PRG setup program. Each day when the menu program is loaded, SETUP can check to see whether it's time for billing.

Bob's Better Books bills on the first working day after the first of the month. The date of the last billing is stored in the field LASTBILL in CONTROLS. Each time the setup program is loaded, we compare the date of the last billing with the current date. If the months are different—it's time to send out bills. Instead of entering the main menu, we go directly to MENU7.PRG—the billing menu. The code to be added to the end of the setup program, SETUP.PRG, is shown below:

```
if month(CONTROLS->BILLDATE) # month(date( ))
   do MENU7
endif
```

You should also add the following after USE CONTROLS:

```
if year(BILLDATE) = 0
  replace BILLDATE with date( )
end if
```

DESCRIPTION	FIELDNAME	FIELDTYPE	WIDTH	DECIMALS
Customer name	NAME	Character	30	
Attention	ATTN	Character	30	
Street address	ADDRESS	Character	25	
City	CITY	Character	20	
State	STATE	Character	2	
Zip code	ZIP	Character	5	
Telephone number	PHONE	Character	14	
Customer since	DATE	Date	8	
Customer ID code	CUSTID	Character	6	
Credit standing	CREDIT	Character	1	
* Current balance	BALANCE	Numeric	8	2
* Date of balance	BILLDATE	Date	8	
* Last posted charges	M1CHG	Numeric	8	2
* 1 month earlier	M2CHG	Numeric	8	2
* 2 months earlier	M3CHG	Numeric	8	2
* 3 months earlier	M4CHG	Numeric	8	2
* 4 months earlier	M5CHG	Numeric	8	2
* 5 months back	M6CHG	Numeric	8	2
* Last posted payments	M1PAY	Numeric	8	2
* 1 month back	M2PAY	Numeric	8	2
* 2 months back	M3PAY	Numeric	8	2
* 3 months back	M4PAY	Numeric	8	2
* 4 months back	M5PAY	Numeric	8	2
* 5 months back	M6PAY	Numeric	8	2
* Base balance	HISTORY	Numeric	8	2

Record Size . . . . . 262 Bytes

File to be indexed on: CUSTID   TO CUSTID

NAME   TO CUSTNAME

Figure 11–3: Revised CUSTOMER database plan.

When we enter the menu program (Figure 11–1), our first action is to execute the SETUP7.PRG program. This program is shown in Figure 11-7. As usual, our first action is to clear the screen and tell the user what's going on. Then we open (and close) the files needed for the menu option. This menu option does not make use of information from the inventory; so the inventory file and its index are closed (saving two open files).

DESCRIPTION	FIELDNAME	FIELDTYPE	WIDTH	DECIMALS
Last Customer Added	CUSTID	Numeric	6	
Last Customer Edited	LASTEDIT	Character	6	
Last Inventory Rec	INVRECORD	Character	13	
Update Step Number	UPDATESTEP	Numeric	1	
Last Purchase Order	PONUMBER	Numeric	6	
Date of P.O.	PODATE	Date	8	
Last Invoice Number	INVOICE	Character	6	
* Date of Last Bill	LASTBILL	Date	8	
* Previous Bill Date	BILLDATE	Date	8	
		Record Size ..... 63 Bytes		

Figure 11–4: Revised CONTROLS database plan.

DESCRIPTION	FIELDNAME	FIELDTYPE	WIDTH	DECIMALS
Customer ID Code	CUSTID	Character	6	
Info about Payment	COMMENTS	Character	20	
Date of Payment	DATE	Date	8	
Amount of Payment	AMOUNT	Numeric	9	2
		Record Size ..... 44 Bytes		
File to be indexed on: CUSTID		to PAID		

Figure 11–5: Database plan for PAID.

DESCRIPTION	FIELDNAME	FIELDTYPE	WIDTH	DECIMALS
Invoice Number	INVOICE	Character	6	
Customer ID Code	CUSTID	Character	6	
Date of Invoice	DATE	Date	8	
Quantity Shipped	QTYDEL	Numeric	3	
Price Charged	PRICE	Numeric	6	2
		Record Size ..... 30 Bytes		
File to be indexed on: CUSTID		TO INVOICED		

Figure 11–6: Database plan for INVOICED.

```
* SETUP7.PRG

clear
? 'Loading Payments and Invoices Files'
select CUSTOMER
   if reccount() = 0
      return to master
   endif
set index to CUSTNAME,CUSTID
select INVENTORY
    use
select 4
   use INVOICED index INVOICED alias CHARGES
   CHARGES = eof()
select 5
   use PAID index PAID alias CREDITS
   CREDITS = eof()
if month(CONTROLS->BILLDATE) # month(date())
    do BANNER with "Monthly Billing Cycle"
    text
        It is time to proceed with the monthly billing operation.

        To over-ride the automatic billing operation answer
        "Y" to the following question
    endtext
    do QUERY with "Interrupt automatic billing (Y/N)?",23,2,ANSWER
    if ANSWER = 'N'
        do MENU7X
    endif
endif
```

Figure 11–7: SETUP7.PRG.

Once the billing files are open, SETUP7.PRG compares the current date to the last billing date. If these are different months, we clear the screen and display the billing messages with the text command. It is possible that we have some other urgent use for the computer; so, a way to override the automatic billing is provided. If we override, the program proceeds to the billing menu. From there, we can return to the main menu by selecting menu option 0.

If we do not override the automatic billing process, the program MENU7X.PRG is activated. This program is shown in Figure 11–8. The data that we need to conduct the billing operation is currently in the monthly transaction files PAYMENTS (MENU6) and INVOICES (MENU5). MENU7X copies the information from these two files into the two monthly billing files, PAID and INVOICED. Once the data has been copied, the two source files are cleared out so that payments and invoices for the coming month can be entered.

To move the monthly invoices from INVOICES to INVOICED, we select CHARGES (the alias for the open file INVOICED) and open the file INVOICES. We copy only the fields of interest (CUSTID, INVOICE, DATE, QTYDEL, and PRICE) to INVOICED. Note that you must use the full pathname for the target file if you are using sub-directories. Then we clear out the INVOICES file with the **zap** command. Finally, we open the INVOICED file and index on the customer ID code CUSTID.

To move the monthly payments from PAYMENTS to PAID, we select the work area CREDITS (the alias for the open file PAID) and close the file with the **use** command. Given that we are copying the entire file PAYMENTS, we can use the **copy file** command. This command is much faster than using the standard dBASE **copy** command. Once again, the full pathname of the target file must be used if you are using sub-directories. When the file has been copied, we use it and clear it out with the **zap** command. Finally, we open the PAID file and index on the customer ID code CUSTID.

Next, we select the CONTROLS file and move the contents of BILLDATE to LASTBILL, and change BILLDATE to the current date. When doing such *ripple* replacements, be careful to perform the replacements in the proper order.

After the invoices and payments have been posted to the work files, it is time to update the CUSTOMER file. This process can be time-consuming if you have any number of customers at all. So for this menu selection we want to keep the user informed about the status of the updating process. We display the total number of customer records on the screen. Then, each time a customer record is processed, we display the record number on the bottom of the screen. The picture of processing status is accurate because the customer records are processed in their physical order.

The records were processed in physical order because it is always faster to process in physical order than in **index**ed order, and in this case there is no value to the **index**ed order.

For each record in the customer file, we select the CREDITS file and **seek** the first payment record for that customer. The **sum** command stores the total value of the customer's payments to the memory variable MPAID. The operation is repeated for the CHARGES file with the total value of the customer's charges stored to the memory variable MOWED. Note that we **set console off** during the **do** loop. The **sum** command affects the screen.

When we've acquired the total charges and total payments, we return to the customer file and perform the **replace** operation. It is important that the replacements be performed in the proper sequence—otherwise you will lose your reference. The three **replace** commands were needed, owing to the 255-character command limit for dBASE.

When the updating process has run its course, we enter the billing menu (Figure 11-2). This menu has four options: a monthly activity summary, print all customer statements, print individual customer statements, and print an ageing report. These printouts can be prepared as often as desired during the month. The data will not (and cannot) be changed until the first working day of the next month.

```
* MENU7X.PRG

clear
do BANNER with 'Billing Update Cycle'
? 'Posting Invoices'
    select CHARGES
    use INVOICES
    copy fields CUSTID,INVOICE,DATE,QTYDEL,PRICE to \BOOK\DATA\INVOICED
    zap
    use INVOICED alias CHARGES
    index on CUSTID to \BOOK\DATA\INVOICED
? 'Posting Payments'
    select CREDITS
    use
    copy file PAYMENTS.DBF to \BOOK\DATA\PAID.DBF
    use PAYMENTS index PAYMENTS
    zap
    use PAID alias CREDITS
    index on CUSTID to \BOOK\DATA\PAID
select CONTROLS
    replace LASTBILL with BILLDATE, BILLDATE with date()
? 'Updating History'
select CUSTOMER
set order to 0
go top
? 'There are',ltrim(str(reccount(),6)),'customer records'
set console off
do while .not. eof()
    @ 23,2 say 'Processing Record'+str(recno(),5)
    select CREDITS
        seek CUSTOMER->CUSTID
        sum AMOUNT while CUSTID = CUSTOMER->CUSTID to MPAID
    select CHARGES
        seek CUSTOMER->CUSTID
        sum PRICE * QTYDEL while CUSTID = CUSTOMER->CUSTID to MOWED
    select CUSTOMER
    replace HISTORY with HISTORY - M6PAY + M6CHG,M6CHG with;
            M5CHG,M5CHG with M4CHG,M4CHG with M3CHG,M3CHG with;
            M2CHG,M2CHG with M1CHG,M1CHG with MOWED
    replace M6PAY with M5PAY,M5PAY with M4PAY,M4PAY with M3PAY,;
            M3PAY with M2PAY,M2PAY with M1PAY,M1PAY with MPAID
    replace BALANCE with HISTORY +M6CHG+M5CHG+M4CHG+M3CHG+M2CHG+M1CHG;
            -M6PAY-M5PAY-M4PAY-M3PAY-M2PAY-M1PAY

    skip
enddo
set console on
```

Figure 11–8: MENU7X.PRG.

MONTHLY ACTIVITY SUMMARY

One of the standard reports that can be provided from the billing menu is the monthly activity summary (menu selection 1). A representative sample of an activity summary is shown in Figure 11–9. The program to produce this report is the MENU71.PRG program, shown in Figure 11–10.

```
Page: 1          Monthly Activity Summary    April  8, 1985

                          Starting  Payments   Current   Current
Customer Name             Balance   Received   Charges   Billing
------------------------------------------------------------------
52ND STREET BOOK SHOP      71,007    70,007                 1,000
A-1 BOOKS                   4,000                            4,000
AARDVARDK ASSOCIATES        3,000                            3,000
ABC BOOK SELLERS            5,000                            5,000
ABC BOOK SELLERS            6,000                            6,000
ACME BOOKS                  7,000                            7,000
ACRIMONY                    9,000                            9,000
ACTION BOOKS               10,000                           10,000
ARTS ARTY BOOKNOOK          2,000                            2,000
ATLANTA BOOKS AND RECORDS   8,000                            8,000
SOFTWORDS, INC             11,000                           11,000
TATE-ASHTON                12,000                           12,000

TOTALS                    148,007    70,007                 78,000
```

Figure 11–9: Sample activity report.

The monthly activity summary is a printing program. After we clear the screen and display the program banner, we display a reminder to the user to *be sure that the printer is on!* The program uses four memory variables: TOTALBAL, TOTALPAY, TOTALCHG, and PAGE. These four variables are initialized to 0 with the single **store** command.

Once inside the loop we print a page heading for each page of the report. The page number is printed on line 6 column 1 by the procedure PAGE. This procedure would have been useful in all previous printed outputs that had page numbers. The procedure is shown in Figure 11–11. The procedure as shown makes use of the fact that the page number is a "public" variable—at least as far as the procedure is concerned. This is a very good example of the use of procedures. We replace several non-essential lines in a program with one line that accomplishes the same result. The program appears simpler since we can concentrate on what it is doing without the distractions of cosmetic items. At the same time, we have a useful subroutine that we can use over and over.

The body of each page is printed by the inner loop. This loop continues until we reach either the end of the file or the bottom of the page. When we reach the end-of-file, we print the bottom line data at the bottom of the last page.

```
* MENU71.PRG


clear
do BANNER with 'Monthly Activity Summary'
? 'Be sure the printer is turned on!'
store 0 to TOTALBAL,TOTALPAY,TOTALCHG,PAGE
set device to print
do while .not. eof()
   do PAGE with 6,1
   @ 6,15 say 'Monthly Activity Summary   '+CDATE
   @ 8,29 say 'Starting  Payments'
   @ 8,50 say 'Current     Current'
   @  9,1 say 'Customer Name            Balance  Received'
   @ 9,50 say 'Charges      Billing'
   @ 10,1 say replicate ("-",68)
   do while prow() < 55 .and. .not. eof()
      @ prow()+1,1  say NAME
      @ prow(),30  say BALANCE-M1CHG+M1PAY picture "@Z( ###,###"
      @ prow(),40  say M1PAY picture "@Z( ###,###"
      @ prow(),50  say M1CHG picture "@Z( ###,###"
      @ prow(),60   say BALANCE picture "@Z( #,###,###"
      TOTALBAL = TOTALBAL + BALANCE - M1CHG + M1PAY
      TOTALPAY = TOTALPAY + M1PAY
      TOTALCHG = TOTALCHG + M1CHG
      skip
   enddo
   if eof()
      @ prow()+2,1  say 'TOTALS'
      @ prow(),30 say TOTALBAL picture "@Z( ###,###"
      @ prow(),40 say TOTALPAY picture "@Z( ###,###"
      @ prow(),50 say TOTALCHG picture "@Z( ###,###"
      @ prow(),59 say TOTALBAL-TOTALPAY+TOTALCHG picture "@Z( ##,###,###"
   endif
   eject
enddo
set device to screen
```

Figure 11–10: MENU71.PRG.


```
procedure PAGE
parameter ROW,COL
PAGE = PAGE + 1
@ ROW,COL say 'Page:  ' + ltrim(str(PAGE,3))
return
```

Figure 11–11: PAGE procedure.

The information printed for each customer includes the last month's balance. This is obtained by subtracting this month's charges and adding this month's payments to the current balance. On each pass through this loop, we update the memory variables TOTALBAL, TOTALPAY, and TOTALCHG. Remember that TOTALBAL is a value derived from the current BALANCE, PAYMENTS, and CREDITS.

The values are displayed with the help of two picture functions and a picture template. A picture function applies to the entire item being displayed. A picture template allows you to operate on each character (or digit) individually. The # function restricts each digit in the display to a numeric symbol. The size of the display is controlled by the number of #s. The comma will insert a comma into the display only if the number has non-zero digits to the left of the comma position. The **Z(** after the @ sign is a **picture** function. The @ sign indicates the letters and symbols following are picture functions. A blank space indicates that the following characters are picture templates. The **Z** function prevents any display if the number is exactly 0. The **(** symbol places parentheses around the number if it is negative.

PRINTING CUSTOMER STATEMENTS

This is the principal program for printing monthly customer statements. The actual printing is done by MENU7P.PRG, which is also used by the next menu selection. This program, MENU72.PRG, is shown in Figure 11–12. MENU72.PRG prints an invoice for every customer.

```
* MENU72.PRG

BANNERMSG = "Printing Customer Statements"
    RECORDS  = 0
    do  while .not. eof()
        do MENU1S
        RECORDS = RECORDS + 1
        @ 23,2
        @ 23,2 say 'Printing '+ltrim(str(RECORDS,5))+;
                    ' of '+ltrim(str(reccount(),6))
        do MENU7P
        select CUSTOMER
        skip
    enddo
```

Figure 11–12: MENU72.PRG.

The program is simple and straightforward. We enter this program already positioned to the first record in the CUSTOMER file. As we print the statements, we keep the user entertained (and informed) by displaying customer information with the customer display program MENU1S.PRG and overlay that display with a statement on how many records have been printed of the total.

We entered the program using the CUSTNAME index so that statements are printed in alphabetical order. Each statement is printed with the use of the MENU7P.PRG printing program. After each statement has been printed, we reselect the customer file and advance to the next record.

The Print Program

The statements are printed by MENU7P.PRG, which prints a single statement—for the selected customer record. The program is shown in Figure 11–13. A typical customer statement prepared by this program is shown as Figure 11–14.

The program uses information from each of the three files CUSTOMER, CREDITS, and CHARGES, to produce a customer statement. Each customer's statement can have several pages (unlikely, but possible). The print routine uses both direct-address printing and relative printing using the double question mark (**??**). This requires that we use both **set print on** and **set device to print**. The console is **set off** because of the use of the **sum** command and the **??**. This addition allows us to control the screen display.

Customer payments are itemized on the statement by selecting the CREDITS file and seeking the customer's ID code. The **do** loop prints payment records. Customer charges are printed by selecting the CHARGES file and positioning to the first charge record for the customer ID code. Note that, before entering the **do** loop, we store a printer row value to the memory variable ROW. While printing from the loop, we used the variable ROW to control the printhead position.

The Header Program

The header for the customer statement is printed with the help of MENU7PH.PRG. This program is shown in Figure 11–15.

PRINTING INDIVIDUAL STATEMENTS

This menu selection (3) allows us to select a customer by name and get a printed copy of the customer's latest statement. It's a good idea to provide such an option. If you don't, you will be unhappy when you need one copy of someone's statement and you have to print 500 customer statements to get the one that you need. The customer is selected and the statement is printed by means of the MENU73.PRG program (Figure 11–16), which calls the procedure FINDCUST.

```
* MENU7P.PRG

set console off
set device to print
set print on
store 0 to PAGE
do MENU7PH
select CREDITS
   @ prow()+2,1 say 'Customer Payments and Credits since '
   ?? CONTROLS->LASTBILL
   seek CUSTOMER->CUSTID
   do while CUSTID = CUSTOMER->CUSTID
        @ prow()+2,10    say AMOUNT picture "@Z( ###,###.##"
        ?? ' ',DATE, COMMENTS
        skip
   enddo
   @ prow()+2,10    say CUSTOMER->M1PAY picture "@Z( ###,###.##"
   ?? "   *** Total Payments ***"
select CHARGES
   @ prow()+2,1 say 'Customer Charges since '+dtoc(CONTROLS->LASTBILL)
   seek CUSTOMER->CUSTID
   do while CUSTID = CUSTOMER->CUSTID
        @ prow()+2,14 say 'Amount      Invoice      Dated'
        ROW = prow()+2
        do while CUSTID = CUSTOMER -> CUSTID .and. prow() < 55
           MINVOICE = INVOICE
           sum PRICE * QTYDEL while INVOICE = MINVOICE to AMOUNT
           @ ROW,10    say AMOUNT picture "@Z( ###,###.##"
           ?? '   ',MINVOICE,'   ',DATE
           ROW = ROW + 1
        enddo
        if CUSTID = CUSTOMER->CUSTID .and. prow() >= 55
           eject
           do MENU7PH
        endif
   enddo
        OLDBALANCE = CUSTOMER->BALANCE - CUSTOMER->M1CHG + CUSTOMER->M1PAY
        @ prow()+2,10    say CUSTOMER->M1CHG picture "@Z( ###,###.##"
        ?? "  *** Total Charges ***"
        @ prow()+1,10    say CUSTOMER->M1PAY picture "@Z( ###,###.##"
        ?? "  *** Total Credits ***"
        @ prow()+1,10    say OLDBALANCE picture "@Z( ###,###.##"
        ?? "  Balance as of",CONTROLS->LASTBILL
        @ prow()+2,10    say  CUSTOMER->BALANCE picture '@Z( ###,###.##'
        ?? "  Amount Now Due"
        eject
set console on
set device to screen
set print off
```

Figure 11–13: MENU7P.PRG.

```
TO:        52ND STREET BOOK SHOP              April 26, 1985
           126 E. 18TH ST.                        Page: 1
           NEW YORK, NY  10003
           ATTN: SHIPPING

FROM:      BOB'S BETTER BOOKS
           3800 Honolulu Avenue
           La Crescenta, California    91214      (213)204-5570

                    TERMS: NET 10 DAYS

Customer Payments and Credits since 03/02/85

        1,887.17   03/09/85 PAYMENT RECEIVED
        1,887.17   03/12/85 PAYMENT RECEIVED
        3,774.34   *** Total Payments ***

Customer Charges since 03/02/85

          Amount      Invoice      Dated
        1,539.50      100034      01/22/85
        1,539.50   *** Total Charges ***
        3,774.34   *** Total Credits ***
        6,734.84   Balance as of 03/02/85
        4,500.00   Amount Now Due
```

Figure 11–14: A typical customer statement.

```
* MENU7PH.PRG


@ 3,(65-len(CDATE)) say CDATE
@ 3,1  say 'TO: '
@ 3,10 say CUSTOMER->NAME
@ 4,10 say CUSTOMER->ADDRESS
do PAGE with 4,59
@ 5,10 say trim(CUSTOMER->CITY)+', '+CUSTOMER->STATE+'  '+CUSTOMER->ZIP
if CUSTOMER->ATTN # space(30)
    @ 6,10 say 'ATTN: '+CUSTOMER->ATTN
endif
@ 8,1  say 'FROM:'
@ 8,10 say "BOB'S BETTER BOOKS"
@ 9,10 say '3800 Honolulu Avenue'
@ 10,10 say 'La Crescenta, California   91214'
@ 10,52 say '(213)204-5570'
@ 12,25 say 'TERMS: NET 10 DAYS'
```

Figure 11–15: MENU7PH.PRG.

THE AGEING REPORT

The ageing report (menu selection 4) is used to give you some feeling for how each customer pays bills. Unfortunately, not everyone is as prompt as you and me about

```
* MENU73.PRG

BANNERMSG = "Print Customer Statements"
    do while .T.
        clear
        do BANNER with BANNERMSG
        MNAME = space(30)
        do FINDCUST with "Customer Name",MNAME
                            if MNAME = space(30)
                                exit
                            endif
        do MENU1S
        do MENU7P
        select CUSTOMER
    enddo
```

Figure 11–16: MENU73.PRG.

paying. One tool for gaining visibility into a customer's financial habits is the program for menu selection 4, MENU74.PRG. A representative report from this program is shown in Figure 11–17. The program itself is shown as Figure 11–18.

```
Page: 1                  Monthly Ageing Report for April 1985

                            February       March       April
52ND STREET BOOK SHOP      19800.00      6545.22     3774.34   Payments
                            6545.22      3774.34     1881.65   Charges
A-1 BOOKS                   1200.37      2754.78      177.35   Payments
                            2754.78       177.35     1364.00   Charges
AARDVARDK ASSOCIATES        8967.55      3994.27     6453.71   Payments
                            3994.27      6453.71    19910.97   Charges
ABC BOOK SELLERS             787.33      1833.67      673.00   Payments
                            1833.67       673.00     7867.78   Charges
ABC BOOK SELLERS            2265.62      1871.98     1273.47   Payments
                            1871.98      1273.47     1542.88   Charges
ACME BOOKS                 17551.23     21854.34    19765.65   Payments
                           21854.34     19765.65    22878.31   Charges
ACRIMONY                     844.37       927.56      841.44   Payments
                             927.56       841.44      912.00   Charges
ACTION BOOKS                   0.00         0.00        0.00   Payments
                               0.00         0.00     8450.00   Charges
ARTS ARTY BOOKNOOK          7422.00       884.74     1663.99   Payments
                             884.74      1663.99     6521.16   Charges
ATLANTA BOOKS AND RECORDS     77.65       844.19      323.67   Payments
                             844.19       323.67      123.45   Charges
SOFTWORDS, INC               234.56       823.99      645.67   Payments
                             823.99       645.67      712.22   Charges
TATE-ASHTON                 1922.08      8745.66     1250.55   Payments
                            8745.66      1250.55     1100.00   Charges
```

Figure 11–17: Sample printout.

This program is relatively simple. Only one file, the main customer file, is used. The interesting feature of the program is the printed headings for the months covered by the report. These headings will change each month. The headings themselves are taken directly from the data.

```
* MENU74.PRG

clear
do BANNER with "Ageing Report"
set device to print
store CONTROLS->BILLDATE to DATE1,DATE2
PAGE = 0
do while month(DATE2) = month(DATE1)
    DATE2 = DATE2 - 28
enddo
DATE3 = DATE2
do while month(DATE3) = month(DATE2)
    DATE3 = DATE3 - 28
enddo
MONTH1  = cmonth(DATE1)
MONTH2  = cmonth(DATE2)
MONTH3  = cmonth(DATE3)
HEADING = space(10-len(MONTH3))+MONTH3+space(10-len(MONTH2))+;
          MONTH2+space(10-len(MONTH1))+MONTH1
do while .not. eof()
    do PAGE with 6,1
    @ 6,pcol()+5 say 'Monthly Ageing Report for '+cmonth(DATE1);
                 +str(year(DATE1),5)
    @ 8,29 say HEADING
    do while prow() < 55 .and. .not. eof()
        @ prow()+1,1  say NAME
        @ prow(),31   say M3PAY
        @ prow(),41   say M2PAY
        @ prow(),51   say M1PAY
        @ prow(),61   say 'Payments'
        @ prow()+1,31 say M3CHG
        @ prow(),41   say M2CHG
        @ prow(),51   say M1CHG
        @ prow(),61   say 'Charges'
        skip
    enddo
    eject
enddo
set device to screen
```

Figure 11–18: MENU74.PRG.

The current billing period provides the basis for extracting the heading information. The **do** loop subtracts 28 days from the date on each pass. (This is the size of the smallest month.) Twenty-eight is the largest number that we can use for subtracting dates. We want to use the largest possible number for program speed.

Once the three calendar months have been extracted and stored to the variables MONTH1, MONTH2, and MONTH3, we assemble the HEADING. Each piece of the heading is assembled by concatenating blank spaces from the **space( )** function with the variable containing the name of the month. By operating in this fashion, we can right-justify the titles. We obtained the proper number of leading blanks by subtracting the number of characters in the month name from 10. The remainder is the number of blanks needed.

CHAPTER TWELVE
Utility Programs

Every program system should have a set of utility programs to perform routine maintenance operations—such as backing up files and resetting the index files. There is always some chance that the disk will fail or lightning will strike the power pole in the neighborhood. Utility programs should be available to provide at least some level of protection for the database files.

It would be nice if the hardware and software available for backing up data files were always adequate for the task. Even the manuals don't always provide clear guidance—especially for the beginner. If the datafiles are too large to fit onto a floppy disk, you should carefully consider a tape backup system. These are valuable for more than the obvious reasons. If backup is a tedious task for the user, it will not be done frequently enough to be useful. If there are a number of large files, the backup procedure onto floppies will be a tedious, time-consuming nuisance. Rule number 1: If the business has large files, buy a tape backup.

If you have only a few large files, the backup procedure onto floppies may be manageable. It is much more manageable if you can use the DOS commands BACKUP and RESTORE. These commands are preferable to the equivalent dBASE routines in this chapter since the DOS commands are substantially faster. If your computer has at least 320K of main memory, you can "call" the DOS commands directly from the dBASE menu. If your business has files that are larger than 360K, you will be time and money ahead to purchase at least an expansion card and additional memory. If you have the 320K of memory, modify the backup and restore routines to resemble menu selection 4. A little money spent on hardware can make your software faster and simpler.

My own experience with backing up data is that today's hardware is so good that one slowly begins making backup copies less and less frequently. When calamity strikes, the backup copy is so out of date as to be virtually useless. Backing up files is vital if a computer system is to be used for direct support of a business. Unless the backup method is quick and painless, it will not be used.

The programs that follow should be studied for their use of dBASE techniques and features. I recommend that anyone who is attempting to use a computer for the daily operation of a business (or department) purchase the necessary hardware to make the process of backing up data quick and painless. This hardware includes a backup tape unit and additional memory to bring the total main memory to at least 320K. If you have such a configuration, you should use the backup and restoration programs supplied with the tape unit. You can make the backup operation automatic by including the statement **run TBACKUP** (assuming the program name is

TBACKUP.COM) just before the **quit** command in the main menu program.

DATABASE PLANS

The utilities system uses two database files: FILES.DBF and UTILITY.DBF. The former is to be loaded by the developer. These files make the software a little simpler and easier to understand. The database plans for the two files are shown in Figure 12–1. The content of the FILES database file is shown in Figure 12–2. This data consists of the principal files used in the complete menu system.

Database Plan for: FILES.DBF			
DESCRIPTION	**FIELDNAME**	**FIELDTYPE**	**WIDTH**
File Name	FILE	Character	40
Display Message	MESSAGE	Character	20
Record Size	RECSIZE	Numeric	4
	Data size . . . . . 65 Bytes		
Database Plan for: UTILITY.DBF			
DESCRIPTION	**FIELDNAME**	**FIELDTYPE**	**WIDTH**
Data Area	DATA	Character	80
	Data size . . . . . 81 Bytes		

Figure 12–1: Database plans for utility programs.

FILE	MESSAGE	RECSIZE
customer index custid, custname	Customer	262
controls	Controls	63
inv index isbn	Inventory	144
publish index pubcode	Supplier	133
onorder index isbn-o	On Orders	47
sales	Master Sales	30
salesdet	Sales Detail	29
openord	Open Orders	7
invoices	Invoices	60
backord	Back Orders	60
payments index payments	Payments	44
paid index paid	Credits	44
invoiced index invoiced	Charges	30

Figure 12–2: Content of FILES database file.

The Utilities Menu

This menu, shown as Figure 12–3, is used to back up, restore, and reset the principal data files used in the bookseller's programs. In addition, there is a program to format floppy disks using the DOS FORMAT command. The program to produce this menu, MENU8.PRG, is shown in Figure 12–4.

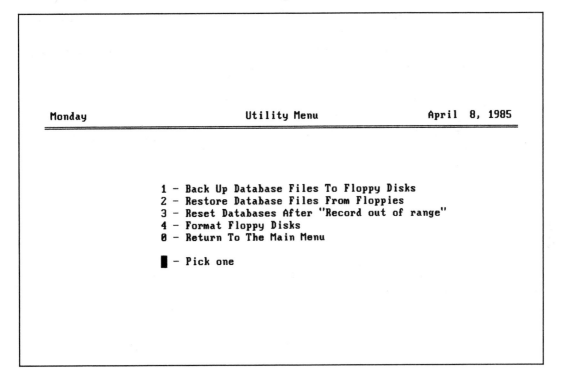

Figure 12–3: Utilities menu.

The setup required by this menu system is to close all open database files and their associated index files, accomplished by the **close databases** command. Upon exiting from this menu system, we reinitialize the system with the SETUP program from Chapter Four.

BACKING UP DATABASE FILES

The disk backup program, MENU81.PRG, is shown in Figure 12–5. This program, to back up the database files used in the program system, must deal with the situation where a database file is larger than the space available on a floppy disk. This means that the file must appear to span floppy disks. In this case, the standard DOS COPY command or its dBASE equivalent **copy file** cannot be used. If the computer has 320K or more of main memory, the DOS command BACKUP can be used instead. BACKUP is significantly faster and the program is simpler. Nevertheless, there is much to be learned about dBASE programming commands from this program.

```
* MENU8.PRG

do while .T.
   close databases
   clear
   do BANNER with 'Utility Menu'
   @  8,20 say '1 - Back Up Database Files To Floppy Disks'
   @  9,20 say '2 - Restore Database Files From Floppies'
   @ 10,20 say '3 - Reset Databases After "Record out of range"'
   @ 11,20 say '4 - Format Floppy Disks'
   @ 12,20 say '0 - Return To The Main Menu'
   @ 14,20 say '  - Pick one'

   do CHOICE with 20,'01234'

      if CHOICE = '0'
          do SETUP
          return
      endif

   do MENU8&CHOICE
enddo
```

Figure 12–4: MENU8.PRG.

Upon entering the program, our first step is to call a message program. This program, MENU81A.PRG, is shown in Figure 12–6. This sub-program displays a message about what the program does and provides the user a chance to abort. The message is displayed with the **text** and **endtext** commands.

If the user doesn't abort the program, the controlling memory variables DISK and SPACEREM are initialized and the files UTILITY and FILES are opened. Then we call the procedure NEXTFILE, which is shown in Figure 12-7. This procedure extracts the name of the next database file to be backed up from the file directory FILES. The substring function is used to pull the filename from the content field FILE. This filename is then opened in work area 3.

The **do** loop continues until all the files on the main disk are backed up. When they are, the end-of-file for FILES is reached. Once inside of the loop, we evaluate the memory variable SPACEREM. This variable keeps track of the amount of space remaining on the backup floppy disk. The program assumes that the backup floppy disk is in the A drive and that we are backing up from the hard disk drive C. When the space remaining on the floppy disk is less than the size of the database header plus the size of one record, we call the procedure GETDISK.

H__SIZE

This procedure is called from **NEXTFILE** to determine the size of the database file

```
* MENU81.PRG

do MENU81A
                  if ANSWER = 'Y'
                        return
                  endif
DISK    = 10
SPACEREM = 0
MFILE   = space(6)
H_SIZE  = 0
select 1
    use UTILITY
select 2
    use FILES
    do NEXTFILE
do while .not. eof()
                        if SPACEREM < H_SIZE + recsize()
                              do GETDISK
                              @ 4,0 clear
                        endif
    select &MFILE
    COPYRECS = int((SPACEREM-H_SIZE)/recsize())
    STARTREC = recno()
    copy next COPYRECS to A:&MFILE
    select FILELIST
        append blank
        if STARTREC = 1
           replace FILE with trim(MFILE)+'.001', MESSAGE with FILES->MESSAGE
        else
           replace FILE with trim(MFILE)+'.002', MESSAGE with FILES->MESSAGE
        endif
        ? 'Now backing up',MESSAGE
    NEWFILE = trim(FILE)
    rename A:&MFILE..DBF to A:&NEWFILE
    select &MFILE
    if .not. eof()
        SPACEREM = SPACEREM - H_SIZE - (COPYRECS * recsize())
        skip
    else
        SPACEREM = SPACEREM - H_SIZE - ((recno()-STARTREC) * recsize())
    endif
    if eof()              && finished copying this file
        select FILES
        skip
        do NEXTFILE
    endif
enddo
save all like DISK to BOOK\DATA\DISKS
```

Figure 12–5: MENU81.PRG.

```
* MENU81A.PRG

clear
do BANNER with "Backing Up Database Files"
text
        This program copies the database files to floppy disks.

        The floppies can either be blank or can contain earlier
        backups of the file to be copied.

endtext
do QUERY with 'Do you want to abort the backup operation',23,2,ANSWER
```

Figure 12–6: MENU81A.PRG.

```
procedure NEXTFILE
        if .not. eof()
            MFILE = substr(FILE,1,at(space(1),FILE))
            select 3
            use &MFILE
            do H_SIZE with H_SIZE
            select FILES
        endif
return
```

Figure 12–7: NEXTFILE.

header, which is approximately 34 bytes plus an additional 32 bytes for each field. We use the **field( )** function in a loop to determine the number of fields in a file. This function returns the name of the field which corresponds to a number passed in the function argument. For example, **field(3)** returns the name of field 3. If the argument is larger than the number of fields, the function returns a **null** (nothing). The **do** loop in the procedure searches for the last valid field number, which is used to calculate the header size (see Figure 12–8).

```
procedure H_SIZE                       && calculate header size
   parameter H_SIZE
   F_COUNT = 1
   do while F_COUNT <= 127
      if len(trim(field(F_COUNT+1))) = 0
         exit
      endif
      F_COUNT = F_COUNT+1
   enddo
   H_SIZE = 34 + 32 * F_COUNT
return
```

Figure 12–8: H__SIZE procedure.

GETDISK

This procedure, shown in Figure 12–9, makes sure that there is adequate space on the floppy disk selected for use as a backup. When we enter the program, we increment the disk counter DISK. Then we enter the loop. If this disk has been used for an earlier backup operation, it will contain the file DISKID.MEM. This file "labels" the disk in the backup sequence. It contains a memory variable, DISKID, which contains a number that is 11 or greater. We test for the existence of this file with the **file( )** function. If it is on the disk, we open the file and bring its memory variables into memory with the command **restore from A:DISKID additive**. The modifier **additive** prevents dBASE from destroying all existing memory variables in the process of reading in the variable from the .MEM file.

```
procedure GETDISK
   DISK = DISK + 1
   private MFILE
   do while .T.
      if file('A:DISKID.MEM')
           restore from A:DISKID additive
           if DISK # DISKID
               do ERRORMSG with 'Wrong Disk ID - Please Insert '+str(DISK,2),23,2
               loop
           endif
           a 23,2
           select 4
           use A:FILELIST          && catalog of backup files on A
           do while .not. eof()    && clear backup files from drive A
              MFILE = trim(FILE)
              erase A:&MFILE
              skip
           enddo
      endif
      do SPACEREM with 'A','C',SPACEREM
      a 23,2
      if SPACEREM < 300000    && new disk should be nearly empty
         do ERRORMSG with 'Insufficient Disk Space - Try another disk' ,23,2
      else
         DISKID = DISK
         save all like DISKID to A:DISKID
         select FILES
         copy structure to A:FILELIST
         select 4
         use A:FILELIST
         exit
      endif
   enddo
return
```

Figure 12–9: GETDISK procedure.

If the DISKID does not match the current value of DISK, we want the user to insert the proper disk in the sequence. Once the proper sequence disk has been inserted, we open the backup file directory on the floppy. This directory, named A:FILELIST, has the same structure as FILES and contains the filenames of the files that are backed up on the disk. The next step is to step through this file—one record at a time—and delete the files from the disk. This step is necessary because the dBASE **erase** command doesn't handle wildcard filenames.

Next we need to verify the space remaining on the disk. This is accomplished by the procedure SPACEREM, which is shown in Figure 12-10. We've arbitrarily decided that if the disk has less than 300,000 free bytes, we want another disk.

The last step is to initialize the disk as a backup disk. To do this, we write the disk label A:DISKID.MEM and create a fresh directory A:FILELIST. These actions are taken even if they already exist to make sure that they exist and that the directory FILELIST is empty.

SPACEREM

This is a simple procedure used to determine the space remaining on the target drive (the floppy disk in drive A). The drive identifiers for the target drive, the source drive (current drive), and a variable in which to store the number of bytes remaining on the target drive are all passed to the procedure (see Figure 12-10).

The function **diskspace( )** provides us with the amount of free disk space on the default drive. The procedure temporarily changes the default drive setting to be the target drive, acquires the amount of free space, and then switches us back to the original (source) drive. Perhaps the next release of dBASE will allow us to pass the desired disk drive as an argument to the **diskspace( )** function.

```
procedure SPACEREM
    parameter TARGET,SOURCE,SPACEREM
    set default to TARGET
    SPACEREM = diskspace()
    set default to SOURCE
return
```

Figure 12-10: SPACEREM procedure.

At this point we have a valid floppy disk installed in the A drive. We're ready to begin backing up the program database files. We select the file to be backed up. This filename is stored in the variable MFILE. Now we want to know how many records are to be copied. The record size is stored in the current record in FILES. To determine the number of records to be copied, we subtract H__SIZE from SPACEREM and divide the remainder by the record size. Next we store the record number to the variable STARTREC. Now we copy the records to a file with the same name on the A drive.

Our next step is to add this file to the backup directory A:FILELIST. We use the file identifiers 001 and 002 to identify the file as being the first part of a database file or a later part. The backup file still has the .DBF file identifier. We change this to match the filename stored in the backup directory with the rename command. Note the two periods in the filename being renamed. Since we are using a macro inside of a larger "word," we need a way to identify the end of the macro. This is done with a period. The second period in the name is the beginning of the file identifier.

Next, we again **select** the file being copied and calculate the space remaining on the disk. This calculation is done based on the actual number of records copied. If we have not reached the end of the file being copied, we issue a **skip** command to advance to the next record to be copied. If we are still not at the end of file we loop back to the beginning of the **do** loop.

If the file has been completely copied, we select FILES, advance a record, and get the next file to be backed up. When finished with the process, we exit from the loop and save the variable DISK to the file DISK. If you are not using subdirectories for your data and programs, omit the subdirectory name \DISKS\ from the command.

RESTORING DATABASE FILES

Menu selection 2 is one we hope you will never need to use. If you need to use it, it means something horrible has happened to the files stored on your hard disk. The program to restore backup files from the floppy disk is MENU82.PRG, which is shown in Figure 12–11.

It is important that the backup disks be used in the proper sequence and that all backup disks be used. When the backups were made, the total number of backup disks was stored as a memory variable DISK in the memory file DISKS. Our first step is to restore the variable from the memory file. Next we set up the control variable DISK and set the initial value to 10.

Once inside the loop, we call the subroutine MENU82A.PRG, shown in Figure 12–12, which makes sure that the backup disks are used in proper sequence and also provides a way for the user to escape from the program if it becomes necessary. The user is prompted to enter a specific backup disk. The disk label (the file DISKID.MEM) is opened and the content of the stored variable DISKID is compared with the control variable DISK. Only when these two variables, DISK and DISKID, match can we proceed to the next step.

When we have the correct backup disk, we open its directory FILELIST. FILELIST contains the names of the backup files. The standard (.DBF) file identifier has been changed to either .001 or .002, depending on whether the file contains the beginning records of a database file or is a continuation. The inner loop makes sure that all records in this particular disk directory are processed before we ask for the next backup disk.

```
*MENU82.PRG

clear
do BANNER with 'Restoring Database Files'
restore from DISKS additive
DISKS = DISK
DISK = 10
Do while DISK < DISKS
     do MENU82A
     select 1
     use A:FILELIST
     a 4,0 clear
     do while .not. eof()
          MFILE  = trim(FILE)
          NEWNAME = substr(FILE,1,at('.',FILE)) + 'DBF'
          ? 'Restoring',MESSAGE
          if substr(FILE,at('.',FILE),4) # '.001'
             select 2
             use &NEWNAME
             append from A:&MFILE
          else
             copy file A:&MFILE to BOOK\DATA\&NEWNAME
          endif
          select FILELIST
          skip
     enddo
enddo
do MENU83
```

Figure 12–11: MENU82.PRG.

Each record in FILELIST contains the name of the backup file as it exists on the backup disk. This filename is stored to the variable MFILE. Its target filename is stored to

NEWNAME by using the **substring** function to search for the period that begins the file identifier and substituting .DBF for the .001 or .002 file identifier. To let the user know that something is going on, we display the content of the MESSAGE field.

If the file identifier for the backup file is .001, we use the **copy file** command to move the file from the backup disk to the data disk. In the example we have assumed that the file is to be copied to a subdirectory. If subdirectories are not used, omit the \BOOK\DATA\ from the target name. Note that we are renaming the file as it is copied.

If the file identifier for the backup file is .002, part of the backup file already exists on the data disk. A copy command would overwrite this part of the file. To avoid this eventuality, we select work area 2 and open the data file. The backup records are added to the file with the **append from** command.

```
* MENU82A.PRG

DISK = DISK + 1
ə row()+1,0 clear
do while .T.
     ə 20,0 say 'Please insert disk number '+str(DISK,2)
     ə 21,0 say 'Press the space bar when the disk has been inserted'
     wait 'or press the "A" key to abort' to ABORT
     ə 20,0 clear
     if ABORT $ 'aA'
          do SETUP
          return to master
     endif
     if .not. file('A:DISKID.MEM')
          do ERRORMSG with 'This is not a Backup Disk',23,2
          loop
     endif
     restore from A:DISKID additive
     if DISKID # DISK
          do ERRORMSG with 'Incorrect Backup Disk',23,2
          loop
     endif
     exit
enddo
```

Figure 12-12: MENU82A.PRG.

When this operation has run its course and all the backup files have been restored, we must run the next program, MENU83.PRG, to reset all of the system index files. Incidentally, you should notice that the index files (and program files) were not backed up. The index files can be reconstructed from the datafiles and the program files need only be backed up once.

RESET DATABASE FILES

The program to reset database files is MENU83.PRG, shown in Figure 12-13. The purpose of the program is to reset the dBASE record header counter and to reindex the associated index files for all open files. Accidental loss of power because of thoughtless acts by the power company or your own tripping over the power cord can result in damaged data or index files. When this occurs, you need to restore these files to a working condition—even if it means the loss of some data.

The most common symptom of a damaged file is the error message "Record out of range." To restore files to a working condition, use the **pack** command. This command cleans up the data file and resets the dBASE record counter. It also initiates an automatic reindexing of all open index files.

```
* MENU83.PRG

clear
do BANNER with 'Resetting Database Files'
@ 4,24 say 'Resetting            Records'
select 2
use FILES
do while .not. eof()
     @ recno()+4,24 say MESSAGE
     FILENAME = FILE
     select 1
     use &FILENAME
     ?? reccount()
     @ 18,0
     set talk on
     pack
     set talk off
     select FILES
     @ recno()+5,0 clear
     skip
enddo
```

Figure 12–13: MENU83.PRG.

For this menu selection, we open our catalogue of system datafiles and, one by one, open the files and their associated indexes and **pack** them. Because this process is time-consuming, we entertain the user by displaying the total number of records in the file. With **set talk on**, the current status of the operation is apparent. A representative screen display from this program is shown in Figure 12–14.

This recovery program allows you to use a damaged database file at the cost of losing some data. *dBASE Programmer's Utilities* from Ashton-Tate offers a program, dREPAIR, which will repair most damaged database files without loss of data. More information on repair and recovery of database files can be found in *Salvaging Damaged Database Files* by Paul Heiser.

FORMAT FLOPPY DISKS

For many operations it is convenient to have formatted floppy disks. If your computer has at least 320K of RAM you can use the **run** or **!** command. This is often referred to as the "bang" command. **Run** allows you to run external programs such as a word processor or any of the DOS command programs. If you have the capability to do so, change the programs MENU81 and MENU82 to take advantage of this command.

```
Monday                    Resetting Database Files        April  8, 1985
                     ==================================================
                          Resetting            Records
                          Customer                12
                          Controls                 1
                          Inventory               12
                          Supplier                 8
                          On Orders               16
                          Master Sales             5
                          Sales Detail            15
                          Open Orders              4
                          Invoices                11
                          Back Orders              2
                          Payments                 1
                          Credits                 18
                          Charges                  5
```

Figure 12–14: Sample screen display from MENU83.PRG.

The MENU84.PRG program demonstrates the **run** command. This program, shown in Figure 12–15, arbitrarily assumes that the system files are on the B drive. As you can see, the program is almost entirely descriptive text and warnings. If your computer has sufficient memory you can (and should) use dBASE as an operating shell. It is far easier to program than the DOS shell and you can make much more interesting (and responsive) menu systems.

```
* MENU84.PRG

clear
do BANNER with "Format Floppy Disks"
if .not. file('B:FORMAT.COM')
     ? 'Formatting Program FORMAT.COM is not on the system directory'
     wait
     return
endif
TEXT

        This program formats blank floppy disks so that they can
        be used to backup database files.

        Any existing data on the floppy disk will be destroyed by
        the formatting process.

        Press either....<Return> to continue
                        "A"       to abort
endtext
wait ' ' to ANSWER
if upper(ANSWER) # 'A'
     a 11,0 clear
     run FORMAT A:
endif
```

Figure 12–15: MENU84.PRG.

SECTION THREE

Special Topics

CHAPTER THIRTEEN
Data-Entry Techniques

Data entry is the most time-consuming aspect of working with a database, as it is primarily a manual process. Fortunately, dBASE III PLUS provides a variety of tools to assist the user with data entry. The five basic dBASE commands for keyboard data entry are:

append
browse
change
edit
insert

Append and **insert** create new data records and provide the means for entering data into those records. **Browse** can create new data records as well as editing the contents of existing records. **Change** and **edit** provide a means for changing the contents of existing records.

These commands are very powerful. Each employs a full-screen form to facilitate data entry. What is meant by "full screen" is that the cursor is under the user's control. The cursor can be moved anywhere on the form. This feature provides flexibility for data entry.

As powerful as these commands are, the dBASE command language provides you with the means to provide the user with capabilities that even improve on these standard data-entry capabilities. Data entry can be enhanced through:

- Custom screen forms
- Indirect data entry
- Entry into two database files at a time
- Error checking
- Editing through a menu

The commands for data-entry programming in dBASE III PLUS include:

append blank	**input**
@ x,y say	**set format to**
@ x,y get	**clear**
replace	**clear gets**
accept	**read**

Of the above, **accept** and **input** are of marginal use. These commands are carryovers from dBASE II. They do allow you to prompt the user to enter data into character and numeric variables. However, the command is executed on the next available screen position (you have little control over position), and the user must enter the correct data type and must always terminate the entry by pressing the **Return** key.

CUSTOM SCREEN FORMS

A typical data-entry screen provided by the **append** and **edit** commands is shown as Figure 13–1. This screen uses the fieldname as the prompt for each field "blank." The fieldnames and the "blank" for the content of each field are in a column. If you have more than 22 fields, not all the fields are displayed at the same time. The screen scrolls up after the twenty-second field has been entered. dBASE allows you to define custom screen forms that you can use in place of the standard displays. An example of such a form is shown in Figure 13–2. The primary commands for creating full-screen data-entry forms are:

clear
@row,col say *expression*
@row,col get *variable*
read

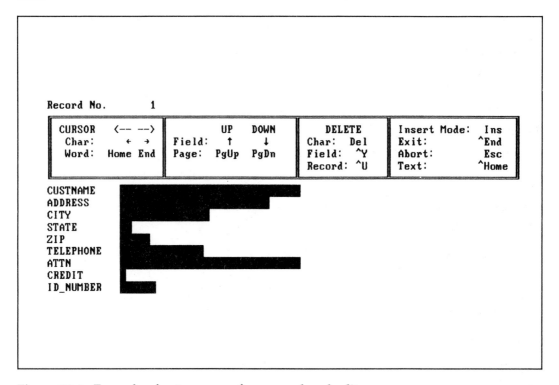

Figure 13–1: Example of entry screen for append and edit.

Clear erases the screen. The two commands beginning with the @ symbol are for display and data entry respectively. These commands allow you to specify the starting row and column where data is to be positioned on the screen. The screen has

25 rows, numbered 0 to 24, and 80 columns numbered 0 to 79. Do not use row 0, which is used for dBASE status messages, unless you **set scoreboard off**.

Each @ . . . **say** command can display a single expression. The expression may be any of the four dBASE data types—character, date, logical, or numeric. Each @ . . . **get** command can display the contents of a single field or memory variable. The variable is normally displayed in reverse video. Variables displayed by **get**s can be edited with the **read** command. **Read** positions the cursor to the first on-screen variable displayed by a **get**. The cursor keys are used to position the cursor to any area displayed by a **get**. These variables are edited by simply typing in new data to replace the existing data.

The screen form shown in Figure 13–2 was produced by the program MENU1S.PRG (discussed in Chapter Five). A variation on this program (that many find effective) is the format file. A format file is similar to a program except that it can contain only the three commands: @ . . . **say**, @ . . . **get**, and **note** (or *). A format file can be used in conjunction with the four full-screen commands **append**, **change**, **edit**, and **insert**. A format file to produce the screen display of Figure 13–2 is shown as Figure 13–3. The file extension .FMT identifies format files. The command **set format to** *filename* opens the format file in the current work area. While this format file is open in the work area, any use of the four full-screen editing commands will produce the screen display of Figure 13–2 rather than the standard (default) display of Figure 13–1. If the open database file is changed, you must close the format file. To close a format file, either open another format file in the work area or use **close format**. You can have a separate format file open for each open database file (subject, of course, to the limit of 15 open files).

The **read** command can be used with format files. If the format has been set to produce a special screen "form," the screen will be created and the current record can be edited with **read**. There are several features of a format file worth noting.

- We are not restricted to the order in which we created the fields; they can be displayed in any order. We can tailor the screen so that the particular items we want to change appear first.

- We don't have to display all the fields. This means that we only have to name the items we want to "edit."

- We can "edit" any variable named with a **get**. We can enter and edit memory variables as well as fields.

- We can put any descriptive text we want on the screen.

- We use only two dBASE III PLUS commands in a FORMAT file: @ **x,y say** and @ **x,y get**. These commands can be augmented with the optional **picture**. As shown in Figure 13–3, the **say** and **get** commands can be combined on a single command line:

@ row,col say *expression* get *variable*

Figure 13–2: Example of custom data-entry screen.

```
@  5,50 say 'I.D. Number    '+CUSTID
@  7,50 say 'Customer Since '+dtoc(DATE)
@  5,2  say 'Customer Name ' get NAME    picture '@!'
@  7,2  say 'Street Address ' get ADDRESS picture '@!'
@  9,2  say 'City......... ' get CITY    picture '@!'
@ 11,2  say 'State........ ' get STATE   picture '@!'
@ 11,24 say 'Zip Code...... ' get ZIP    picture '99999'
@ 13,2  say 'Telephone..... ' get PHONE  picture '(999) 999-9999'
@ 15,2  say 'Attention..... ' get ATTN   picture '@!'
@ 13,50 say 'Credit Standing' get CREDIT picture '@!'
```

Figure 13–3: Format file to create the display in Figure 13–2.

PICTURES

Pictures are used to provide "special effects" for both data entry and display. A picture can force all entered characters to uppercase. Or a picture can limit data entry for a character field to numeric digits. A separate picture can be used with each **say** and **get**.

@ row,col **say** . . . picture " . . . " **get** . . . picture " . . . "

Picture Functions

There are two optional parts for a picture: the picture function and the picture template. If **picture** is specified, at least one of these must be used. A picture function applies to the entire variable. A picture template uses one template symbol for each character (or digit) in the variable. A picture function must begin with the @ symbol. For example, the picture function @! forces all characters in a variable to uppercase.

@ 11,2 say 'State . . . . ' get STATE picture '@!'

The table of picture functions is shown as Figure 13-4.

Picture Functions	
C	displays CR after a positive number
X	displays DB after a negative number
(	encloses negative numbers in parentheses
B	left-justifies numeric data
Z	displays zero numeric value as a blank string
D	American date format
E	European date format
A	alphabetic characters only
!	capital letters only
R	allows literals in the template, not assumed to be part of data
S<n>	limits field width display to n characters
	enables horizontal scrolling within n characters

Figure 13-4: Picture functions.

Picture Templates

The example below shows the use of a template containing a 9 in each character position. This particular template limits the data entry to the digits 0 through 9.

@ 11,24 say 'Zip Code . . . ' get ZIP picture '99999'

The table of template symbols is shown as Figure 13-5. When characters and symbols that are not template symbols are used in a template, they become a permanent part of the data unless the R picture function is used. In the example below, the symbols ( ) and – are not template symbols. They become a permanent part of the data stored in the file.

@ 13,2 say 'Telephone' get PHONE picture '(999)-999-9999'

For numeric variables, the template can fix the size of the displayed variable. This feature has the side benefit of setting limits to the size of a number that can be stored. Fields are automatically displayed with size limits. This is not true for memory variables, which are normally displayed with space for ten digits. To limit the display of a variable to a specific number of digits, use a # for each digit.

@ . . . get NUMBER picture '###.##'

Template Symbols	
9	allows only digits for character data, digits, and signs for numeric data
#	allows only digits, blanks, and signs
A	allows only letters
L	allows only logical data
N	allows letters and digits
X	allows any character
!	converts letters to uppercase and has no effect on other characters
$	displays dollar signs in place of leading zeros
*	displays asterisks in place of leading zeros
.	specifies decimal position
,	displays comma if there are numbers to its left
Y	restricts entry to Y and N, forces uppercase

Figure 13–5: Template symbols.

Range Checking

You can employ range checking to limit data entries to a specific range of values for numeric and date fields. For example, suppose that we have the field COST and we want to limit the range of possible entries to positive values. This can be done with:

@ . . . get COST range 0

As a second example, we have a field named WIDGET, and we want to limit data entry into this field to numbers between and including 5 through 9. This is done with:

@ . . . get WIDGET range 5,9

In both of these examples, any attempt to enter a number outside of the specified range will result in an error message on screen row 0. This message specifies the correct range and tells you to press the space bar to continue. This message is called the "scoreboard." If you want to hide the allowed range from the user (or yourself), the "scoreboard" can be turned off with the command **set scoreboard off**.

The range can also be set by means of the contents of fields or memory variables. The range setting is the value of the field or variable content at the time the command was invoked. You cannot have (at least not yet) a dynamic range setting. Let's suppose that you have two fields in your database, COST and PRICE. To ensure that you always at least break even, we can use the COST as a lower-range limit for PRICE.

@ . . . get PRICE range COST

FORMAT files are separate files. Opening a file takes a fraction of a second—noticeably longer on MS-DOS systems with floppy-disk drives. On some systems when you **set** the format you will perceive a noticeable hesitation. If this is the case you will probably want to move the FORMAT into your program once the program has been developed.

INDIRECT DATA ENTRY

When updating an inventory, the user has to add the quantity received to the quantity on hand, and then enter the result of the addition to the database. We want the user to simply enter the quantity received into the computer and have the computer do the addition and make the appropriate change to the database. This is an example of indirect data entry

We used this technique extensively in the examples in earlier chapters. A simple example of this technique is shown by these few lines of dBASE code:

```
PARTNO = space(10)
QTYRCVD = 0
@ 12,10 say "Enter part Number"   get PARTNO
@ 14,10 say "Qty Received"        get QTYRCVD
read
replace QTY with QTYRCVD for PARTNUMBER = PARTNO
```

Indirect data entry relieves the user of the need to make unnecessary decisions and calculations. By so doing, we reduce the chances for error.

ENTERING DATA INTO MULTIPLE DATABASES

There are times when it is convenient (and natural) to enter data into multiple database files through a single data-entry screen. The inventory database of Chapter Seven makes use of this technique.

Data can be entered into multiple database files at one time through a single data-entry screen. All data files to be edited must be in use, and each must be positioned to the desired record. The program or format file must identify each field by alias->fieldname. A program segment illustrating this operation is shown in Figure 13-6. The files in use are INV alias INVENTORY and SUPPLIER alias SUPPLIER.

ERROR CHECKING

Data entry offers the user the greatest opportunity of making errors in the database. In a large number of cases, protection against entry error can be provided. We cannot protect against the user entering a legitimate—but wrong—value.

```
@ 5,2  say 'Title   '         get INVENTORY->TITLE    picture '@!'
@ 6,2  say 'Author  '         get INVENTORY->AUTHOR   picture '@!'
@ 7,2  say 'Subject '         get INVENTORY->SUBJECT  picture '@!'
@ 14,30 say "Information on Publisher"
@ 16,3  say 'Publisher ' get SUPPLIER->NAME    picture '@!'
@ 17,3  say 'Attention ' get SUPPLIER->ATTN    picture '@!'
@ 18,3  say 'Address   ' get SUPPLIER->ADDRESS picture '@!'
read
```

Figure 13–6: Data entry into two database files from one screen.

The **picture** clause can be used to provide some limited protection against errors. As described above, **picture** can be used to check each character entered and to force a character to be uppercase or a number. This feature can be used to prevent a telephone number from being entered as 555-12A1. The masking aspect of **picture** can be used to fill in parts of an entry—such as the slashes (/) in a date entry. **Picture** can be used as a "first line of defense" against errors.

The next line of defense is range checking. For the case where a numeric or a date entry is limited to a continuous range of values, the **range** clause should be employed. This operation is fast and is automatically in effect every time the cursor is moved into the variable.

If a value is truly two-valued, you can use a logic field for the variable. dBASE will not allow entry of any symbol other than True/False (Yes/No). You should be careful here, however. Many two-valued functions are in reality three-valued: Yes, No, and Unknown. As an example, when entering student data we encounter an item "Was student retained?" Well, it's clear that the student either was or wasn't retained. But— and it's a big but—the person entering the data might not know which is the case. All normal displays except for standard full-screen operations will show these records as "False." If there is any possibility that an item is really a three-valued function, you should use a character field for the item.

The last line of defense is to write dBASE code to either check data as it's entered or to verify the data afterward. If the former course is chosen, we lose some of the value of full-screen operations—we must prohibit the user from "backing up" and changing an earlier entry. After-the-fact validation (validation between records) is often preferable since it takes advantage of the fact that most data entries are not in error. About the only time that you should use in-line checking is when a value depends on another value (dynamic screen entry).

To illustrate the use of in-line error checking in a program, we offer the example shown in Figure 13-7. In this example, the items to be entered are NAME, ROOM, GRADE, and RETAINED (the latter indicates whether or not the student failed last year). All four fields are character fields. We validate that the last three items are, at least, legitimate values. Figure 13–8 takes the same problem and uses batch checking to validate the same values. As you can see, the batch operation is slightly more complex; however, it appears simpler and more flexible to the user.

Though serviceable, Figure 13-7 eliminates the major advantage of full-screen entry: the freedom to change your mind, to back up an item and change the entry. After each **read**, you cannot go back to a previous item. **Read** only allows you access to "open" **gets** that have been displayed since the last **read** command.

```
@ 3,1  say "STUDENT'S NAME" get NAME
do while .not. ROOM $ ' 1, 3,15,22,31,4A'
   @ 5,1  say 'ROOM' get ROOM
   read
enddo
do while .not. GRADE $ 'K123456'
   @ 5,20 say 'GRADE' get GRADE
   read
enddo
do while .not. upper(RETAINED) $ 'YN'
   @ 5,40 say 'RETAINED (Y/N)?' get RETAINED
   read
enddo
```

Figure 13-7: Sample of in-line error checking.

The best way to handle error checking for this kind of entry problem is shown in Figure 13-8. Note that there really isn't a lot of difference. We allow the user to enter the data. The "batch test" occurs after the data has been entered. The user is only prompted to reenter erroneous data. Although Figure 13-8 has more lines of code, it is far preferable to the original program.

```
@ 3,1  say "STUDENT'S NAME" get NAME
@ 5,1  say 'ROOM' get ROOM
@ 5,20 say 'GRADE' get GRADE
@ 5,40 say 'RETAINED (Y/N)?' get RETAINED
do while .not. ROOM $ ' 1, 3,15,22,31,4A'
   @ 5,1  say 'ROOM' get ROOM
   read
enddo
do while .not. GRADE $ 'K123456'
   @ 5,20 say 'GRADE' get GRADE
   read
enddo
do while .not. upper(RETAINED) $ 'YN'
   @ 5,40 say 'RETAINED (Y/N)?' get RETAINED
   read
enddo
```

Figure 13-8: Improved error-checking approach.

ENTRY SCREENS

In-line checking of data entry, like that shown in Figure 13–7, should be limited to situations where the "form" presented to the user varies with the answer to a specific question. In this case, we are not so much checking the validity of a response, but looking for a cue as to what to do next.

To illustrate this point, let's consider a problem facing many American school districts these days. An increasing number of students are from non–English-speaking families. Schools are required to classify students from non–English-speaking families by the student's proficiency in English. If the student's home language is a part of the student's database record, we can ignore English-proficiency questions for students whose home language is English. The program segment shown in Figure 13–9 illustrates how data entry can be facilitated.

In this simple example, the user is presented with the opportunity to enter the home language and English proficiency only if the response to the question, "Is the home language English?," is negative.

```
@ 3,1  say "STUDENT'S NAME" get NAME
@ 5,1  say 'ROOM' get ROOM
@ 5,20 say 'GRADE' get GRADE
@ 5,40 say 'RETAINED (Y/N)?' get RETAINED
@ 7,1  say 'Is the home language English (Y/N)?' get QUERY
read
@ 7,0                  && clear line
if QUERY $ 'Nn'
   @ 7,1 say 'HOME LANGUAGE'            get LANGUAGE
   @ 9,1 say 'ENGLISH PROFICIENCY LEVEL' get PROFICIENT
else
   replace LANGUAGE with 'ENGLISH'
endif
```

Figure 13–9: Dynamic screen entry.

There are a number of cases where the response to a screen entry can alter a "form" for a user. Another example of tailoring screen entry to take the relevance of data into account would be to avoid asking single persons for their spouse's name.

EDITING THROUGH A MENU

We can make a menu of the items displayed for editing. This can be convenient when the display consists of a large number of items, and the items to be changed vary considerably from record to record. This technique also allows us to make a greater use of codes since we work with only a single item with each **read**. (Note that this is markedly different from putting a **read** with each "in-line" entry).

```
do while .T.
  ITEM = space(1)
  @ 3,1  say "1 - STUDENT'S NAME"  get NAME
  @ 5,1  say '2 - ROOM'            get ROOM
  @ 5,20 say '3 - GRADE'           get GRADE
  @ 5,40 say '4 - RETAINED (Y/N)?' get RETAINED
  clear gets
  @ 18,1  say 'Enter a * when finished'
  @ 20,1  say 'Enter Item Number to be edited' get ITEM
  read
  do case
    case ITEM = '*'
        exit
    case ITEM = '1'
        @ 3,1  say "1 - STUDENT'S NAME" get NAME
        read
    case ITEM = '2'
        @ 5,1  say '2 - ROOM' get ROOM
        read
        do while .not. ROOM $ ' 1, 3,15,22,31,4A'
           @ 5,1  say '2 - ROOM' get ROOM
           read
        enddo
    case ITEM = '3'
        @ 5,20 say '3 - GRADE' get GRADE
        read
        do while .not. GRADE $ 'K123456'
           @ 5,20 say '3 - GRADE' get GRADE
           read
        enddo
    case ITEM = '4'
        @ 5,40 say '4 - RETAINED (Y/N)?' get RETAINED
        read
        do while .not. upper(RETAINED) $ 'YN'
           @ 5,40 say '4 - RETAINED (Y/N)?' get RETAINED
           read
        enddo
  endcase
  @ 18,0 clear           && clears bottom of screen
enddo
```

Figure 13–10: Example of menu editing.

Figure 13-10, which is based on our school example, illustrates the use of a menu for editing. One of the advantages of a menu-selection approach to editing is that the "editing" software for each entry can be very elaborate. We can actually search other files and make very extensive uses of "coding" with this approach. This is an extremely powerful technique that is rarely used.

Browsing

Browse is a wonderful command. It provides a quick and convenient technique for entering data into columnar form. This command was designed to be used in the interactive mode and provides options that are considered undesirable if we use it from within a program.

Suppose that we have the following fields: PARTNAME, PARTNO, PRICE, and QUANTITY. We want to use the **browse** command to edit the PRICE column. An appropriate use of the command might look like:

browse fields PARTNAME,PARTNO,PRICE freeze PRICE nomenu noappend

The argument **fields** followed by a field list limits the display to the fields contained in the field list. **Freeze** PRICE limits editing to the field PRICE (this field must be contained in the field list). **Nomenu** prevents a user from having access to the command capabilities of **browse**. **Noappend** prevents **browse** from entering into the **append** mode.

Even with these enhancements, I feel that **browse** is marginally acceptable as a programming command. There are, however, cases where you will find it to be invaluable. In general, it is best to avoid the high-level dBASE data-entry and editing commands.

In-Line Checking and Validation

The **readkey( )** function, introduced with dBASE III PLUS, makes it possible to do data entry with *in-line* error checking. Programs to make use of this feature will be more complex than simple data-entry programs which use batch data-validation. However, once you master the technique, you can use it effectively—and profitably. Your programs will be better accepted than those written by others who are still using the batch techniques.

To demonstrate, let's use the problem of Figure 13–10. Code which solves the problem is shown as Figure 13–12. Look at the additional complexity. First we paint the screen, then **clear gets**. From this point on, each **read** handles just one variable. We must keep track of where we are, because each **read** takes us to the "next" variable. In order to know which is next, we assign an identifier to the variable and monitor the key used to exit from the **read**. The latter is accomplished with the help of the **readkey( )** function.

Readkey( ) is a remarkably simple function which provides you with a numeric code to indicate the key used to end the **read** operation. The value of the **readkey( )** code depends upon the key used to *exit* from the **read** and whether or not any data was changed during the **read**. Codes returned by the function are shown in Figure 13–11. As you can see, if any data was changed during the **read**, the value returned is 256 plus the no-change key code. Of course, since the **Esc** key discards changes, the code value is always 12 for this key.

Last Key Pressed	Exit Without Change	Exit With Change
Right Arrow	0	256
Left Arrow	1	257
Up Arrow	4	260
Down Arrow	5	261
Home	2	258
End	3	259
PgUp	6	262
PgDn	7	263
Ctrl-Left Arrow	8	264
Ctrl-Right Arrow	9	265
Ctrl-Home	33	289
Ctrl-End	14	270
Ctrl-PgUp	34	290
Ctrl-PgDn	35	291
Backspace	0	256
(Return) Enter	15	271
Escape	12	12
F1	36	292
Anything else	15	271

Figure 13–11: Readkey( ) code values.

```
* assumes a database with fields NAME, ROOM, and GRADE
clear
set talk off
@ 5,10 say "Student's Room " get ROOM  picture '@!'
@ 7,10 say "          Grade" get GRADE picture '@!'
clear gets
FIELD = 1
do while .T.
   do case
      case FIELD = 1
         @ 3,10 say "Student's Name " get  NAME picture '@!'
      case FIELD = 2
         @ 5,10 say "          Room " get  ROOM picture '@!'
      case FIELD = 3
         @ 7,10 say "          Grade" get GRADE picture '@!'
   endcase
   read
   do case
      case FIELD = 2 .and. .not. ROOM $ ' 1,22,11,4A'
         @ 18,2 say 'Invalid Room Number'
      case FIELD = 3 .and. .not. GRADE $ '1,2,3'
         @ 18,2 say 'Invalid Grade'
      otherwise
         @18,2 say space(30)
         READKEY = iif(readkey() > 255, readkey() - 256, readkey())
         do case
            case str(READKEY,2) $ ' 0, 4, 8, 2'
               FIELD = iif(FIELD > 1, FIELD - 1, FIELD)
            case str(READKEY,2) $ ' 1, 5, 9, 3,15' .and. FIELD  < 3
               FIELD = FIELD + 1
            case str(READKEY,2) $ ' 1, 5, 9, 3,15'
               exit
            case str(READKEY,2) $ '12,14,33,34,35'
               exit
            case READKEY = 6
               FIELD = 1
            case READKEY = 7
               FIELD = 3
         endcase
   endcase
enddo
```

Figure 13–12: Demo program for in-line validation.

CHAPTER FOURTEEN
The Report Command

The dBASE III PLUS **report** command deserves this chapter of its own. **Report** is often misunderstood and underrated, and our inability to make full use of it may be one of the reasons that we learn to program with dBASE in the first place. As you will see, **report** can be used to replace many of the simple reporting programs developed for BOB'S BETTER BOOKS.

Report allows you to extract and display data from one or more database files in a columnar format, as shown in Figures 14–1 and 14–2. Reports such as these are produced from *report forms*, which are disk files that contain the answers to a series of simple questions regarding the content and format of each report. Each *report form* is saved as a disk file and has a .FRM extension.

PREPARING THE REPORT FORM

All database files that will be used in the report must be open at the time you prepare the report form. Report forms are created and modified by the following identical commands:

```
create report
modify report
```

These are among the most powerful and easy-to-use of all the dBASE commands. The report form is created with the help of five *pull-down* menus, which are used to describe the page layout, provide subtotalling and grouping information, and describe the content of the report. To use these menus, move the lightbar so that the desired option is highlighted. To *select* the highlighted option, press the **Return** key. dBASE provides you with help information at the bottom of the screen. You can toggle between the key assistance help screen (bottom of Figure 14–3) and a mock-up of the report page by means of function key **F1**.

The Options Menu: Page Layout

Page layout is controlled by the options menu shown in Figure 14–3. This screen is used to enter a report title, set margins, change the page size, and set the line spacing. It determines the *page layout* as well as what is to go into the report. Let's look at how we use **create report** to enter this information. When you create a report, you must be using the database that you will be reporting on.

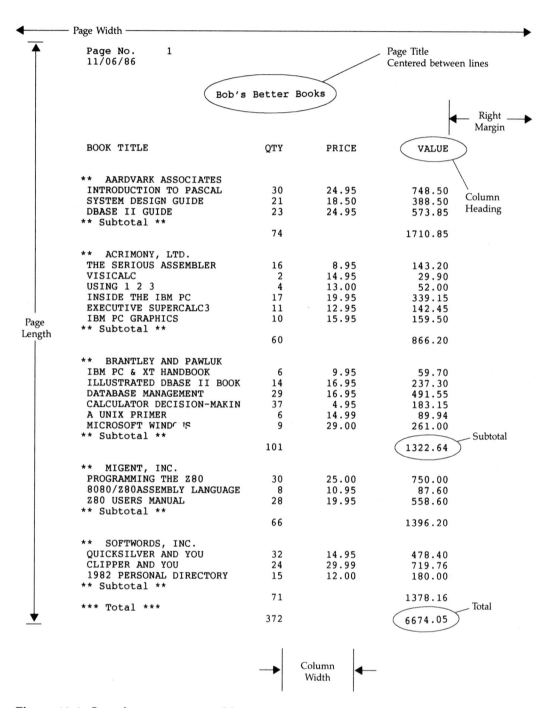

```
  Page No.    1
  11/06/86
                                                    Page Title
                                                    Centered between lines

                    Bob's Better Books

                                                              Right
                                                              Margin

    BOOK TITLE              QTY      PRICE        VALUE


    **   AARDVARK ASSOCIATES
    INTRODUCTION TO PASCAL   30      24.95        748.50
    SYSTEM DESIGN GUIDE      21      18.50        388.50      Column
    DBASE II GUIDE           23      24.95        573.85      Heading
    ** Subtotal **
                            74                   1710.85

    **   ACRIMONY, LTD.
    THE SERIOUS ASSEMBLER    16       8.95        143.20
    VISICALC                  2      14.95         29.90
    USING 1 2 3               4      13.00         52.00
    INSIDE THE IBM PC        17      19.95        339.15
    EXECUTIVE SUPERCALC3     11      12.95        142.45
    IBM PC GRAPHICS          10      15.95        159.50
    ** Subtotal **
                            60                    866.20

    **   BRANTLEY AND PAWLUK
    IBM PC & XT HANDBOOK      6       9.95         59.70
    ILLUSTRATED DBASE II BOOK 14     16.95        237.30
    DATABASE MANAGEMENT      29      16.95        491.55
    CALCULATOR DECISION-MAKIN 37      4.95        183.15
    A UNIX PRIMER             6      14.99         89.94
    MICROSOFT WINDOWS         9      29.00        261.00
    ** Subtotal **                                           Subtotal
                           101                   1322.64

    **   MIGENT, INC.
    PROGRAMMING THE Z80      30      25.00        750.00
    8080/Z80ASSEMBLY LANGUAGE 8      10.95         87.60
    Z80 USERS MANUAL         28      19.95        558.60
    ** Subtotal **
                            66                   1396.20

    **   SOFTWORDS, INC.
    QUICKSILVER AND YOU      32      14.95        478.40
    CLIPPER AND YOU          24      29.99        719.76
    1982 PERSONAL DIRECTORY  15      12.00        180.00
    ** Subtotal **
                            71                   1378.16
    *** Total ***                                            Total
                           372                   6674.05
```

Page Width

Page Length

Column Width

Figure 14–1: Sample report grouped by customer.

```
Page No.          1
11/6/86
                        CUSTOMER LIST
                      BOB'S BETTER BOOKS
                 10150 W. JEFFERSON BOULEVARD
                 CULVER CITY, CALIFORNIA  90230

NAME AND ADDRESS                        PHONE NUMBER
======================================= =============


52ND STREET BOOK SHOP                   (212)266-4410
SHIPPING
126 E. 18TH ST.
NEW YORK,  NY  10003


A-1 BOOKS                               (303)925-1234
77 E. COPPERFIELD
ASPEN, CO  81611


AARDVARK ASSOCIATES                     (201)267-1000
KAREN
121 STONE CT.
NORTHVALE,  NJ  07647


ABC BOOK SELLERS                        (214)344-3740
9715 MINERS AVENUE
DALLAS,  TX  75231


ABC  BOOK SELLERS                       (313)425-7711
CAROLINE SIMMONS
12510 FRONTIER
LIVONIA,  MI  48154


ACME BOOKS                              (312)741-3380
ALBERT LONGMAN
115 S. WEST ST.
ELGIN,  IL  60120


ACRIMONY                                (503)284-9876
MORT EASTON
2512  NE COLUMBIA
PORTLAND,  OR  97232
```

Figure 14-2: Sample report with data items combined in column.

To enter data into a menu item, use the **Left** or **Right Arrow** key to select the menu. Then use the **Up** and **Down Arrow** keys to select an item within the menu. Press

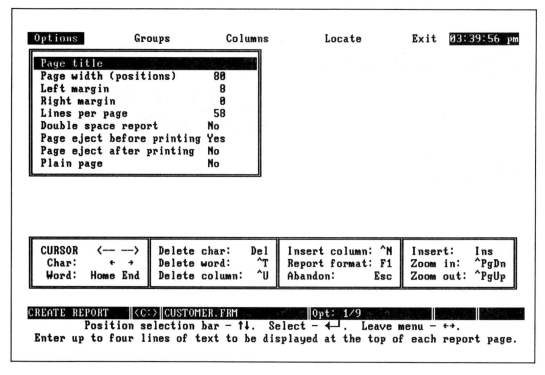

Figure 14–3: Options menu.

the **Return** key to enter the selection. Type in the new information. Then, press the **Return** key to exit from the selection.

Page title: The page title consists of up to four lines. Each line can be up to 60 characters long and will be automatically centered *between the margins*. If the body of the report does not take up the full space (margin to margin), the title will *not* be centered over the body of the report. Adjust either the content of the report or the right margin to get the title to appear centered.

To enter the title, use the arrow keys to highlight *Page title*. Press **Return**. You'll be presented with the screen shown as Figure 14–4. The cursor is placed automatically at the beginning of a box 36 characters wide. As you enter a title line that is longer than 36 characters, the line will scroll to the left. This is to allow you full use of the title width. When finished with the title, press **PgDn**.

Page width: The page width is the number of *character positions* for the total width of your page, including margins (shown in Figure 14–1). The default page width is 80 characters. Change this value if you are using either wide paper or small print. dBASE will not allow you to use more characters in your report than the page width value.

Left margin: The default left margin is 8 character spaces, indicated on screen by the > > > > symbols on the first line in the box for REPORT FORMAT (see Figure 14–7). Each > stands for one character position in the left margin.

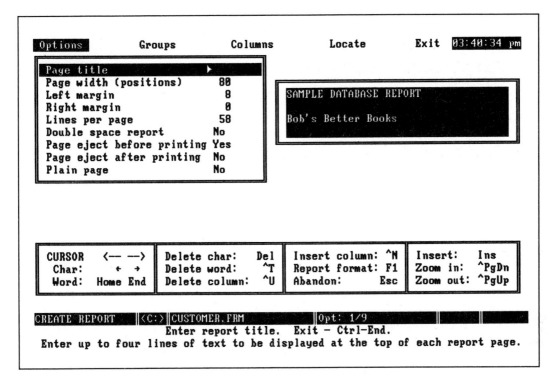

Figure 14–4: Entering report title.

Right margin: The right margin is also given in character positions. The default right margin is zero (no right margin). When you assign a right margin, dBASE displays < < < < symbols in the same way the left margin symbols are used.

Lines per page: Practically speaking, this value sets the bottom page margin. The lines-per-page value is the total number of lines, including the page header, that dBASE will print for each page of the report. The page header includes the page number, date, page title, and column headings (as shown in Figure 14–1). The report begins one line down from the top of the page. Most printers use 11-inch paper and are set to six lines per inch (66 lines per page). The standard setting of 58 lines provides a seven-line bottom margin.

You *cannot* use this setting to change the paper length. That is done by your printer. To use paper that is not 11 inches, you must change *both* this setting and the form length adjustment on your printer.

Top margin: No adjustment is provided for the top margin. To move the report "down" on the paper, you must adjust the starting position of the paper in the printer.

Double space report: Normally, one record (or a part of one record) is printed on each line of the report. As we'll see later, you can use more than one line for each record (see Figure 14–2). A *yes* entry for this item will insert a blank line between records.

Page eject before printing: dBASE normally ejects one page from the printer before beginning the report. This makes sure that your report will always begin at the top of a page (just in case you have a partially printed page in the printer).

Page eject after printing: The last page in the report is not normally ejected. This feature allows comments to be printed at the end of the report.

Plain page: Each page of the report is normally printed with a full page heading: page number, date, and page title. If you select *Plain page*, the page number and date will not be printed at all, while the page title will be printed on the first page only.

The Groups Menu

This menu (shown in Figure 14–5) allows us to *group* like items together in a report. If you look at Figure 14–1, you will see that the records for each customer are grouped together. To take advantage of this feature, the database must be arranged so that the records in a group are adjacent to one another.

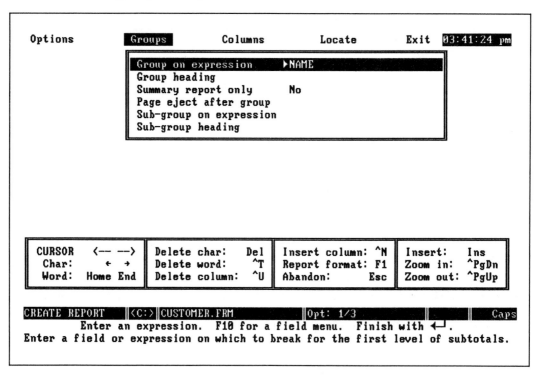

Figure 14–5: Groups menu.

Group on expression: This selection is used to identify the field (or fields) that the report is to be grouped by. The database is usually sorted or indexed on this field. In Figure 14–1, the records were grouped by the contents of the field CUSTOMER.

When records are grouped, any numeric columns that are to be totalled will be automatically subtotalled by the group (as in Figure 14–1).

Group heading: The content of the grouping field is automatically printed at the beginning of the group. You may insert additional text just before this automatic group heading. For example, if we had entered **Customer Name:** for the group heading, it would be printed just before and on the same line as the customer's name.

Summary report only: A summary report consists of only the grouping field and the subtotals, if any. It's a good way to get a quick overview of a large report. A summary report using the same data as Figure 14–1 is shown as Figure 14–6.

Page eject after group: This feature is used when you want each group to begin on a fresh page.

Sub-group on expression: Sub-groups are simply groups which occur within larger groups. When sub-groups are identified, numeric columns that are to be totalled will be automatically sub-subtotalled by sub-group.

Sub-group heading: This is text that is to be displayed just before the sub-group field data.

The Columns Menu

This menu, shown in Figures 14–7 and 14–8, is used to define each of the columns in the *body* of the report. Columns are defined one at a time. When a column is defined, you must use the **PgDn** key to advance to the next column. Use the **PgUp** key to back up to a previous column definition.

Contents: This item determines *what* is to go into the column. This will usually be a field from the current database or an expression involving one or more fields from that database. You must be using the database that you want to report on when you create (or change) the report form.

If you forget the name of a field, press **F10**. This adds help information to the column definition screen, as shown in Figure 14–7. As you can see, the help is provided by two on-screen boxes. The first lists the field names in the database. If there are more fields than can be displayed at a time, you can scroll through additional fieldnames by pressing the **PgDn** key. One of these fields will be highlighted. Information about the highlighted field is displayed in the second box. Use the **Up** and **Down Arrow** keys to move the lightbar to another fieldname.

Heading: A column heading is optional. If you elect to enter a column title, you are provided with a box in which to enter the heading. This box (as shown in Figure 14–8) has space for four lines. If you enter the heading into the first line, there will be three blank lines between the heading and the data. To eliminate these blank lines, enter the column title on the bottom line. When you do, you will find that the column heading (as displayed in the column menu) has three semicolons in front of it (;;;NAME). The semicolon acts like a carriage return.

```
Page No.       1
11/06/86


                        Bob's Better Books


    BOOK TITLE                    QTY        PRICE          VALUE


    **   AARDVARK ASSOCIATES
    **   Subtotal **
                                   74                     1710.85


    **   ACRIMONY, LTD.
    **   Subtotal **
                                   60                      866.20


    **   BRANTLEY AND PAWLUK
    **   Subtotal **
                                  101                     1322.64


    **   MIGENT, INC.
    **   Subtotal **
                                   66                     1396.20


    **   SOFTWORDS, INC.
    **   Subtotal **
                                   71                     1378.16
    ***  Total ***
                                  372                     6674.05
```

Figure 14-6: Summary report.

Width: This value is the number of character spaces to be allocated to the column. The standard value is exactly the width of the column contents or the column heading (whichever is wider). You can elect to use either more or fewer character spaces. If you use additional spaces, they will be added to the right for character fields and to the left for numeric fields. This provides you with one way to adjust the spacing between columns. If the column width is less than the width of the contents, the contents will "wrap" within the column boundaries and be printed on multiple lines.

Decimal places: This value is the number of decimal places to be displayed in the column. It is normally the number of decimal places in the field (fields) involved in the column. However, you can choose to use either more or fewer decimals than the database contains.

Total this column: This item is available *only* if the column content is numeric. If

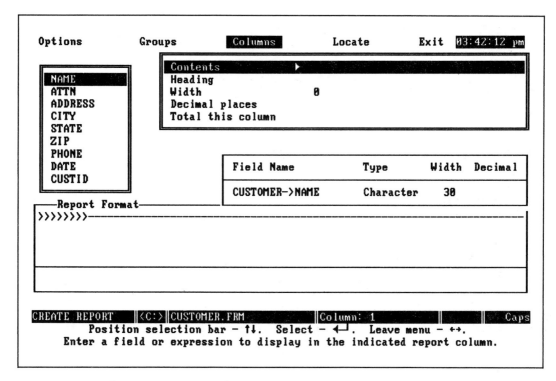

Figure 14–7: Columns menu with field help information.

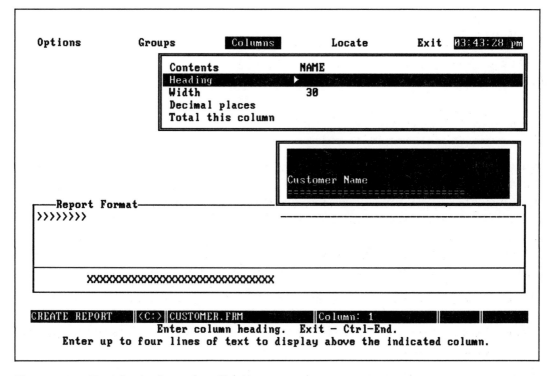

Figure 14–8: Entering column heading.

a column is to be totalled, all groups and sub-groups in the report will be automatically totalled and subtotalled. The width of the field must be enough to accomodate the total.

The Locate Menu

This menu is provided to help with column definition. Menu selections consist of the contents of each defined field. You can go directly to the column definition for any previously-defined field by simply highlighting the column you want to review and pressing the **Return** key.

The Exit Menu

This menu provides you with two choices: to save the report form that has just been defined or to abandon it.

Printing Items Vertically

It is often desirable to put several data items into a single column, as shown in Figure 14–2. The trick is to tell dBASE that the column is smaller than the data that is to go into the column, so that data will "wrap" within the column. The customer database file contains a number of fields, including:

NAME	Character	30
ATTN	Character	30
ADDRESS	Character	25
CITY	Character	20
STATE	Character	2
ZIP	Character	5
PHONE	Character	14

To prepare the report shown in Figure 14–2 from this database we use the following characteristics of the **report** command:

- Data wraps if it is wider than the column width.
- Text can be entered if enclosed by quotes.
- Character fields can be concatenated (added together).
- Semicolons will force the data to the next line.

The first column of Figure 14–2 contains NAME, ATTN, ADDRESS, CITY, STATE, and ZIP. We'll put all this into one column by entering

NAME + ATTN + ADDRESS + ';' + TRIM(CITY) + ', ' + STATE + ' ' + ZIP

as the column content. dBASE will protest a little since the width of this item is larger than the page width. Ignore the protest and set the column width to 30. Why 30? This is the width of the widest field that we want displayed. Data will wrap at the column width, and we want each field to be displayed without wrapping. The NAME field fills the first line of the column; ATTN the second. The ADDRESS field begins the third line, but has only 25 characters—not enough to fill the line. The semicolon (enclosed in quotes) moves the output to the next report line, placing CITY at the beginning of line 4.

The **trim( )** function is used to discard "trailing" blank spaces from data items. The contents of CITY are not the same length. *El Paso* is shorter than *San Francisco.* Here it discards trailing blanks from CITY, allowing us to place a comma immediately after the city name (see Figure 14-2). This comma and a single blank space separate CITY from STATE. The comma and the space are inserted into the expression by enclosing them in quotes.

The report is double-spaced to separate the records in the report, but double spacing doesn't affect the line spacing within the record.

Substituting Text

Text substitution is another trick to use here. The ATTN column is often blank, and this prints out as a blank line within the record. To prevent dBASE from printing the blank, substitute

iif(ATTN = space(30), chr(0), ATTN)

for ATTN in the column content expression. You can read this substitution as "print ATTN only if the field isn't empty." **Chr(0)** is a null, which takes no space.

A more common use of text substitution is to expand data. For example, you have a one-character field to represent a person's sex: M for male, F for female. To print the words *Male* and *Female* in the report, we enter the following expression for the column content:

iif(SEX= 'F', 'Female', 'Male')

Use this technique for "exception" reporting. For example, suppose that you have a check register database which includes a logic field (CANCEL) to indicate whether or not a check has "cleared." We want the report to display the word "open" for checks that haven't cleared and nothing for checks that have. It's easier to spot the open items in a printout when you use this technique. Use

iif(.not. CANCEL, "open", " ")

for the column contents.

Column Headings

The column heading appears to be limited to four lines, but you can use the semicolon to obtain column headings that are longer. Simply insert a semicolon whenever you want a new heading line.

THIS;IS;A;SIX;LINE;TITLE

produces a column heading that looks like:

```
THIS
IS
A
SIX
LINE
TITLE
```

Grouping Data Items

We can combine multiple fields into a single data item for grouping. For example, we have a database of grade-school children, which includes the fields NAME, ROOM, GRADE. We can use a report to prepare class rosters: alphabetical listings of the students in each room and grade.

Some of the rooms have students from two grades. Use the **index** (or **sort**) command to arrange the records so that they appear alphabetically within the desired groupings:

. index on ROOM + GRADE + NAME to class

Next, prepare the report form. The proper entry for *group on expression* is:

ROOM + GRADE

A "better" entry for this data item would be:

"Room: "+ ROOM + " Grade: "+ GRADE

The text inside the quotes doesn't affect the grouping because it doesn't change from record to record. Only the content of the specified fields can change. This is a "better" grouping expression because of the way dBASE prints it. The first expression, ROOM+GRADE, is printed (for grade 6, room 21B) as:

* 21B6

while the second expression comes out as the more desirable:

Room: 21B Grade: 6

Reporting From Multiple Databases

Your report can contain information from more than one database file, if you link the database files together by the **set relation** command. When specifying a data item from another database file, use the *alias* for the work area of the other file, the -> (- and >) and the fieldname.

alias->fieldname

Records can be grouped by a field in a linked database. The selected database must be sorted (or indexed) on the field which is used to link to the other database. Any field in the linked database can be specified as the grouping field. Remember: All databases to be used in a report must be open when the report form is created, and the database setup, position, index files, relationships, and so on must be in place when the report is executed. The database view must be established by your program.

Let's examine an elementary school database system. The STUDENT file contains NAME, ROOM, and GRADE. The TEACHERS file contains NAME, ROOM, and GRADE also. Both files, of course, contain other fields. They are both indexed on GRADE and ROOM. To link these files together, we use

```
. select STUDENTS
. set relation to GRADE+ROOM into TEACHERS
```

We choose to have the report grouped by the TEACHER's name. To do this, the entry in Group on expression becomes

```
TEACHERS -> NAME
```

which gives us exactly the same result as if we had grouped directly on GRADE+ROOM—except that the teacher's name will appear at the beginning of each class roster, instead of the room and grade.

THE REPORT COMMAND

The **report** command itself provides you with a set of options. The command options allow you to:

- specify *which* records are to be included
- print a special *page heading*
- specify that the report is to be *printed*
- specify that the report is to go to a *disk file*

Selecting Records

To specify which records are to be included in the report, add a **for** or **while** clause to the **report** command. To include only the New York, NY, records in the report of Figure 14–2, use

```
. report for CITY='NEW YORK' and STATE='NY'
```

Page Headings

Report allows you to define page headings in addition to the title. The additional heading is printed at the top of the page, beginning on the line which normally contains the page number. There is no specific limit to the number of lines that can be used for the heading, although the **report** command is limited to 255 characters. Headings allow you to include specific pertinent text at the top of each report without having to modify the report. To include special headings use the "heading" option with the **report** command:

```
. report form filename heading expression
```

The heading must be a character string. It can be characters enclosed by delimiters, fields, memory variables, or any combination of the above. Heading lines are normally centered and printed beginning with the top line of the report. Let's print the letterhead "Bob's Better Books," complete with address, as the heading for a report. Use the command (but enter it on one line):

. report form sales heading "Bob's Better Books; 10150 W. Jefferson Boulevard; Culver City, California; 90230"

The semicolons act as carriage return/line feeds, printing the item following the semicolon on the next line. The beginning of the report looks like:

Page No. 1

Bob's Better Books
10150 W. Jefferson Boulevard
Culver City, California
90230

02/04/85

Note that the date is printed on the first line following the heading and that the first line of the heading is printed on the same line as the page number.

To move the heading to the left margin, use the **chr( )** function for carriage return: **chr(13)**. This command won't work properly if you have used the **set margin** command to set the left margin. To place the letterhead above at the left margin, use

. report form sales heading ";" + chr(13) + "Bob's Better Books;" + chr(13) + "10150 W. Jefferson Boulevard;" + chr(13) + "Culver City, California;" + chr(13) + "90230"

which produces the following result:

Page No. 1
Bob's Better Books
10150 W. Jefferson Boulevard
Culver City, California
90230
02/04/85

To remove the page number and the date from the report, use the word *plain* in the command. Unfortunately, the addition to the command also prevents the page heading from being displayed, and the report title is printed only on the first page of the report.

Reporting To a Printer

A report is always displayed on screen. The modifier TO PRINT sends the report to the printer.

. report to print

Saving Report Output on Disk

You can also send the report to a disk file, providing the luxury of editing the report with a word processor. To send a report to disk, use

. report to *filename*

The filename can be any legitimate disk filename you desire. dBASE adds TXT as the file extension.

PUTTING IT ALL TOGETHER

To demonstrate some of the capabilities of **report**, let's use the command to print a sales order similar to the one in Figure 14-10. This report was "set up" by the program file RPT1.PRG (see Figure 14-11). The report form is set up with the format features shown in Figure 14-9.

Title	none
Page layout	defaults
Group/subtotal on	SONUMBER
Summary report	No
Eject after group	Yes
Group/subtotal heading	Sales Order Number

Column (Field) Content	Title	Width
ISBN	ISBN Number	14
INVENTORY->TITLE	Title	30
QTY	QTY	3
PRICE	Price	7
QTY * PRICE	Cost	8

Figure 14-9: Format features for sales order.

```
SALES ORDER 100051    DATED: 02/02/85
Page Number   1

TATE-ASHTON                        CUSTOMER P.O.  a-12345
OLIVIA
3800 HONOLULU
LA CRESCENTA, CA  91214

ISBN NUMBER      QTY      PRICE      TITLE

0-02-501980-5    75       16.95      HOW TO SAVE ON YOUR INCOME TAX
0-8359-1246-9    76       19.95      DBASE II FOR EVERY BUSINESS
0-89588-124-1    77       17.95      BUSINESS GRAPHICS FOR THE PC
```

Figure 14-10: Sample sales order.

```
* RPT1.PRG

set margin to 0
A = chr(13)+space(8)
B = "Bob's Better Books;"
C = "10150 W. Jefferson Boulevard;"
D = "Culver City, California  90230;;;"
E = A+CUSTOMER->NAME+';'
F = A+CUSTOMER->ADDRESS+';'
G = A+trim(CUSTOMER->CITY)+", "+CUSTOMER->STATE+'  '+CUSTOMER->ZIP
H = ";;Customer Purchase Order "+SALES->PONUMBER
select CUSTOMER
     set index to CUSTID
select SALES
     set relation to CUSTID into CUSTOMER
select SALESDET
     set relation to ISBN into INVENTORY
report form SALES to print noeject heading ";;"+B+C+D+E+F+G+H ;
        while SONUMBER = SALES->SONUMBER
eject
set margin to 10
```

Figure 14–11: RPT1.PRG.

First, we must set margin to 0 in order to prevent the report margins from adding to the dBASE set margin value. Next, we set up memory variables to contain the various lines of the heading. Without the use of variables, the command length of the **report** command would exceed the maximum of 255 characters.

We select the various database files that we will be using and establish the relationships between these files. This report draws on data from three database files. It is presumed that the sales and sales detail files have already been positioned to the correct records.

The **report** command routes its output to both the printer and the screen. The **noeject** option prevents **report** from issuing an initial page eject. The **heading** option uses the memory variables A through H to produce the page heading. The two initial semicolons are used to position the first line of the letterhead to two lines from the top of the page. Each of the first several memory variables is terminated with a semicolon. This step forces a line feed. The three variables E, F, and G begin with variable A, which contains the ASCII carriage return code and eight blank spaces. The carriage return is used to force these variables to the left edge of the paper, and the spaces are used to reposition the variables to the left margin. The carriage return overrides dBASE margins in both **set margin** and the left report margin.

This chapter has briefly shown the wonders of the **report** command. As you have seen, this command has a language and a set of capabilities all its own. **Report** has enormous power; it can be used to replace quite complex procedural programs.

CHAPTER FIFTEEN
Time and Date

dBASE offers a number of tools to help you deal effectively with both time and date. Dates, in particular, are usually essential elements of most business database applications. Without the proper software tools, such as the date data type, working with dates can be particularly messy.

Part of the problem with dates stems from the manner in which we have chosen to deal with them as a society. Dates, in the United States, are usually written as *month, day, year*. In Europe (and the American military) dates are usually expressed as *day, month, year*. In Japan, dates are used in the form *year, month, day*. In addition, the symbols used to separate the three parts of a date vary with culture and country. At least three different symbols are in common use: the slash, hyphen, and comma.

Standard sorting and comparison operations for character data begin with the left-most character and proceed, character by character (or digit by digit), from left to right. If dates are entered as character data (i.e., into character fields) they cannot be properly sorted unless they have been entered in the sequence *year, month, day*. The sorting operation would normally serve to group dates by month, creating the situation where May 5, 1985 would come before June 1, 1960. Similar problems arise when you attempt to compare two dates. Only the Japanese can work naturally with dates entered as character items.

The other factor complicating date operations is the number of days in a month, which can vary from 28 to 31—depending on the month, the year, and the century. Many people are unaware that leap years (when February has 29 days) occur every four years—except on century years. Every fourth century year is a leap century (a leap year that falls on a century year). Thus, the years 1600, 2000, and 2400 are leap centuries, and the years 1900 and 2100 are not.

THE DATE

dBASE III PLUS offers a *date* data type, which can apply to fields as well as memory variables. This data type allows us to work with dates in a natural manner—we don't have to conform to the computer. All date variables are automatically eight bytes in length. Dates appear to be in the standard date format MM/DD/YY; the date September 23, 1986 appears to be stored as 09/23/86.

Dates are actually stored in the form YYYYMMDD (for example, September 9, 1986 is stored as 19860923), making it reasonable for the computer to apply standard sorting, indexing, and comparison operations directly to the field. dBASE takes care of all of the conversions necessary to transform the date as it is actually stored to the date as seen by the user. The slashes are presented for our convenience, but they are not actually stored in the database.

Whenever dates are entered into date fields or date variables via any standard full-screen operation, the date is automatically validated. When an invalid date (for example, September 32) is entered, it will not be accepted. An error message will be displayed at the top right of the screen—the "scoreboard." To proceed further, the user must press the **Spacebar** to acknowledge the invalid entry and then enter a valid date.

Date Arithmetic

You can perform routine arithmetic operations with date variables. Subtracting one date from another gives you the number of days between the two dates. You can add a number to a date. The number is taken as a number of days, and the result is a new date. You can also subtract a number of days from a date, and again, the result is a new date.

Date1–Date2 = Number of days between Date1 and Date2
Date1 + N (days) = New Date1
Date1–N (days) = New Date1

Changing the Date

dBASE III PLUS makes no provision to change the computer's system date (or time). You can change the system date from within dBASE only if your computer has at least 320K of RAM. When this is the case, use the dBASE command **run** with the DOS shell command DATE:

run DATE

Fussing with the date is a nuisance. If your computer is to be used in the course of business, you should buy an expansion clock-calendar card. These cards, which usually have other useful features such as additional memory, have a small battery that will keep track of the time and date even when the computer is turned off. A computer should not be used in a business application unless it has a battery-operated clock calendar.

Date Functions

An array of functions has been provided to help you get the most mileage out of dates. The functions help you perform standard date operations, including the following:

- produce the current date
- extract the year from a date
- extract the month from a date
- extract the day of the month from a date
- extract the day of the week from a date
- produce the name of the month for a date
- produce the name of the day for a date
- transform dates to character strings and vice versa

The Current Date: date( )

The current date as set by your computer's system clock is available through the function **date( )**. Treated as a date data type by dBASE, this date normally occurs in the standard American format of mm/dd/yy, unless the format has been set to one of the alternate date formats with the **set date** command. Examples of the use of the **date( )** function are:

```
MDATE = date( )
NEXTDATE = date( ) + 7
? date( )
replace ORDERDATE with date( )
```

The Year Function: year(date)

The **year** function extracts the four-digit numeric value for the year (for example, 1986). Use this function for display purposes or for making calculations based on the year. Some examples of the use of the **year** function are:

```
? 'Equipment was purchased in', year(purchdate)
? 'Approximate age is', year(date( ) )– year(purchdate)
```

The Month Function: month(date)

Use the **month** function to obtain the numeric representation of the month for the specified date. This function is most useful in calculations and comparisons involving dates. Examples of the month function are shown below:

```
?   'Data are for month', month(date)
if month(date) = 4
? 'Income tax time'
endif
```

The Day Function: day(date)

The **day** function returns the number for the current day of the month. Again, the function is most valuable for calculations and comparisons involving dates. Examples of the **day** function are shown below:

```
? 'The day of the month', day(date( ))
DAY = day(date( ) )
```

Day of the Week Function: dow(date( ))

The **dow** function returns a one-digit number (1 through 7) which represents a day of the week. Sundays are represented by a 1, Mondays by a 2, and so on. This function is particularly useful in making calculations and comparisons. It is invaluable in scheduling and appointment-calendar programs. Examples of the **dow** function are shown below:

```
*   'weekdays are represented by the numbers 2 through 6'
if dow(date( )) = 1 .or. dow(date( )) = 7
?'This is a weekend'
endif
```

Name of the Day of the Week: cdow(date( ))

The **cdow** function return the name of the day of the week (e.g., Monday) for the date inside of the parentheses. This is useful for producing natural language displays. The following example illustrates the **cdow** function:

```
* the date is 10/23/86 (Tuesday)
? 'Today is a', cdow(date( ))
Today is a Tuesday
```

Name of the Month Function: cmonth(date( ))

The **cmonth** function is the companion of the **month** function. It produces the name of the month for the specified date (e.g., September). Examples of its use are:

```
?'The month is', cmonth(date( ))
?   "We haven't received payment on your account since", cmonth(date)
```

Transforming To and From a Date Variable

As was mentioned earlier, date data types are stored in the form yyyymmdd. To use these variables in conjunction with standard text strings we must convert from a date to a character date type. This is accomplished by the **dtoc** (date to character) function, which transforms a date to a character string of the form MM/DD/YY. To display the text string

```
Today is 03/15/85
```

use the **?** command with the **dtoc** function.

```
? 'Today is'+dtoc(date( ))
```

To transform a character sequence to a date data type, use the **ctod** (character to date) function. Use this function when creating a date variable from the keyboard or a program. To illustrate the creation of a blank date variable, use:

MDATE = ctod(" / / ")

Why do you have to do this? dBASE doesn't require that you declare variables. In most languages, you must declare (specify the type and size) each variable that is to be used in a program before you can use it. In dBASE the declaration is made informally whenever you store an item to the variable. dBASE makes certain reasonable assumptions about the data type based on the data being stored. Items enclosed in quotes are assumed to be character strings. Numbers not enclosed in quotes are assumed to be numbers. Dates are composed of numbers and (at least in the U.S.) the slash (/), which is also used to indicate division. If we don't put the date in quotes, it is indistinguishable from a legitimate arithmetic operation. If we do enclose the number in quotes, it can be a legitimate character sequence. The **ctod** function changes the character sequence into a date variable.

Out of This Century

There are many reasons for dealing with dates that fall out of this century. Historical records of events, births, and deaths may fall into earlier centuries. Financial records of loans, annuities, and insurance policies can fall into the next century. A 30-year home mortgage, for example, will be paid off in 2017.

dBASE, in its normal full-screen editing mode, treats dates as all belonging to the twentieth century. To work with dates from other centuries, use the command:

set century on

With the "century" set on, all dates will be displayed using a four-digit format for the year. To return to a two-digit year display, use:

set century off

Date Formats

dBASE normally works with dates in the American style of DD/MM/YY. Another special **set** command allows you to choose from among the following six date formats:

American	mm/dd/yy
ANSI	yy/mm/dd
British	dd/mm/yy
French	dd/mm/yy
German	dd.mm.yy
Italian	dd-mm-yy

To have dates displayed in the French manner, for example, use the following **set** command:

set date french

If you always want to work with dates in other than the American manner, include the **set date** command in the CONFIG.DB file. (See Appendix C.)

Comparing Dates

Dates are compared using the standard relational operators: $<\ >\ =\ \#$. The only problem you may encounter is comparing a date to a blank date. All comparisons involving blank dates are false. To test for "blankness," use the year, day, or month functions. For example, to determine if the variable DATE is empty (blank), use:

? year(DATE) = 0

A blank date will always return a 0 in conjunction with the year function. This is a reliable technique for determining that a date field or variable is empty.

Indexing on Dates

dBASE will allow you to index a date field directly. The only problem with this is that you must use a date variable in conjunction with either **find** or **seek**. For example, we can index a file on the DATE field named RCVD:

index on RCVD to R__DATE

To position to a particular date record, we can use the **seek** command with the **ctod** function.

seek ctod('12/25/85')

A more useful technique for indexing on DATE fields is to translate the date into a character string (Clipper™ calls this a **date to string** function). To index the date field RCVD, we use:

index on str(year(RCVD),4)+str(month(RCVD),2)+str(day(RCVD),2) to R__DATE

This provides us with the ability to search for the beginning of the year or month by incorporating only as much of the date as we need. Note that leading date zeros (09) must be represented by spaces in this expression. To find the first record in June, 1985 we can use

seek '1985 6'

This approach becomes even more valuable when we want to index on expressions such as CUSTID and DATE together. The string operation shown above can be concatenated with another character field and still maintain date order.

TIME

The time function **time( )** provides direct access to the time stored in your computer's system clock. This function returns the time in the form *hh:mm:ss*. The output of the function is a 24-hour clock (3 p.m. is displayed as 15:00:000). Because the time function output is a character data type, you can insert time directly into a character string. For example,

The time is now 11:45:15

can be produced by the command

? "The time is now", time( )

Arithmetic

dBASE does not offer time arithmetic. When it is necessary to work with the time, use substring operations to separate time into its separate parts (hours, minutes, and seconds). It is most convenient to convert time to seconds (the basic unit) first. To calculate the number of seconds since midnight, use

SECONDS = (val(substr(time( ),1,2)) * 3600) +;
               (val(substr(time( ),4,2)) * 60) + val(substr(time( ),7,2))

Once you have the number of seconds, you can calculate the number of minutes since midnight as

MINUTES = SECONDS/60

Finally, to determine the number of hours (e.g. 15.35), use

HOURS = SECONDS/3600

Figure 15-1 shows a procedure to calculate the time between 12:49:16 and 15:22:37 (3:22:37 p.m.).

```
TIME1    = '12:49:16'
TIME2    = '15:22:37'
SECONDS1 = (val(substr(TIME1,1,2)) * 3600) +;
           (val(substr(TIME1,4,2)) * 60) + val(substr(TIME1,7,2))
SECONDS2 = (val(substr(TIME2,1,2)) * 3600) +;
           (val(substr(TIME2,4,2)) * 60) + val(substr(TIME2,7,2))
DELTA    = SECONDS2 - SECONDS1
MINUTES  = INT(DELTA/60)
SECONDS  = DELTA - MINUTES * 60
HOURS    = INT(MINUTES/60)
MINUTES  = MINUTES - HOURS * 60
```

Figure 15-1: Procedure for calculating time.

Time in AM/PM

Let's assume that you want to display clock information on your screen. Furthermore, you want to display it in conventional 12-hour clock time (such as 2:45 p.m.). The program code shown in Figure 15–2 will convert the time character string to an am/pm character string:

```
do case
    case time()<'12'
      AMPM=time()+' am'
    case time()='12'
      AMPM=time()+' pm'
    case time()>'12'
      AMPM=str(val(time())-12,2)+right(time(),6)+' pm'
endcase
```

Figure 15–2: Code to convert time to am/pm.

CHAPTER SIXTEEN
Debugging and Special Effects

Debugging is the process of getting a program to work the way that you want it to work. Whatever your level of programming skill, debugging ranges from achieving the trivial to attempting the impossible. It is always frustrating.

There are two basic kinds of errors you can make when writing a program: mechanical errors and design errors. Of the two, mechanical errors are preferable. Usually the program won't "run" until you have found and fixed all mechanical errors. Design errors are insidious—your program will "run," but gives you the wrong result. Even worse is the case where you get an incorrect answer only part of the time.

MECHANICAL ERRORS

Examples of mechanical errors include misspelled commands, mistakes in the command structure, and non-allowed operations. The first two are usually called syntax errors. dBASE III PLUS will detect and partially diagnose most of the possible mechanical errors. It's up to you to complete the diagnosis and correct the error. This is called debugging.

Spelling a command incorrectly (dispay instead of display) provides a common example of a mechanical error. dBASE reacts to any error by halting your program's execution and displaying the following messages:

∗∗∗ Unrecognized command verb
Called from—C:menu23.prg
Called from—C:menu2.prg
Called from—C:menu.prg
Cancel, Ignore, or Suspend? (C, I, S)

dBASE neither aborts the program nor attempts to second-guess your error. It simply halts the program, provides you with an idea as to what's wrong, and offers you three options: cancel the program, ignore the error and continue, or suspend the program. You are provided with the name of the program which has failed. If the failure occurs in a procedure file, however, you are not informed as to which of the procedures has failed—the error message gives you only the name of the file. You must determine which procedure has failed.

Debugging such mechanical errors is a nuisance—a "time fine" we pay for being careless. Mechanical errors are easy to find. There are even computer programs that you can buy which will read your dBASE programs and provide you with a listing of all mechanical errors—misspelled commands, mismatched delimiters, mismatched

if/endifs, **do/enddo**s, **case/endcase**s, and so on. *dBASE Programmer's Utilities* from Ashton-Tate contains just such a program. More often, however, we have to do slightly more work to debug an error. Another common error is mismatched data types, as shown in the following example:

```
data type mismatch
                                   ?
display for ROOM = "6" .and. Grade = 5
   Called from—B:EXAMPLE1.PRG
   Called from—B:EXAMPLE.PRG
   Cancel, Ignore, or Suspend? (C, I, S)
```

In this example, one of the options was to suspend the program execution. If we select this option, everything is exactly as at the instant of failure, except that the command line containing the error has not been executed. All of the memory variables are as they were before this command line. Often, the status of a memory variable is not what we want it to be—the contents of variables could often provide us with clues as to where our errors lie.

While suspended, you can enter commands at the dot prompt level. This lets you explore your environment, examining files and memory variables, to help you track down your error. When you have finished exploring, you can return to the program with the command **resume** or terminate the program with the command **cancel**.

In the sample error above, it isn't quite so clear what's wrong. dBASE has told us which program the error is in. It has also told us that the error is to the left of the question mark placed above the command line. But we don't know which of the two data items (ROOM or GRADE) is mismatched. In this example we can track down (that is, debug) the problem with **display memory** or with the help of the **?** command and the **type( )** function.

The **type( )** function returns a letter indicating the data type of field or variable (C, D, N, or L) or a U if the variable does not exist.

```
?   type("ROOM"), type("GRADE")
   C C
```

Our test tells us that both fields exist and that both fields are character fields. The syntax used in the command for the contents of the GRADE field indicates a numeric field—there are no delimiters. Missing delimiters (or mismatched delimiters) are a common cause of syntax errors. We can "fix" this problem by putting delimiters around the 5 of GRADE.

Not all dBASE error messages provide as much help as the two examples above. For example, let's attempt to run the following section of dBASE III PLUS code:

```
select 1
use EXAMPLE
select 2
use EXAMPLE
```

dBASE does not allow you to open the same file in two work areas at once. If you try the above routine from a program, you will be told

Alias name already in use.
                    ?

use EXAMPLE
Called from C:test.prg.
Cancel, Ignore, or Suspend? (C, I, S)

and given a chance to escape from the program. This particular error demonstrates why you should close all unneeded files at the end of each program: you are not allowed to have a file open in two work areas simultaneously. Tracking down this error is relatively easy; you know exactly what to look for.

There are other mechanical errors that can also result in your being kicked out of the program and returned to the keyboard or even to the operating system. Some of these errors may not—at least not consistently—give you any clue at all as to what has happened. All you know is that the program didn't finish, and sometimes you might not even know that, if the program was designed to return to the keyboard and did not provide status displays.

One of the most common causes of bizarre computer behavior is forgetting the second half of a paired command: an **enddo**, an **endif**, or an **endcase**. When this happens, the logic of the program can become skewed, and these errors will rarely result in an error message that is helpful. When unexpectedly ejected from a program, verify that:

- each **if** has an **endif**.
- each **do while** has one **enddo**.
- each **do case** has one **endcase**.
- a procedure file does not contain a return.

Again, purchased error-checking programs can be a godsend when these errors occur. Finding where you have put a **do/endif** in a large program, when it's late and you're tired, isn't always easy.

DESIGN ERRORS

When you give dBASE III PLUS a series of perfectly valid commands with no mechanical errors involved and the program still does not produce the intended result, you have a design error. Let's look at the simple program in Figure 16–1. This is the skeleton of a program to print class rosters from a school database of STUDENTS, GRADE, ROOM, and so forth.

When we run this program, we get nothing: no class rosters—just a dot prompt. There are no mechanical errors. dBASE has done exactly what we told it to do. When dBASE finishes indexing, the database is positioned to the end-of-file record, and the end-of-file flag has been set. The **do while .not. EOF( )** statement does exactly what we told it to do, but there are no results because we gave it the wrong com-

```
use SCHOOL
index on GRADE + ROOM + NAME to ROSTER
set margin to 30
do while .not. eof()
     do HEADING
     CLASS = GRADE + ROOM
     display off NAME to print while CLASS = GRADE + ROOM
enddo
set margin to 0
```

Figure 16–1: Sample of a program with design error.

mands. In this case, adding the command **go top** before the **do while** command will solve the problem.

Debugging usually requires that you look at the program carefully and apply a bit of common sense. Most errors are simple and straightforward. When things get messier, there are a number of remedies that you can try.

THINGS TO TRY

Make your own diagnostic messages. In this case, you can add commands to display memory variables or a series of text strings on the screen, such as "reached point A." Modifying your program temporarily to include this special screen output is particularly advantageous when you are being ejected suddenly without notice.

The following technique can be used to monitor the content of an accumulator in a **do** loop. Suppose you are not getting the correct subtotals during a process. Presumably, the subtotal is to print at the end of a loop. You can monitor the process as it goes through the loop and locate where it goes wrong by displaying the accumulator content at every step.

Add a **suspend** command to suspend program execution temporarily, allowing you to examine the state of your database files and memory variables. When satisfied with the state of affairs, use the command **resume**.

Use the standard debugging tools which dBASE III PLUS provides in addition to the error messages and **suspend/resume**. The following commands can help track down your problem.

set step on
set echo on
set talk on
set debug on

Set echo on displays the program command lines on the monitor. **Set talk on** displays the dBASE III PLUS response to each command. **Set step on** allows you to step through your program one command line at a time. **Set debug on** routes the output to a printer when full-screen operations are encountered. These commands are most efficient for debugging when used together, because they allow you to view the operation of your program one command at a time. But if you attempt to carry the **step** process through a counting loop, the experience will be tedious. Remember, you can insert these items as command lines in your program during a debugging process.

One useful idea is to place the four commands in a procedure named DEGBUGON and the four counterparts in a procedure named DEBUGOFF. This adds a quick on/off debug capability to your program, which can also be used while in **suspend**.

Set debug on/off is provided to help you in debugging programs that have full-screen operations. **Set debug on** routes the normal output of **echo**, **talk**, and **step** to the printer instead of the screen and keeps the screen from becoming cluttered with the combination of "debugging" output and your program's normal screen display.

The Command History

Another dBASE tool to help you debug your programs is the command history. When using dBASE from the keyboard, you can move back to a previous command by pressing the **Up Arrow** key. Each time you press the key you "back up" one command in the keyboard command history. To view this command history, use the command:

display history

If you suspect that your program isn't branching properly (the response to an **if** statement isn't what you think it should be), use this procedure to examine the commands issued by your program.

The command history is normally limited to commands issued from the keyboard. You have to take special action to maintain a history of commands issued from a program. Use the command **set dohistory on/off** to turn program command logging on and off (it's normally off).

History normally records the last 20 commands. You can change this value with the **set history to** command to anything between 0 and 16,000. To set history so that you can record the last 50 commands, use:

set history to 50

The value of this command lies in testing how your program branches. Normally, you will have **dohistory** turned off, and you can read your program without bothering to run a history. The overhead isn't great, but recording history does make your program run slower, so don't use this feature unless you need it.

All in all, debugging is overrated. Most of your problems will be mechanical: typing errors, misspellings, and missing delimiters. These are easily found and can be checked by a large number of commercial programs.

Time spent in debugging can be greatly reduced by developing your programs a little at a time, using small modules. Try using a top-level program that looks something like

```
do PART1
do PART2
do PART3
do PART4
```

and so on. If you take this small-module approach and develop your program in stages, you are less likely to end up with a serious debugging problem. It isn't a bad idea to hold program modules to one screen, although this approach may initially cause your program to run a little slower since you will be opening and closing a number of program files. Once you have everything working, put it all back together into a single file, or assemble it into a single program with the help of the pseudo-compiler dBCODE and the linker dBLINKER.™

SPECIAL EFFECTS

Screen displays and printed reports are what others see as the product of our coding efforts. dBASE III PLUS does not as yet take advantage of any special characteristics or capabilities of your printer and only a few of the capabilities of your monitor. This is sure to change in the future.

You can gain control of special capabilities of the video monitor and your printer by using the **chr( )** function. This function is similar to the CHR$ function in BASIC. dBASE normally filters out any control characters (the non-printable ASCII characters) that we might try to enter into fields or memory variables. The **chr( )** function allows us to incorporate control characters into variables and to direct these central characters to the printer and/or the monitor.

The Printer

Today's printers have a large number of special features that can be used to enhance the appearance of your printed output. The appearance of the hardcopy will affect the way that clients or coworkers view your applications programs. The "slicker" the printed page appears, the more demand there will be for your services. Special printer controls can be invoked either by setting switches on the printer itself or by the use of special control codes that you can embed in your software. Most modern printers allow you to control:

- print density and weight (boldness)
- horizontal and vertical tabs
- page layout (left, right, top, and bottom margins)
- line spacing
- font selection and underlining
- color selection (for color printers)

Print Characteristics

Many printers allow you to select among a number of print characteristics, including such items as *pitch* and *weight*. Pitch is usually taken to mean the number of characters per inch (print density). Weight is the "darkness" of the print, which is usually done by overprinting each character a number of times.

These characteristics can be used to provide your printed output with more pizzazz— or they might be used to fit all of the items onto a page. To demonstrate how to control the printer from dBASE, we use an Epson® FX-85 as our example printer. The Epson FX-85 mode-selection techniques are similar to those of most other printers, but the specific command sequences will be different.

The FX-85 is normally set up to print in a single-strike mode at 10 characters per inch (in typewriter terminology called pica). You can send commands from your program to set the print size to one of the six Epson options shown in Figure 16–2.

Print Density	ASCII Sequence	dBASE III PLUS Code
Pica (10 cpi)	Esc P	Chr(27)+'P'
Elite (12 cpi)	Esc M	Chr(27)+'M'
Compressed (17 cpi)	SI	Chr(15)
Expanded (5 cpi)	SO	Chr(14)
Expanded Elite (6 cpi)	SO	Chr(14)
Expanded Compressed (8.5 cpi)	SO	Chr(14)

Figure 16–2: Print size controls for Epson FX-85.

The Epson printer manual, like other printer manuals, gives examples of printer control in BASIC. The BASIC command to set the printer to print in the *elite* mode is:

```
LPRINT CHR$(27);"M"
```

The equivalent dBASE command (assuming that you have **set print on**) is:

```
? chr(27)+'M'
```

The escape is a standard beginning sequence to alert a peripheral device that the data following is control information. The printer knows when the control characters end and your text begins. In the last example, to add the text "How are you," the command could read:

```
? chr(27)+'MHow are you'
```

or

```
? chr(27)+'M'+'How are you'
```

If the text to be printed is in a field or memory variable, you can combine the control with the field data as:

```
? chr(27)+'M'+FIELDNAME
```

The normal print-density commands need only be sent at the beginning of the print session. They stay in effect until you send a control sequence to select another print density or you turn the printer off. They need not be sent at the beginning of every line (see the manual for exceptions).

The print controls can also be sent using the @ . . . **say** command. For this to have an effect, you must have sent the command **set device to print.** The controls can be sent with the first line to be printed:

```
@ 5,10 say chr(27)+'M'+FIELDNAME
```

The following command sequence illustrates the use of the controls in printing from dBASE, by printing the letterhead for Bob's Better Books (shown in Figure 16–3). The letterhead is to be printed in elite with the company name expanded.

```
set device to print
set margin to 0
@ 5,18 say chr(27)+'M'+chr(14)+"Bob's Better Books"
@ 6,26 say '10150 W. Jefferson Boulevard'
@ 5,25 say 'Culver City, California 90230'
set device to screen
```

```
Bob's Better Books
10150 W. Jefferson Boulevard
Culver City, California  90230
```

Figure 16–3: Sample letterhead printout.

Other printing characteristics that you might want to invoke are underline, subscript, superscript, and italics. The dBASE control sequences for the Epson FX series of printers are shown below.

Print Characteristic	dBASE III PLUS Sequence
Underline On	Chr(27)+" –1"
Underline Off	Chr(27)+" –0"
Superscript On	Chr(27)+" S0"
Subscript On	Chr(27)+" S1"
Super/Subscripts Off	Chr(27)+" T"
Italics On	Chr(27)+" 4"
Italics Off	Chr(27)+" 5"

Figure 16–4: Print characteristic controls for Epson FX printers.

While these particular sequences are for the Epson FX series, most printers have similar features. The general approach to control is also similar from printer to printer. To gain a fuller understanding of the capabilities and control of a particular printer, refer to the printer's manual.

There are any number of additional capabilities offered by today's printers. Nearly all offer the capabilities described above as well as various tab and margin controls. Some printers offer extended graphics and line-drawing capabilities that you can invoke to print forms and charts. For a complete description of what your printer can do, consult your manual. Remember: The **chr( )** function is the key to using your printer's special capabilities.

It is important to remember that there may be control sequences that require sending an ASCII null character (^@ or **Chr(0))** to the printer. You cannot transmit this character from dBASE III PLUS. Because many computers and applications packages also cannot transmit a null character, most printer manufacturers offer an alternative control sequence. Again, consult your printer's manual.

Multiple Printers

You can make easy use of multiple printers. This can become particularly important if your application routinely uses a few different printed forms. Changing printer paper is a bother, and today's dot-matrix printers are inexpensive. There are any number of applications in which it is desirable to have two printers: one for a commonly-used form, the other for plain paper. Use the **set printer to** command to switch between printers, which must be connected to different printer ports on your computers. The **set printer to** command lets you switch between the ports lpt1, lpt2, lpt3, com1, and com2.

Suppose we have two printers on one computer. One is connected to the parallel printer port lpt1. The other is connected to the serial port com1. To switch printer output to the serial printer, use:

set printer to com1

To return to the printer on the parallel port, use:

set printer to lpt1

This capability is particularly convenient when you want to switch between a local printer and a network printer.

The Video Monitor

Your video monitor can produce some quite dazzling effects. You've seen a number of very nice screens on commercial software packages, and there is no reason at all why your screens cannot have the same professional appearance. As with the printer, the **chr( )** function is the key to many of these screen effects. However, dBASE III PLUS provides a number of set commands to control special screen characteristics. Some of the special effects you can control are:

- normal video
- reverse video
- intensity
- underlining
- blinking
- color
- line drawing
- graphics

The IBM PC video monitor system uses the extended ASCII code as shown in Appendix A. With the extended ASCII code, you can produce visual symbols for almost all values from 0 to 255. These additional symbols allow you to display words and their correct foreign-language symbols and to create special visual effects such as drawing lines, boxes, arrows, and so forth.

Color, Underlining, Blinking, and Intensity

The screen displays are a user's first introduction to your programs. You can make your displays far more interesting and attractive by the use of color or other features of the monitor. Color, underlining, blinking, and intensity are called *attributes*. The screen attributes of monochrome and color monitors are listed below.

Monochrome	Color
Underline	Color
Blinking	Blinking
Intensity	Intensity
Reverse video	Reverse video

Your monitor has 25 rows with 80 characters per row. That is a total of 2000 characters. Each character position uses two bytes, one for the character, the second for its attribute. The attribute byte has four characteristics: the background color of the character cell (the color of a blank space), the foreground color of the cell (the color of a nonblank character), the intensity of the foreground, and whether or not the foreground character blinks. This means that there are 8 background colors and 16 foreground colors. When dBASE writes to the screen, it writes both the character and an attribute. Attributes written by dBASE are controlled by the **set color** and **set intensity** commands.

As far as your program goes, the difference between monochrome and color monitors is in underlining and color. Color monitors allow you to select various color combinations but do not have an *underline* attribute. The same commands are used to control the monochrome monitor and the color monitor. It can be challenging to write a program that is attractive (or even visible) on both monitors. dBASE can detect which type of monitor is being used, which allows you to select attributes based on the monitor. This is done with the **iscolor** function, which returns TRUE if a "color" monitor is in use. A note of caution: The function also returns TRUE for most monochrome graphics cards—such as the ones used in the Compaq® computers. These cards display "color" as shades of green or amber, which defeats much of the value of the **iscolor** function. It remains a challenge to write programs which are attractive on all monitors. Probably the best option available is to provide your user with the ability to select color combinations.

The **set color to** command controls screen attributes for three conditions: standard characters, enhanced characters, and the border. Standard characters are used for the normal display of screen text in response to commands such as **?**, **list**, **display**, and so on. Enhanced characters are normally used for data-entry areas with **edit**, **change**, **browse**, and so on. The border is the unused area at the edge of the screen. You cannot set the border color with all color systems. The IBM EGA, for example, will not allow you to control the border color. The syntax of the **set color to** command is:

set color to standard,[enhanced],[border]

Both standard and enhanced have attribute pairs. The foreground attribute is specified first and is separated from the background attribute by a slash.

foreground/background

Attributes are different for color and for monochrome. If you are using attributes other than simple black and white, take care to test your choices on all three kinds of monitors.

The **set intensity** command is actually misnamed. This command does not control the intensity at all; it merely overrides the enhanced attribute selection and makes it the same as the standard selection. Intensity is controlled by adding a plus sign (+) to the foreground attribute. Blinking is selected by adding an asterisk (∗) to the foreground attribute. To return to the dBASE default attributes, use the **set color** command without a following argument:

set color to

The Color (Graphics) Monitor

Colors must be selected from the color codes shown in Figure 16-5.

The following command sets the screen display so that the screen background is blue with white letters. The enhanced areas will have a brown background with black letters, and the border is green. Note the blank space before the slash in the area to define the enhanced screen:

set color to W/B, /GR,G

Color	Letter Code
Black	N
Blue	B
Green	G
Cyan	BG
Blank	X
Red	R
Magenta	RB
Brown	GR
White	W

Figure 16–5: Color table.

To control the "brightness," or intensity, of the foreground color, add a plus sign (+) to the color code:

set color to W+/B, /GR,G

You cannot change the background intensity of a character—only the foreground. Incidentally, GR+ (high intensity brown) looks like yellow.

To cause an item to blink on and off, add an asterisk to the code for the foreground color. The example below shows the enhanced screen areas with blinking, high-intensity black letters on a brown background:

set color to W/B, + */GR

The Monochrome Monitor

The monochrome monitor allows underlining, blinking, brightness control, and reverse video. This is all that you have to work with. The only useful color definitions for monochrome monitors are **space** for black and **w** for white. The normal configuration is:

set color to w/ , /w

To set the underline attribute, use the letter U to specify the attribute. The following command allows you to use the underline instead of reverse video for screen editing:

set color to w/ ,u

Blinking and intensity controls are used in the same way for the monochrome monitor as for the color monitor.

General Comments

If you want to use color (or other attributes) in your programs, be sure to use the

iscolor function, and specify attributes for both kinds of monitors. Examine the effect of your color selections on a computer with a monochrome graphics monitor.

A useful trick with the color controls is to set the data-entry area foreground and background to the same color. This makes the data being entered invisible, which is important for entering passwords or other "secret" information. An onlooker cannot tell what characters have been entered by looking at the screen. To set both foreground and background to blue in the enhanced area, use:

set color to rg+/ ,b/b

Set Intensity and Delimiters

As was mentioned, the **set intensity** command does not affect the intensity, but overrides the reverse video (enhanced) attribute setting. "Intensity" is normally on. If you turn the "intensity" off, you will need some means of identifying the boundaries for data-entry areas. dBASE III PLUS does provide the ability to delineate data-entry areas by other than reverse (enhanced) video.

set delimiters on/off
set delimiters to "[ ]"

This command allows you to set off the data areas with colons or other characters such as brackets or quotes. **Set delimiters** is independent of reverse video. If you set delimiters on, the field areas will be automatically bracketed by colons, as shown below:

Enter the customer's name :

Ordinarily, the reverse video is an effective a way of identifying field areas. Unfortunately, on some color monitors it is difficult to read the first and last characters in a reversed block, due to the resolution of the monitor. When this is the case, it may be effective to use delimiters to set off the data-entry areas.

Line-Drawing Characters

Your menus and other displays can be made much more attractive by using the special graphics characters provided for line drawings. These characters are shown in Figure 16–6. There are two sets of line-drawing characters: the double line and the single line.

dBASE III PLUS provides the capability to draw boxes using either single or double lines with the @ x,y command.

To draw a single-line box from screen coordinates 5,11 to 13,45, use:

@ 5,11 to 13,45

To draw a double-line box from coordinates 7,9 to 20,75, use:

@ 7,9 to 20,75 double

Vertical Bar	Chr(186) ‖	Chr(179) │	
Horizontal Bar	Chr(205) =	Chr(196) –	
Top Left Corner	Chr(201) ╔	Chr(218) ┌	Chr(214) ╓	Chr(213) ╒
Top Rt Corner	Chr(187) ╗	Chr(191) ┐	Chr(183) ╖	Chr(184) ╕
Lower Lt Corner	Chr(200) ╚	Chr(192) └	Chr(211) ╙	Chr(212) ╘
Lower Rt Corner	Chr(188) ╝	Chr(217) ┘	Chr(190) ╜	Chr(189) ╛
Top Junction	Chr(203) ╦	Chr(194) ┬	Chr(210) ╥	Chr(209) ╤
Bottom Junction	Chr(202) ╩	Chr(193) ┴	Chr(208) ╨	Chr(207) ╧
Left Junction	Chr(204) ╠	Chr(195) ├	Chr(198) ╞	Chr(199) ╟
Right Junction	Chr(185) ╣	Chr(180) ┤	Chr(181) ╡	Chr(182) ╢
Center Junction	Chr(206) ╬	Chr(197) ┼	Chr(216) ╪	Chr(215) ╫

Figure 16–6: Characters for line drawing.

Special Screen Effects

The screens used in the sample programs for Bob's Better Books were kept simple to keep the screen display program code from overwhelming the content. It has become popular to use light-bar menus. These can be written in dBASE using variables and the @ . . . **say** and @ . . . **get** commands. Doing so, however, is satisfactory only on IBM Personal Computer AT® and faster computers. There are a number of very nice menu bar programs that can be purchased at a reasonable price. It just isn't worth the effort to do a bad job when you can buy a good one for just a few dollars.

Interesting screen effects, such as dimming the entire screen or changing the attributes of a part of the screen, can all be easily accomplished with the help of assembly-language programs to be called from dBASE III PLUS using the **load** and **call** commands. Again, there are a variety of programs to choose from. Examples include the *dBASE Programmer's Utilities* from Ashton-Tate and *Tom Rettig's Library* from Tom Rettig Associates.

An important side effect of these programs is the fact that cursor position and screen color settings in dBASE are unchanged when calls are made to outside programs.

THE KEYBOARD

Function Keys

The special function keys on your keyboard can have any number of uses. Use these keys for special effects, such as filling in today's date. You can store character sequences to any of these keys except for the **F1** key, which is reserved by dBASE III PLUS for Help.

The function keys come preset with dBASE III PLUS commands such as **edit** and **display**. Unless you will be assigning specific values to these keys, you should disable them by loading **chr(0)**—preventing a user from producing an unexpected result. When **chr(0)** has been loaded into a function key, pressing that key will have no effect. You can also store control codes and the extended ASCII graphics characters to the function keys. Examples of special code sequences in function keys are shown in Chapter Five and again in Chapter Ten.

To store a character sequence to a function key, use the **set function** command followed by the key number and the sequence to be stored. The example below stores the command **edit** to the function key **F2**. When **F2** is pressed, the **edit** command is issued.

set function 2 to "edit;"

The semicolon indicates a carriage return. If the semicolon is omitted, you must press **Return** for dBASE III PLUS to execute the command.

To store a date in a function key so that it can be used for entering into a date field, the date must be configured as a six-digit character sequence. For example, to store the date 10/31/87 to a function key which is to be used for entry into date variables, we would use:

set function 4 to "103187"

Do not load the slashes which separate the sections of the date. Load the key in exactly the manner that you would enter the data from the keyboard.

The Keyboard Buffer

You must have noticed that you can "type ahead" when entering data from the keyboard. This can occasionally cause a problem. dBASE normally grabs characters as fast as you enter them, but if it's busy doing a particular task, the characters are stored in a buffer (called the *typeahead buffer*) until they can be used. You can control the size of the buffer and clear its contents. To clear out the typeahead buffer, use the command:

clear typeahead

The size of the typeahead buffer is controlled by a special set command. You can choose any value between 0 and 32,000 characters (the normal value is 20). According to the manual, you change the buffer size only while **escape** is on. Although this is not necessarily true, it is safest to follow the manual if you are writing programs for other users. This means that you would use the following code sequence to change the size of the typeahead buffer:

```
set escape on
set typeahead to 2
set escape off
```

Typeahead buffer sizing is subjective. Personally, I would recommend that you leave it alone and clear the buffer just prior to each menu selection and just prior to each new data-entry screen.

CHAPTER SEVENTEEN

Programmer's Tools

RunTime,™ *compilers*, and *assembly code* are three important tools to help you develop programs for yourself or for sale to others. Each has a special place in the dBASE III PLUS development library. These tools reduce the size of your programs, protect your code, and speed up your programs. They can give your programs a more professional look and feel.

RUNTIME

There are really three pieces to RunTime: the pseudocompiler dBCODE, the dBASE linker dBLINKER, and the RunTime environment. Both dBCODE and dBLINKER are furnished with dBASE III PLUS and can be used with dBASE, without the RunTime environment. These two programs can do a lot for you and, if you're going to program in dBASE, you should become familiar with them—even if you never use RunTime itself.

The dBASE RunTime package dBRUN™ lets you run dBASE programs. RunTime is a special Ashton-Tate product that is exactly like dBASE, except that it has no interactive command mode—its only purpose is to run dBASE programs. The RunTime concept has been around since dBASE II. RunTime allows you to develop programs in dBASE, which are then coded and linked, using dBCODE and dBLINKER. The resulting program is then sold or distributed in a package that includes dBRUN—enabling the purchaser to run the program without having dBASE. dBRUN, by the way, is less expensive than dBASE itself. You can only run dBASE programs that have been coded with dBCODE from RunTime, although you can run both coded and uncoded files within dBASE.

An important side benefit of this technique is that few customers can edit your coded programs or get in and make "unauthorized" changes to your database files. This makes it unlikely that you'll get a call from a client, saying "Your program doesn't work anymore!" followed by "I didn't do anything."

The dBASE III PLUS Pseudocompiler dBCODE

dBCODE is a *pseudocompiler* that transforms your dBASE III PLUS programs into a special code that is easier for dBASE to read. It also removes blank spaces, comments, and unused lines. The coded program is smaller and slightly faster than your original dBASE program. dBCODE is called a pseudocompiler because the code that it generates can only be used within a dBASE environment—dBASE itself or dBASE RunTime.

When a program is encoded by either a pseudocompiler or a true compiler, the resulting program code is called *object code*. The code that the program was written in is called *source code*. If we write programs in dBASE, the dBASE programs are the source code.

To illustrate the use of the coder, we'll encode the library program MENUPROC (see Figure 17-1). dBCODE reads your dBASE III PLUS program (the source code) and creates a new program which is the encoded version of the source (the object code). To use dBCODE, you must rename the source program by changing its file extension from PRG to SRC, because dBCODE assigns the file extension PRG to the output program. The coder dBCODE is used from DOS.

```
C>rename MENUPROC.PRG MENUPROC.SRC

C>dbc MENUPROC


dBCODE  (2.05) MS-DOS/PC-DOS ***
COPYRIGHT (c) ASHTON-TATE 1984, 1985
AS AN UNPUBLISHED LICENSED PROPRIETARY WORK.
ALL RIGHTS RESERVED.
  Creating MENUPROC.prg ... Completed.
*** END RUN   dBCODE

C>dir MENUPROC.*

 Volume in drive C is PC-AT
 Directory of  C:\BOOK\PROGRAMS

MENUPROC SRC    12544  11-20-86   5:21p
MENUPROC BAK    12544  11-20-86   4:17p
MENUPROC PRG     5795  11-20-86   5:22p
         3 File(s)  22853632 bytes free

C>
```

Figure 17-1: Coding MENUPROC with dBCODE.

After coding, there are two versions of the program: the source program and the object program. The object program will be smaller than the original. In the above example, the source program had more than 12,000 bytes while the coded version had less than 6,000 bytes. There can be considerable variation in the percentage reduction from program to program. Those programs containing a lot of text material and string data will not reduce as much as those which consist only of commands. The average size reduction seems to be around 40 percent. The complete set of programs for Bob's Better Books uses about 87K of source code, while the encoded programs total about 48K.

You can encode several source programs at a time by providing dBCODE with a list of the files to be coded. This list can be a disk file. For example, let's assume we want to encode the programs MENU1, MENU2, . . . MENU5. Our first step is to create a list, which we'll call FILELIST.TXT. This file can be created with any word processor that will produce a straight ASCII file:

MENU1
MENU2
MENU3
MENU4
MENU5

If files to be coded have the file extension SRC, the extension need not be included. Since all output files have the extension PRG we cannot have source files with the same name but different extensions (permitted in uncoded dBASE). All of our source files will be renamed with the SRC file extension.

To encode the files whose names are listed in FILELIST we use the program dBCODE with the r option:

C> dBC –rFILELIST.TXT

Each program in the list will be separately coded. There will be an output program for each source program in the list.

The dBASE III PLUS Linker dBLINKER

The linker dBLINKER lets you assemble a set of programs, such as the 80-odd programs in Bob's Better Books, into a single dBASE III PLUS program. This eliminates a host of problems and can reduce, if not eliminate, our concern over the total number of open files. This is a truly important point: *By coding and linking programs, you can have more data files and indexes open at any given time.*

You can link only those programs which have been encoded by the dBCODE program. To make use of the linker, we need to give it the names of the object files to be linked, as well as the name of the composite program. The list of files is contained in a disk file, just as in the coding example above.

The highest-calling program must be the first program in the list, but the other files can be listed in any order. dBLINKER will assemble all of the listed files into a single disk file, which contains a table with the relative disk positions of each of the programs.

Do not include procedure files in the list. dBASE III PLUS and dBRUN III PLUS™ both assume procedure files to be separate disk files. If included in the linkage list, procedure files will be absorbed into the composite—increasing its size—but will not be of any use.

The list of files for the programs in Bob's Better Books, which we again call FILELIST, would look something like:

MENU
MENU3
MENU5
MENU4
MENU2

. . .

etc

To assemble these programs into a single program called BBBOOKS (for Bob's Better Books), we would use the dBLINKER program which, like dBCODE, is used from DOS.

C> dBLINKER –fBBBOOKS –rFILELIST

The –f option is used to name our output program, while the –r option provides the name of the file containing the list of files to be linked.

COMPILERS

There are a number of dBASE compilers on the market. These programs convert dBASE (or dBASE-like) source code into object code that, after linking, can be run directly from DOS. Compiled programs don't require either dBASE or dBRUN as an operating environment. The two best-known dBASE compilers are Nantucket's Clipper and WordTech's Quicksilver.™ Each has special features to attract programmers to the product.

Compiled programs are usually smaller than the combined size of dBASE plus the dBASE program code. Nearly all compiled programs will execute more quickly than interpretive dBASE code, even if it has been encoded with dBCODE. This extra speed can be used to give your programs a "snap" that makes them more salable than their pure dBASE counterparts. Compiler speed offers a host of advantages. First of all, a compiler can buy you years of experience—compiled code prepared by a beginner can execute as quickly as dBASE code written by an expert. It can also compensate for CPU speed. Compiled code running on an IBM PC will appear to be as fast or faster than the equivalent dBASE code running on an IBM Personal Computer AT.

There are normally some differences between the versions of the dBASE language offered by Ashton-Tate and those of the compiler vendors. In most cases there will be some commands and functions which are not found in the compiler language, while the compilers may offer features not found in dBASE itself. There may also be subtle differences in specific commands. If you jump into a compiler environment, you need to be forewarned that you may need to make some changes in your programs.

If you use a compiler, why have dBASE at all? The answer is simple. dBASE is the standard. Most of us develop the basic programs and routines in dBASE, with its rich interpretive environment and debugging facilities, and then transfer the nearly-complete program to the compiler. Most of the time, we make changes to the basic dBASE code to take advantage of some special features offered by the compiler.

Compiling

To demonstrate, let's compile the program Bob's Better Books using Nantucket's Clipper Compiler. To use Clipper to compile a set of programs, all you have to do is type **clipper** and the name of the highest program in the set. The compiler reads your programs and assembles its own list of programs to be included. Note that procedure files are included by the compiler.

```
C>clipper menu
The Clipper Compiler, Autumn '86
Copyright (c) 1985, 1986 Nantucket Corp., All Rights Reserved.

Compiling MENU.PRG
Compiling SETUP.PRG
line     19:   SET not recognized
set help off
        ^

Compiling MENUPROC.PRG
line    307:   rest of line ignored
           return to MASTER
                  ^

Compiling MENU7.PRG
Compiling SETUP7.PRG
Compiling MENU7X.PRG
2 errors detected
Code Pass 1
Code Pass 2
Code size 7392, Symbols 2032, Constants 3408

C>
```

Figure 17–2: Clipper's attempt to compile Bob's Better Books.

As you can see, the program did not compile. It was developed to demonstrate the commands and functions of dBASE III PLUS, not to work with any of the available compilers. But now look and see what Clipper has done for us. Even though it hasn't successfully compiled these programs, it's told us which programs have problems, and where the problems occur. It's a simple matter to go into the program and change it to be compatible with the compiler. There are other problems still to come (we've only been given the errors Clipper found directly)—syntax problems. This set of programs uses a variety of dBASE tricks that Clipper isn't expecting, for example, macro substitution in place of **do case** menu selection.

The process is quite similar when using the WordTech Quicksilver compiler, which is a little closer to standard dBASE and may require fewer modifications. The compile command for WordTech is:

C> DB3C –A MENU

The –A option tells **Quicksilver** to include all programs and subroutines called by the program. As you can see, operating the compilers is simple and straightforward.

Most of us will use one or more of the special features offered by the compilers. For example, both of these compilers offer user-defined functions (UDFs), which let us define additional functions. These UDFs are used in exactly the same way that standard functions are used. With time, most compiler users build libraries of special functions and subroutines that fall outside of standard dBASE. The more you use a compiler, the more your coding techniques will change to take advantage of the special features offered by the compiler.

Linking

The compiled program is an .OBJ (object) file. In this case, it is MENU.OBJ, which includes all of the dBASE III PLUS program (.PRG) files that make up Bob's Better Books. We still have one more step to take before we have an executable program: linking, which combines the .OBJ file with a standard library. The result of this process is an .EXE file, which can be executed directly from DOS.

There are a number of programs that can link a compiled program with a library. One of these is PLINK86 which is offered by Phoenix Software, Inc. A special version of PLINK86 is supplied with Clipper. WordTech supplies a linking program named DB3L. Another linking program, which just about everyone owns, is Microsoft's LINK.EXE, which comes with DOS.

To link the Clipper-compiled program MENU with the Clipper library CLIPPER.LIB, use:

C> PLINK86 FILE MENU

To link the Quicksilver-compiled program MENU with the Quicksilver-supplied libraries, use:

C> DB3L MENU

Wordtech offers an optional, additional step in the linking process to improve the execution speed of the final program code:

C> QS –L MENU

As you can see, the entire process of writing a dBASE III PLUS program, compiling the program into object code, and then linking the object code with the linking libraries is not at all difficult. If you can write the dBASE program, you can do the rest of it, which is entirely mechanical.

ASSEMBLY CODE

Assembly code is often the final solution to programming problems. You can use this tool with dBASE III PLUS—and the dBASE compilers—just as with other languages. Assembly language provides a way around operations that are too slow, awkward, or even impossible in dBASE. They also provide you with a way to achieve special effects in your programs. For example, with assembly, you could instantly change the color of all or part of a screen without disturbing the current display.

dBASE III PLUS provides you with three commands specifically designed to let you use certain assembly programs with dBASE. The assembly programs must be prepared according to specific rules, but they are usually simple, and writing these routines is not difficult, even for a beginner.

Commands related to the use of assembly programs are **load, call**, and **release**.

Load FILENAME

This command reads a specified assembly-language program into memory. You can load up to 16 assembly programs at a time, even though the dBASE manual specifies five. The command assumes a .BIN file type. Each assembly program can be as large as 32,000 bytes, which is a very big .BIN file indeed.

Call FILENAME with MEMVAR

This command activates a previously-loaded assembly program. The optional **with MEMVAR** is used to pass any needed parameters to the assembly program.

Release FILENAME

This command releases a previously-loaded assembly program.

Constructing an Assembly Program For dBASE III PLUS

To construct an assembly program that can be used with dBASE III PLUS, you have to follow some very simple rules. The following example (Figure 17–3) shows required boilerplate for assembly programs. This example is more detailed and complicated than necessary to allow its use with dBASE, Clipper, Quicksilver, and other packages.

While dBASE does not require you to label an assembly module as public, some other programs do, and one of the virtues of the code base is that it can be used nearly everywhere. The commented line **lds** lets you use your program with **Clipper** and a variety of other packages by simply removing the leading colon at assembly time. dBASE sets the **DS:BX** register to point to the beginning of a memory variable passed to the assembly program. Removing the colon causes the same effect for a program to be used with Clipper.

dBASE Constraints

dBASE imposes a limited number of constraints on assembly programs, but you will not find these to be an imposition.

```
        title     ** put a descriptive title here
        public    ** name of routine goes here
_prog   segment byte
        assume  cs:_prog
NAME    proc    far              ; NAME is the procedure name
        push    BP
        mov     BP,SP
        push    DS
        push    ES
        push    BX
;       lds     bx,[bp+6]        ;remove first ; for clipper

; ------------------------------------------------------------


;               body of program goes here


; ------------------------------------------------------------
        pop     BX
        pop     ES
        pop     DS
        pop     BP
        ret                      ; this is a FAR return
NAME    endp                     ; NAME is the procedure name
_prog   ends
        end
```

Figure 17–3: Basic assembly-language module.

- Exit from the assembly program with a **far return**.

- Restore the stack and code registers upon exiting.

- Do not use a program offset.

- Do not change the size of a memory variable used to pass data to or from the assembly module. The end of the dBASE variable is indicated by a binary zero.

- Do not allocate memory outside of the program boundary. dBASE doesn't read your program and hence cannot know of any memory-allocation scheme.

An Example Program

The dBASE III PLUS manual provides us with a simple example of an assembly-language program to be called from within dBASE. This program is designed to change the size and shape of a cursor. We'll change the program just a little, and explain what we're doing. Our version is shown as Figure 17–4.

First of all, we need to know a little bit about the cursor, which is made up of one character with lines. A monochrome monitor uses up to 14 lines (0–13) for the cursor, while a graphics monitor usually is limited to 8 lines (0–7). A normal cursor consists of the two lines at the bottom of the cursor position (6,7 for color and 12,13 for monochrome).

The cursor shape is changed by loading the starting line and ending line positions into the CH and CL registers, setting the AH register to 1, and using **interrupt** 10h. Setting CH to 32 will cause the cursor to disappear. Setting CL to a value less than CH will cause the cursor to wrap around inside the cursor block.

The program shown in Figure 17–4 expects to receive a dBASE memory variable which contains sufficient information to set the cursor. The first byte of the variable will contain the cursor starting line, and the optional second byte will contain the cursor ending line. The example in the dBASE III PLUS manual passes the single value 18 to the program. This will create a block cursor.

Pass parameters as character strings. If you want to pass numeric data, use the **chr** function.

```
        title    cursor control program
        public   cursor
_prog   segment byte
        assume   cs:_prog
cursor  proc     far             ; cursor is the procedure name
        push     BP
        mov      BP,SP
        push     DS
        push     ES
        push     BX
;       lds      bx,[bp+6]       ;remove first ; for clipper
; ----------------------------------------------------
                                 ;bx points to dbase memory var.
        mov      ch,[bx]         ;move byte 1 of memvar to ch reg.
        inc      bx              ;move pointer to byte 2 of memvar
        mov      cl,[bx]         ;move byte 2 of memvar to cl reg.
        mov      ah,1            ;set up to change cursor
        int      10h             ;video interrupt
; ----------------------------------------------------
        pop      BX
        pop      ES
        pop      DS
        pop      BP
        ret                      ; this is a FAR return
cursor  endp                     ; cursor is the procedure name
_prog   ends
        end
```

Figure 17–4: Assembly source code to change cursor shape.

Compiling Your Assembly Program

To compile the source code in Figure 17–4 into a program that can be used with dBASE III PLUS, we use the Microsoft Macro Assembler MASM.EXE, the Microsoft Linker (LINK.EXE), and the program EXE2BIN.

To compile the program, all you need to do is enter

C> MASM CURSOR

and then press the **Return** key four times. You now have an .OBJ file. Stop here if the program will be used with Clipper.

Next, link the program with

C> LINK CURSOR

and again press the **Return** key four times. You now have an .EXE file (don't try to run it from DOS).

Finally, convert the .EXE file to a .BIN file with

C> EXE2BIN CURSOR

and now you're ready to **load** and **call** this program from within dBASE.

Using Your Assembly Program

To use the program, we first have to **load** it:

load CURSOR

Once the program has been loaded into memory, we can call it as often as we like, without reloading. This example program requires that we pass parameters via a character string. There's no checking here—if you make a mistake, it's your problem. Assembly code offers a lot of power, but it lets you shoot yourself in the foot too.

call CURSOR with chr(6)+chr(7)

This will provide you with a two-line cursor at lines 6 and 7.

Parameters can be passed as either character strings or as memory variables. If you want the program to operate on your parameters and return something to you, pass the parameters as a memory variable. Remember, don't change the size of the variable.

BLOCK = chr(3)+chr(7)
call CURSOR with BLOCK

Don't mix character strings and memory variables.

Caution: If you will be using the **run** command or are using a text editor other than **modify command**, you need to set MAXMEM to a value that will keep your assembly modules from being overwritten. If they are overwritten and you attempt to call, the computer may hang. While you are learning to use assembly programs with dBASE, you may find yourself hung a good percentage of the time. Nevertheless, it is a good way to learn assembler. The results are well worth the effort.

It is interesting to note that all of your assembly operations are entirely independent of dBASE. You can change the screen colors or move the cursor from assembly; when dBASE picks up again, it will continue to use the colors that it had been using, and the cursor will be in the last dBASE cursor position.

OTHER PROGRAMMER'S TOOLS

There is a wide assortment of tools that you can buy to help you program in dBASE. Most of these are quite inexpensive. Ashton-Tate's products include the *dBASE Programmer's Utilities* and *dBASE Tools for C.*™ The *Programmer's Utilities* include a variety of assembly programs to save and restore screens, create special effects, prevent interlopers from using your data files, and give you five additional files from within dBASE. Also included in the package are programs to analyze your programs and a program to recover damaged database files, as well as a host of useful utilities. *dBASE Tools for C* offers a graphics library for use with dBASE and a package of useful statistical functions.

There are many others which you may find of particular interest. Tom Rettig, coauthor of the *Advanced Programmer's Guide* from Ashton-Tate, has his own package: *Tom Rettig's Library*. Luis Castro, another coauthor of the *Advanced Programmer's Guide*, offers a package to help with program generation and screen design: *ViewGen*. George Rothbart, of the Research Group, has a popular screen-generating package called *SayWhat?!*. There's no shortage of valuable support products, far too many to cover in this brief discussion. Purchasing utilities is a terrific trade-off of time and money—it's a rare set of utilities that are cheaper to build than buy.

APPENDIX A
ASCII Table

Binary	Hex	Decimal	Character	Code	Symbol	Description
0000000	00	0		^@	NUL	Null
0000001	01	1	☺	^A	SOH	Start of Heading
0000010	02	2	☻	^B	STX	Start of Text
0000011	03	3	♥	^C	ETX	End of Text
0000100	04	4	♦	^D	EOT	End of Transmission
0000101	05	5	♣	^E	ENQ	Enquiry
0000110	06	6	♠	^F	ACK	Acknowledge
0000111	07	7	•	^G	BEL	Bell
0001000	08	8	◘	^H	BS	Backspace
0001001	09	9	○	^I	SH	Horizontal Tabulation
0001010	0A	10	◙	^J	LF	Line Feed
0001011	0B	11	♂	^K	VT	Vertical Tabulation
0001100	0C	12	♀	^L	FF	Form Feed
0001101	0D	13	♪	^M	CR	Carriage Return
0001110	0E	14	♫	^N	SO	Shift Out
0001111	0F	15	✳	^O	SI	Shift In
0010000	10	16	►	^P	DLE	Data Link Escape
0010001	11	17	◄	^Q	DC1	Device Control 1
0010010	12	18	↕	^R	DC2	Device Control 2
0010011	13	19	‼	^S	DC3	Device Control 3
0010100	14	20	¶	^T	DC4	Device Control 4
0010101	15	21	§	^U	NAK	Negative Acknowledge
0010110	16	22	▬	^V	SYN	Synchronous Idle
0010111	17	23	↨	^W	ETB	End of Transmission Block
0011000	18	24	↑	^X	CAN	Cancel
0011001	19	25	↓	^Y	EM	End of Medium
0011010	1A	26	→	^Z	SUB	Substitute
0011011	1B	27	←	^[	ESC	Escape
0111000	1C	28	∟	^\	FS	File Separator
0011101	1D	29	↔	^]	GS	Group Separator
0011110	1E	30	▲	^^	RS	Record Separator
0011111	1F	31	▼	^_	US	Unit Separator
0100000	20	32				

Binary	Hex	Decimal	Character	Binary	Hex	Decimal	Character
0100001	21	33	!	1000011	43	67	C
0100010	22	34	"	1000100	44	68	D
0100011	23	35	#	1000101	45	69	E
0100100	24	36	$	1000110	46	70	F
0100101	25	37	%	1000111	47	71	G
0100110	26	38	&	1001000	48	72	H
0100111	27	39	'	1001001	49	73	I
0101000	28	40	(	1001010	4A	74	J
0101001	29	41	)	1001011	4B	75	K
0101010	2A	42	*	1001100	4C	76	L
0101011	2B	43	+	1001101	4D	77	M
0101100	2C	44	,	1001110	4E	78	N
0101101	2D	45	−	1001111	4F	79	O
0101110	2E	46	.	1010000	50	80	P
0101111	2F	47	/	1010001	51	81	Q
0110000	30	48	0	1010010	52	82	R
0110001	31	49	1	1010011	53	83	S
0110010	32	50	2	1010100	54	84	T
0110011	33	51	3	1010101	55	85	U
0110100	34	52	4	1010110	56	86	V
0110101	35	53	5	1010111	57	87	W
0110110	36	54	6	1011000	58	88	X
0110111	37	55	7	1011001	59	89	Y
0111000	38	56	8	1011010	5A	90	Z
0111001	39	57	9	1011011	5B	91	[
0111010	3A	58	:	1011100	5C	92	\
0111011	3B	59	;	1011101	5D	93	]
0111100	3C	60	<	1011110	5E	94	^
0111101	3D	61	=	1011111	5F	95	−
0111110	3E	62	>	1100000	60	96	`
0111111	3F	63	?	1100001	61	97	a
1000000	40	64	@	1100010	62	98	b
1000001	41	65	A	1100011	63	99	c
1000010	42	66	B	1100100	64	100	d

Binary	Hex	Decimal	Character	Binary	Hex	Decimal	Character
1100101	65	101	e	0000011	83	131	â
1100110	66	102	f	0000100	84	132	ä
1100111	67	103	g	0000101	85	133	à
1101000	68	104	h	0000110	86	134	å
1101001	69	105	i	0000111	87	135	ç
1101010	6A	106	j	0001000	88	136	ê
1101011	6B	107	k	0001001	89	137	ë
1101100	6C	108	l	0001010	8A	138	è
1101101	6D	109	m	0001011	8B	139	ï
1101110	6E	110	n	0001100	8C	140	î
1101111	6F	111	o	0001101	8D	141	ì
1110000	70	112	p	0001110	8E	142	Ä
1110001	71	113	q	0001111	8F	143	Å
1110010	72	114	r	0010000	90	144	É
1110011	73	115	s	0010001	91	145	æ
1110100	74	116	t	0010010	92	146	Æ
1110101	75	117	u	0010011	93	147	ô
1110110	76	118	v	0010100	94	148	ö
1110111	77	119	w	0010101	95	149	ò
1111000	78	120	x	0010110	96	150	û
1111001	79	121	y	0010111	97	151	ù
1111010	7A	122	z	0011000	98	152	ÿ
1111011	7B	123	{	0011001	99	153	ö
1111100	7C	124	¦	0011010	9A	154	ü
1111101	7D	125	}	0011011	9B	155	¢
1111110	7E	126	~	0011100	9C	156	£
1111111	7F	127	△	0011101	9D	157	¥
0000000	80	128	Ç	0011110	9E	158	℞
0000001	81	129	ü	0011111	9F	159	ƒ
0000010	82	130	é	0100000	A0	160	á

Binary	Hex	Decimal	Character	Binary	Hex	Decimal	Character
0100001	A1	161	í	0111111	BF	191	┐
0100010	A2	162	ó	1000000	C0	192	└
0100011	A3	163	ú	1000001	C1	193	┴
0100100	A4	164	ñ	1000010	C2	194	┬
0100101	A5	165	Ñ	1000011	C3	195	├
0100110	A6	166	ª	1000100	C4	196	─
0100111	A7	167	º	1000101	C5	197	┼
0101000	A8	168	¿	1000110	C6	198	╞
0101001	A9	169	⌐	1000111	C7	199	╟
0101010	AA	170	¬	1001000	C8	200	╚
0101011	AB	171	½	1001001	C9	201	╔
0101100	AC	172	¼	1001010	CA	202	╩
0101101	AD	173	¡	1001011	CB	203	╦
0101110	AE	174	«	1001100	CC	204	╠
0101111	AF	175	»	1001101	CD	205	=
0110000	B0	176	░	1001110	CE	206	╬
0110001	B1	177	▒	1001111	CF	207	╧
0110010	B2	178	▓	1010000	D0	208	╨
0110011	B3	179	│	1010001	D1	209	╤
0110100	B4	180	┤	1010010	D2	210	╥
0110101	B5	181	╡	1010011	D3	211	╙
0110110	B6	182	╢	1010100	D4	212	╘
0110111	B7	183	╖	1010101	D5	213	╒
0111000	B8	184	╕	1010110	D6	214	╓
0111001	B9	185	╣	1010111	D7	215	╫
0111010	BA	186	║	1011000	D8	216	╪
0111011	BB	187	╗	1011001	D9	217	┘
0111100	BC	188	╝	1011010	DA	218	┌
0111101	BD	189	╜	1011011	DB	219	█
0111110	BE	190	╛	1011100	DC	220	▄

Binary	Hex	Decimal	Character
1011101	DD	221	▌
1011110	DE	222	▐
1011111	DF	223	▪
1100000	E0	224	α
1100001	E1	225	β
1100010	E2	226	Γ
1100011	E3	227	π
1100100	E4	228	Σ
1100101	E5	229	σ
1100110	E6	230	μ
1100111	E7	231	τ
1101000	E8	232	Φ
1101001	E9	233	θ
1101010	EA	234	Ω
1101011	EB	235	δ
1101100	EC	236	∞
1101101	ED	237	φ
1101110	EE	238	ε
1101111	EF	239	∩
1110000	F0	240	≡
1110001	F1	241	±
1110010	F2	242	≥
1110011	F3	243	≤
1110100	F4	244	⌠
1110101	F5	245	⌡
1110110	F6	246	÷
1110111	F7	247	≈
1111000	F8	248	°
1111001	F9	249	·
1111010	FA	250	·
1111011	FB	251	√
1111100	FC	252	ⁿ
1111101	FD	253	²
1111110	FE	254	■
1111111	FF	255	

APPENDIX B
Commands and Functions

SYNTAX OF COMMANDS

? <exp list>

?? <exp list>

@ <row, col> [SAY <exp> [PICTURE <clause>]] [GET <variable>
[PICTURE <clause>] [RANGE <expN>,<expN>]]/[CLEAR]

@ <row1, col1> [CLEAR] TO <row2, col2> [DOUBLE]

ACCEPT [<prompt>] TO <memvar>

APPEND [BLANK]

APPEND FROM <filename> [FOR <condition>] [TYPE] [<file type>]

ASSIST

AVERAGE <exp list> [<scope>] [WHILE <condition>] [FOR <condition>]
[TO <memvar list>]

BROWSE [FIELDS <field list>] [LOCK <expN>] [FREEZE <field>] [NOFOLLOW]
[NOMENU] [WIDTH <expN>] [NOAPPEND]

CALL <module name> [WITH <expC>/<memvar>]

CANCEL

CHANGE [<scope>] [FIELDS <field list>] [WHILE <condition>]
[FOR <condition>]

CLEAR

CLEAR ALL

CLEAR FIELDS

CLEAR GETS

CLEAR MEMORY

CLEAR TYPEAHEAD

CLOSE ALL/ALTERNATE/DATABASES/FORMAT/INDEX/PROCEDURE

CONTINUE

COPY FILE <filename> TO <filename>

COPY STRUCTURE TO <filename> [FIELDS <field list>]

COPY TO <filename> [<scope>] [WHILE <condition>] [FIELDS <field list>]
[FOR <condition>] [TYPE] [<file type>]

COPY TO <new file> STRUCTURE EXTENDED

COUNT [<scope>] [WHILE <condition>] [FOR <condition>] [TO <memvar>]

CREATE <.dbf filename>

CREATE <new file> FROM <structure extended file>

CREATE LABEL <.lbl filename>/?

CREATE QUERY <.qry filename>/?

CREATE REPORT <.frm filename>/?

CREATE SCREEN <.scr filename>/?

CREATE VIEW <.vue filename>/?

CREATE VIEW <.vue filename> FROM ENVIRONMENT

DELETE [<scope>] [WHILE <condition>] [FOR <condition>]

DIR [<drive:>] [<path> \] [<skeleton>]

DISPLAY [<scope>] [<exp list>] [WHILE <condition>] [FOR <condition>]
[OFF] [TO PRINT]

DISPLAY HISTORY [LAST <expN>] [TO PRINT]

DISPLAY MEMORY [TO PRINT]

DISPLAY STATUS [TO PRINT]

DISPLAY STRUCTURE [TO PRINT]

DO <.prg filename>/<procedure name> [WITH <parameter list>]

DO CASE . . . CASE . . . [OTHERWISE] . . . ENDCASE

DO WHILE . . . <commands> . . . ENDDO

EDIT [<scope>] [FIELDS <list>] [WHILE <condition>] [FOR <condition>]

EJECT

ERASE <filename>/?

EXIT

EXPORT TO <filename> TYPE PFS

FIND <character string>/<n>

GO or GOTO BOTTOM/TOP or <expN>

HELP [<keyword>]

IF . . . [ELSE] . . . ENDIF

IMPORT FROM <filename> TYPE PFS

INDEX ON <keyexp> TO <.ndx filename> [UNIQUE]

INPUT [<prompt>] TO <memvar>

INSERT [BLANK] [BEFORE]

JOIN WITH <alias> TO <new file> FOR <condition> [FIELDS <field list>]

LABEL FORM <.lbl filename>/? [<scope>] [SAMPLE] [WHILE <condition>]
[FOR <condition>] [TO PRINT] [TO FILE <filename>]

LIST [OFF] [<scope>] [<exp list>] [WHILE <condition>] [FOR <condition>]
[TO PRINT]

LIST HISTORY [LAST <expN>] [TO PRINT]

LIST MEMORY [TO PRINT]

LIST STATUS [TO PRINT]

LIST STRUCTURE [TO PRINT]

LOAD <binary filename>[.<extension>]

LOCATE [<scope>] [WHILE <condition>] [FOR <condition>]

LOOP

MODIFY COMMAND <filename>

MODIFY LABEL <.lbl filename>/?

MODIFY QUERY <.qry filename>/?

MODIFY REPORT <.frm filename>/?

MODIFY SCREEN <.scr filename>/?

MODIFY STRUCTURE

MODIFY VIEW <.vue filename>/?

NOTE/* <undelimited character string>

ON ERROR/ESCAPE/KEY <dBASE command>

PACK

PARAMETERS

PRIVATE [ALL[LIKE/EXCEPT <skeleton>]]/[<memory variable list>]

PROCEDURE < procedure name>

PUBLIC < memory variable list>

QUIT

READ [SAVE]

RECALL [< scope>] [WHILE < condition>] [FOR < condition>]

REINDEX

RELEASE < memvar list> [ALL[LIKE/EXCEPT < skeleton>]]
[MODULE < module name>]

RENAME < current filename> TO < new filename>

REPLACE [< scope>] < field> WITH < exp> [, < field2> WITH < exp2>, . . .]
[WHILE < condition>] [FOR < condition>]

REPORT FORM < .frm filename>/? [< scope>] [WHILE < condition>]
[FOR < condition>] [PLAIN] [HEADING < expC>] [NOEJECT] [TO PRINT]
[TO FILE < filename>] [SUMMARY]

RESTORE FROM < .mem filename> [ADDITIVE]

RESUME

RETRY

RETURN [TO MASTER]

RUN < command>

SAVE TO < .mem filename> [ALL LIKE/EXCEPT < skeleton>]

SEEK < expression>

SELECT < work area/alias>/?

SET

SET ALTERNATE on/OFF

SET ALTERNATE TO [< filename>]

SET BELL ON/off

SET CARRY on/OFF

SET CATALOG ON/off

SET CATALOG TO [< .cat filename>/?]

SET CENTURY on/OFF

SET COLOR ON/OFF

SET COLOR TO [< standard> [, < enhanced>] [, < border>] [, < background>]]

SET CONFIRM on/OFF

SET CONSOLE ON/off

SET DATE AMERICAN/ANSI/BRITISH/ITALIAN/FRENCH/GERMAN

SET DEBUG on/OFF

SET DECIMALS TO <expN>

SET DEFAULT TO <drive>

SET DELETED on/OFF

SET DELIMITERS on/OFF

SET DELIMITERS TO [<character string>] [DEFAULT]

SET DEVICE TO SCREEN/print

SET DOHISTORY on/OFF

SET ECHO on/OFF

SET ESCAPE ON/off

SET EXACT on/OFF

SET FIELDS on/OFF

SET FIELDS TO [<field list> ALL]

SET FILTER TO [FILE <.qry filename>/?] [<condition>]

SET FIXED on/OFF

SET FORMAT TO [<.fmt filename>/?]

SET FUNCTION <exp> TO <exp C>

SET HEADING ON/off

SET HELP ON/off

SET HISTORY ON/off

SET HISTORY TO <expN>

SET INDEX TO [<.ndx file list>/?]

SET INTENSITY ON/off

SET MARGIN TO <expN>

SET MEMOWIDTH TO <expN>

SET MENUS ON/off

SET MESSAGE TO <cstring>

SET ORDER TO [<expN>]

SET PATH TO [<path list>]

SET PRINT on/OFF

SET PRINTER TO <DOS device>

SET PROCEDURE TO [<procedure filename>]

SET RELATION TO [<key>/RECNO( )/<expN> INTO <alias>]

SET SAFETY ON/off

SET STATUS ON/off

SET STEP on/OFF

SET TALK ON/off

SET TITLE ON/off

SET TYPEAHEAD TO <expN>

SET UNIQUE on/OFF

SET VIEW TO <.vue filename>/?

SKIP <expN>

SORT TO <new filename> ON <field> [/A] [/C][/D] [,<field2> [/A] [/C]
[/D] . . .] [<scope>] [WHILE <condition>] [FOR <condition>]

STORE <exp> TO <memvar list> [,<memvar list>]

SUM [<scope>] [<exp list>] TO [<memvar list>] [WHILE <condition>]
[FOR <condition>]

SUSPEND

TEXT . . . ENDTEXT

TOTAL ON <filename> TO <key> [<scope>] [FIELDS <field list>]
[WHILE <condition>] [FOR <condition>]

TYPE <filename> [TO PRINT]

UPDATE ON <key field> FROM <alias> REPLACE <field> WITH <exp>
[,<field2> WITH <exp2> . . .] [RANDOM]

USE [<.dbf filename>/?] [INDEX <.ndx file list>] [ALIAS <alias>]

WAIT [<prompt>] [TO <memvar>]

ZAP

FUNCTIONS

Function Name	Function Description	Output Data Type	Input Data Type
&	Macro Substitution	C,D,L,N	C
ABS	Absolute Value	N	N
ASC	Character to ASCII Code Conversion	N	C
AT	Substring Search	C	C
BOF	Beginning-of-File	L	*
CDOW	Day of Week	C	D
CHR	ASCII Code to Character Conversion	C	N
CMONTH	Calendar Month	C	D
COL	Current Screen Column Position	N	*
CTOD	Character to Date Conversion	D	C
DATE	System Date	D	*
DAY	Day of Month	N	D
DBF	Name of Database File in USE	C	*
DELETED	Deleted Record	L	*
DISKSPACE	Free Space (Bytes) on Disk	N	*
DOW	Day of Week	N	D
DTOC	Date to Character Conversion	C	D
EOF	End-of-File	L	*
ERROR	Number for ON ERROR Condition	N	*
EXP	Exponential (ex)	N	N
FIELD	Names of Fields in Database File	C	N
FILE	File Existence	L	C
FKLABEL	Names of Function Keys	C	N
FKMAX	Maximum No. of Function Keys	N	*
FOUND	Result of Database File Search	L	*
GETENV	Operating System Environmental Variables	C	C
IIF	One Expression or Another	C,D,N	C,D,N
INKEY	Keypress during Program Execution	N	C
INT	Integer	N	N
ISALPHA	Evaluate for Letter	L	C
ISCOLOR	Evaluate for Color Mode	L	*
ISLOWER	Evaluate for Lowercase	L	C
ISUPPER	Evaluate for Uppercase	L	C
LEFT	Substring Selection from Left Side	C	C
LEN	Length of Character String	N	C
LOG	Logarithm	N	N

An * indicates that the input data type is not applicable.

Function Name	Function Description	Output Data Type	Input Data Type
LOWER	Upper to Lowercase Conversion	C	C
LTRIM	Remove Leading Blanks	C	C
LUPDATE	Last Update of Database File	D	*
MAX	Determine Greater of Two Values	N	N
MESSAGE	ON ERROR Message String	C	*
MIN	Determine Smaller of Two Values	N	N
MOD	Modulus	N	N
MONTH	Month of Year	N	D
NDX	Names of Open Index Files	C	N
OS	Name of Operating System	C	*
PCOL	Printer Column Position	N	*
PROW	Printer Row Position	N	*
READKEY	Determine Full-Screen Exiting Keypress	N	*
RECCOUNT	No. of Records in Database File	N	*
RECNO	Current Record Number	N	*
RECSIZE	Size of Record	N	*
REPLICATE	Repeat Character Expression	C	C
RIGHT	Substring Selection from Right Side	C	C
ROUND	Rounds Off	N	N
ROW	Current Screen Row Position	N	*
RTRIM	Remove Trailing Blanks	C	C
SPACE	Generates Blank Spaces	C	N
SQRT	Square Root	N	N
STR	Numeric to Character Conversion	C	N
STUFF	Replace Portion of String	C	C
SUBSTR	Substring Selection	C	C
TIME	System Time	C	*
TRANSFORM	Character/Number in PICTURE Format	C	C,N
TRIM	Remove Trailing Blanks	C	C
TYPE	Validates Expression	C	C
UPPER	Lower to Uppercase Conversion	C	C
VAL	Character to Numeric Conversion	N	C
VERSION	dBASE III PLUS Number	C	*
YEAR	Year	N	D

An * indicates that the input data type is not applicable.

Customizing dBASE III PLUS With CONFIG.DB

The configuration file CONFIG.DB is used to customize dBASE to suit your own taste and needs. CONFIG.DB must be located on the same disk and directory as DBASE.OVL, the overlay file. The file can be used to establish your own default values for most of the set commands and the function keys, as well as some processing parameters that cannot be set within dBASE.

To illustrate the use of this file, the following example configuration file accomplishes part of the configuration control established by the setup program SETUP.PRG (see Chapter Four).

```
bell = off
escape = off
device = screen
F2 = chr(0)
F3 = chr(0)
F4 = chr(0)
F5 = chr(0)
F6 = chr(0)
F7 = chr(0)
F8 = chr(0)
F9 = chr(0)
F10 = chr(0)
help = off
margin = 10
menu = on
safety = off
talk = off
PROMPT = $
WP = WP.EXE
TEDIT = WS.COM
command = do MENU
```

The **set** commands are issued with an equation using the command's keyword and the desired setting. **Set talk off** becomes **talk = off** in the configuration file. The function key *set* commands *set function n to setting* become **F***n* = *setting*.

You can issue *one* dBASE III PLUS command from within CONFIG.DB. In the sample, the program system developed in this book is brought up automatically by issuing the command **do MENU** from within the configuration file. If more than one *command* is issued, only the last command is actually executed.

The configuration file allows you to set seven processing parameters that cannot be set at all from within dBASE. These are BUCKET, GETS, MAXMEM, MVARSIZ, PROMPT, TEDIT, and WP. The sample program makes use of the last three of these special setup controls.

PROMPT allows you to substitute a prompt of your own choosing for the dot prompt normally used by dBASE. The prompt is not to be enclosed by delimiters. If you create or edit the configuration file with WordStar,® or any other word processor that allows you to enter control characters into the text, you can use a prompt that is not one of the keyboard characters. For example, you can use a heart, or a happy face, or any other exotic character that is available from the extended ASCII set. If you edit the file with WordStar, place the cursor on the character position occupied by the dollar sign in the above example configuration file—then press **Ctrl-P** followed by **Ctrl-C.** This will give you a heart as the dBASE prompt. In your WordStar file, the result of this operation will be ^C.

WP allows you to substitute an external word-processing program for the internal word processor that is normally used to edit **memo** fields. In this example, we have substituted the editor WordPerfect® for the internal dBASE editor to edit memo fields. The easy way to find out if your favorite editor will work with dBASE is to try it.

TEDIT allows you to substitute an external word processor for the internal word processor used for **modify command**. In this example we have substituted Word-Star for the internal dBASE editor. If you use another editor, you should follow whatever installation procedure—or usage control as necessary—to ensure that it is used in the correct mode. The **modify command** processor *must* be set to edit standard ASCII files. In WordStar this means that it *must* be set to automatically edit in the *non-document* mode.

BUCKET controls the number of 1K blocks of memory dedicated to handling the **picture** and **range** options for **get** commands. The normal memory allocation for these options is 2K. If you have trouble with **picture** and **range**, increase the memory allocation (up to 31K). To set the memory allocation to 4K, use:

BUCKET = 4

GETS limits the number of active GETS. An active GET is one which may be accessed by a **read** command. Normally, the number of active GETS is limited to 128. To increase this number to 217, use:

GETS = 217

MAXMEM controls the amount of memory retained by dBASE when calling another program with the **run** command. The normal memory retained is 256K. Increase

MAXMEM when using more than the normal amount of memory with either BUCKET, GETS, or MVARSIZ.

MVARSIZ controls the amount of memory allocated to dBASE memory variables. The default allocation is 6K. You can increase this allocation to 31K. The additional memory is above and beyond the 256K normally required by dBASE. If you do use added memory and you want to use the **run** command, change the memory retention with MAXMEM.

APPENDIX D
Complete Procedure File

```
* menuproc.prg    procedure file for menu system   1/15/85
* banner    - prints screen heading
* choice    - select menu option
* dupechk   - test for duplicate records called from findcust
* errormsg  - print error message and ring the bell
* findcust  - search for correct customer - handles duplicates
* findisbn  - search for isbn number
* findrec   - search for invoice or backorder record
* getrec    - search for salesorder or invoice
* getdisk   - get next backup disk
* h_size    - find header size in bytes
* inkey     - read next key pressed
* isbntest  - validate an isbn number
* nextfile  - get next file name from file dictionary
* page      - print page number
* qtyedit   - edit qty delivered in order fulfillment
* query     - answer yes/no question
* replcate  - replicate n characters on a line
* rowcheck  - rolls screen up at page bottom
* search    - binary search routine
* spacerem  - space remaining on a disk

procedure BANNER
   parameter BANNER
   @ 2,2
   @ 2,2  say cdow(date())
   @ 2,(80-len(BANNER))/2 say BANNER
   @ 2,78 - len(CDATE) say CDATE
   @ 3,1  say BAR
return

procedure CHOICE
   parameters COL, RANGE
   CHOICE = ' '
   ROW = row()
   do while .not. CHOICE $ RANGE
     @ ROW,COL get CHOICE
     read
   enddo
return
```

```
procedure DUPECHK
   skip
   DUPERECS  = (NAME = trim(MNAME))
   MCUSTID = space(6)
   skip -1
   if DUPERECS
      do while NAME = trim(MNAME) .and. readkey() # 12 .and. MCUSTID = space(6)
         clear
         ? 'There are multiple records for '+MNAME
         display off next 15 CUSTID,NAME,ADDRESS while NAME = trim(MNAME)
         ?
         ? 'To select: enter a customer ID number'
         ? 'To abort:  press the Esc Key '
         ? 'otherwise: press the Return Key'
         a row(), col()+2 get MCUSTID picture '999999'
         read
      enddo
      if MCUSTID = space(6) .and. readkey() # 12    && valid entry
         set order to 2              && customer id index
         seek MCUSTID
         POSITION = recno()          && record number
         set order to 1              && name index
         if .not. found()
                  ?? BELL
                  wait "&MCUSTID is not valid - press Return"
         else
                  go POSITION
         endif
      else
         seek chr(13)                && set end of file
      endif
   endif
return

procedure ERRORMSG
   parameter MESSAGE, ROW, COL
   a ROW,COL
   a ROW,COL say MESSAGE
   ?? chr(7)              && ring the bell
return
```

```
procedure FINDCUST
   parameters LEGEND,MNAME
   do while .T.
      MNAME = space(30)
      @ 23,2  say  LEGEND get MNAME pict '@!'
      read
                        if MNAME = space(30)
                             exit
                        endif
      seek trim(MNAME)
                         if eof()
                             do ERRORMSG with 'No record for '+MNAME, 21, 2
                             loop
                         endif
      @ 21,2
      do DUPECHK
      exit
   enddo
return

procedure FINDISBN
   parameters LEGEND, MISBN
   do while .T.
      private all
      VALIDTEST = .F.
      @ 23,2 say LEGEND get MISBN picture '@!'
      read
      @ 23,40
                        if MISBN = space(13)
                             exit
                        endif
      seek MISBN
                        if found()
                             exit
                        endif

      do ISBNTEST with MISBN, 'BOGIE', VALIDTEST
      do ERRORMSG with ;
          MISBN+ iif(VALIDTEST,' is not in the database',' is invalid'),23,40
   enddo
return
```

```
procedure FINDREC
   parameters LEGEND,  FIELDNAME
   private all
   do while .T.
      VALIDTEST = .F.
      MEMVAR    = space(6)
      @ 23,2 say LEGEND get MEMVAR picture "999999"
      read
                           if MEMVAR = space(6)
                              if .not. eof()
                                 do GOEOF
                              endif
                              exit
                           endif
      * validate number stored in MEMVAR
                           if .not.  mod(val(MEMVAR)-100000,17)=0
                              do ERRORMSG with MEMVAR + ' is invalid',22,2
                               loop
                           endif
         @ 22,2
         do SEARCH with MEMVAR, "&FIELDNAME"
                              if eof()
                                 do ERRORMSG with MEMVAR + ' not found',22,2
                                 loop
                              endif
         exit
   enddo
return
```

```
procedure GETDISK
   DISK = DISK + 1
   private MFILE
   do while .T.
      if file('A:DISKID.MEM')
            restore from A:DISKID additive
            if DISK # DISKID
               do ERRORMSG with 'Wrong Disk ID - Please Insert '+str(DISK,2),23,2
               loop
            endif
            @ 23,2
            select 4
            use A:FILELIST          && catalog of backup files on A
            do while .not. eof()     && clear backup files from drive A
               MFILE = trim(FILE)
               erase A:&MFILE
               skip
            enddo
      endif
      do SPACEREM with 'A','C',SPACEREM
      @ 23,2
      if SPACEREM < 300000     && new disk should be nearly empty
         do ERRORMSG with 'Insufficient Disk Space - Try another disk' ,23,2
      else
         DISKID = DISK
         save all like DISKID to A:DISKID
         select FILES
         copy structure to A:FILELIST
         select 4
         use A:FILELIST
         exit
      endif
   enddo
return
```

```
procedure GETREC
parameters LEGEND, MEMVAR, FIELDNAME
private all
do while .T.
    MEMVAR    = space(6)
    @ 23,2 say LEGEND get MEMVAR picture "999999"
    read
                    if MEMVAR = space(6)
                        exit
                    endif

                    if .not.  mod(val(MEMVAR)-100000,17)=0
                        do ERRORMSG with MEMVAR + ' is invalid',22,2
                        loop
                    endif
    @ 22,2
    go bottom
    OFFSET  = (val(&FIELDNAME) - val(MEMVAR))/17
    if recno() - OFFSET > 0
        go recno() -  OFFSET
    else
        go top
    endif
    locate rest for &FIELDNAME >= MEMVAR
                    if &FIELDNAME = MEMVAR
                            exit
                    endif
    do ERRORMSG with MEMVAR + ' not found',22,2
enddo
return

procedure GOEOF
   if reccount() > 0
      go reccount()
      skip
   endif
return

procedure H_SIZE                      && calculate header size
   parameter H_SIZE
   F_COUNT = 1
   do while F_COUNT <= 127
      if len(trim(field(F_COUNT+1))) = 0
         exit
      endif
      F_COUNT = F_COUNT+1
   enddo
   H_SIZE = 34 + 32 * F_COUNT
return
```

```
procedure INKEY
   parameter KEYCODES
   INKEY = 500              && impossible value

     do while .not. str(INKEY,3) $ KEYCODES
        INKEY = inkey()
     enddo
  return


procedure ISBNTEST
   parameters MISBN,MPUB,TEST
   private CHECKDIGIT, ISBNNUMBER, REM, DASH, GROUP, BOOKID, ISBNTEST, CHECK
   CHECKDIGIT = right(MISBN,1)
   REM        = left(MISBN,11)
   if '-' $ REM
        DASH      = at('-',REM)
        GROUP     = left(REM,DASH-1)
        REM       = right(REM,len(REM)-DASH)
   endif
   if '-' $ REM
        DASH      = at('-',REM)
        MPUB      = left(REM,DASH-1)
        BOOKID    = right(REM,len(REM)-DASH)
   endif
   ISBNNUMBER = GROUP+MPUB+BOOKID
   if len(ISBNNUMBER) = 9 .and. CHECKDIGIT $ '0123456789X'
        CHECK     = iif(CHECKDIGIT = 'X',10,val(CHECKDIGIT))

        X = 1
        do while X <= 9
           CHECK = CHECK + val(substr(ISBNNUMBER,X,1)) * (11-X)
           X = X+1
        enddo
        if mod(CHECK,11) = 0      && is check evenly divisible by 11
          TEST = .T.
        endif
   endif
  return
```

```
procedure LINEFEED
   parameter LFS
   ? replicate(chr(10),LFS)
return

procedure PAGE
parameter ROW,COL
PAGE = PAGE + 1
@ ROW,COL say 'Page:  ' + ltrim(str(PAGE,3))
return


procedure NEXTFILE
         if .not. eof()
             MFILE = substr(FILE,1,at(space(1),FILE))
             select 3
             use &MFILE
             do H_SIZE with H_SIZE
             select FILES
         endif
return
```

```
procedure QTYEDIT
parameter MVAR, FIRSTREC
private FIRSTREC,START,LASTREC,X
set relation to ISBN into INVENTORY
ANSWER  = "Y"
START   = FIRSTREC
do while ANSWER = "Y"
   clear
   do BANNER with "Editing Invoice " + MVAR
   ? ' ISBN Number       Title '
   @ row(),col()+28 say 'Ordered  Shipped   Price'
   ? ' '+BAR
   go START
   X = 10
      do while INVOICE = MVAR .and. X < 27 .and. .not. eof()
         MEMVAR = 'M'+str(X,2)
         store QTYDEL to &MEMVAR
         X = X+1
         ? ' '+ISBN+'   ',INVENTORY->TITLE,str(QTY,8),str(PRICE,18,2)
         @ row(),63 get &MEMVAR picture '###' range 0,QTY
         skip
      enddo
   read
   x=10
   go START
      do while INVOICE = MVAR .and. x < 27 .and. .not. eof()
         MEMVAR = 'M'+str(x,2)
         if &MEMVAR # QTYDEL
            select INVENTORY
            replace QTYONHAND with QTYONHAND - (&MEMVAR - INVOICES->QTYDEL),;
                    SOLDTHISYR with SOLDTHISYR+(&MEMVAR - INVOICES->QTYDEL)
            select INVOICES
            replace QTYDEL with &MEMVAR
         endif
         X = X+1
         skip
      enddo
      if INVOICE # MVAR .or. eof()
         do QUERY with "Do you want to re-edit",23,2,ANSWER
         @ 23,2
         START = FIRSTREC
      else
         START = recno()
      endif
enddo
set relation to
go FIRSTREC
return
```

```
procedure QUERY
     parameters LEGEND, ROW, COL, ANSWER
     ANSWER = ' '
     @ ROW,COL
     do while .not. ANSWER $ 'YN'
          @ ROW,COL say LEGEND get ANSWER picture '!'
          read
     enddo
     @ ROW,COL
return

procedure ROWCHECK
     parameter ROW
     clear gets
       if ROW >= 22
         ?
         ?
       else
         ROW = ROW+1
       endif
return
```

```
procedure SEARCH                      && for ordered, UNindexed database
    parameters SEARCHVAR, SEARCHFLD
    Private all
    JUMPSIZE = reccount()
do while JUMPSIZE > 1
    if SEARCHVAR = &SEARCHFLD
       exit
    endif
    if SEARCHVAR < &SEARCHFLD .and. recno() > JUMPSIZE
      go recno() - JUMPSIZE
    endif
    if SEARCHVAR > &SEARCHFLD .and. recno() + JUMPSIZE <= reccount()
      go recno() + JUMPSIZE
    endif
    JUMPSIZE = int(round(JUMPSIZE/2,0))
enddo
do while .not. bof()
    skip -1
         if &SEARCHFLD < SEARCHVAR
             exit
         endif
enddo
locate rest for &SEARCHFLD >= SEARCHVAR
if .not. &SEARCHFLD = SEARCHVAR
   do GOEOF
endif
return


procedure SPACEREM
    parameter TARGET,SOURCE,SPACEREM
    set default to TARGET
    SPACEREM = diskspace()
    set default to SOURCE
return
```

Index

OF RELATED INTEREST

Periodicals

Ashton-Tate Quarterly is designed to help business and professional users of Ashton-Tate software increase effectiveness and productivity. Regular features include business applications for corporations, small businesses, managers, intrapreneurs, and entrepreneurs; professional advice on planning computer solutions to business problems; practical technical tips; in-depth case studies of Ashton-Tate products in a variety of business settings; book excerpts from Ashton-Tate publications; and other information of interest to Ashton-Tate customers. Published each January, April, July, and October. Subscriptions: $20 (US), $26 (Canada and Mexico), $35 (Overseas).

TechNotes, a monthly journal published by the Ashton-Tate Software Support Center, provides the most current and accurate technical support available to users of Ashton-Tate software. Feature articles, written by Ashton-Tate technicians, provide programming and design tips for developing applications. Monthly columns include Usage Tips, Technical Tidbits, On-Line Services, Anomalies, Known Software Problems, and Work-Arounds. Subscriptions: $50 (US), $65 (Canada and Mexico), $75 (Overseas).

To subscribe to the *Ashton-Tate Quarterly* or *TechNotes*, please send your prepaid order to: Ashton-Tate Periodicals, PO Box 3729, Escondido, CA 92025-0929. Charge orders accepted by phone at 1-800-331-4164 (from California) and 1-800-828-2514 (from all other states).

Books

Advanced Programmer's Guide
Featuring dBASE III, dBASE II, and dBASE III PLUS ISBN: 0-912677-05-8 $28.95
dBASE III PLUS and Local Area Networks   ISBN: 0-912677-80-5 $24.95
dBASE III PLUS for Sales Professionals   ISBN: 0-912677-46-5 $29.95
dBASE III PLUS Programming: Tips and Techniques ISBN: 0-912677-91-0 $19.95
dBASE III PLUS Trail Guide   ISBN: 0-912677-84-8 $29.95
Everyman's Database Primer
Featuring dBASE III PLUS   ISBN: 0-912677-85-6 $19.95

Utilities

dBASE Programmer's Utilities   ISBN: 0-912677-78-3 $89.95
dBASE Tools: The Graphics Library for C   ISBN: 0-912677-81-3 $89.95
dBASE Tools: The Programmer's Library for C   ISBN: 0-912677-79-1 $89.95
dBASE Tools: Pascal Programmer's Library   ISBN: 0-912677-93-7 $89.95

Please call 1-800-437-4329 for more information or to order books and utilities.

When placing your order for magazines or books, please indicate that you're ordering from *dBASE III PLUS for Every Business.*